COMMERCIAL MARITIME LAW

The title 'Commercial Maritime Law' is a misnomer. There is a patchwork of different commercial maritime laws around the world. However, the title is a true reflection of what many legal scholars and practitioners in the field have long desired: a common framework of commercial maritime law. This book unravels the complexities of bridging the gap between common law and civil law and will discuss whether the title will remain a misnomer despite the countless attempts at harmonisation. Internationally renowned legal scholars and practitioners discuss herein the areas in which the common law and civil law are divided; the impact of these differences on the drafting and ratification of international conventions; the search for a common framework; and the procedural aspects of the common law and civil law divide embedded within commercial maritime law.

Commercial Maritime Law

Edited by
Melis Özdel

•HART•
OXFORD • LONDON • NEW YORK • NEW DELHI • SYDNEY

HART PUBLISHING

Bloomsbury Publishing Plc

Kemp House, Chawley Park, Cumnor Hill, Oxford, OX2 9PH, UK

1385 Broadway, New York, NY 10018, USA

HART PUBLISHING, the Hart/Stag logo, BLOOMSBURY and the Diana logo are trademarks of Bloomsbury Publishing Plc

First published in Great Britain 2020

A catalogue record for this book is available from the British Library.

Library of Congress Cataloging-in-Publication data

Names: International Conference on Commercial Maritime Law (2016 : University College, London) | Özdel, Melis, editor.

Title: Commercial maritime law / edited by Melis Özdel.

Description: Oxford ; New York : Hart, 2020. | "This book presents nine papers delivered at the two-day Conference on Commercial Maritime Law held at University College London in May/June 2016 ... The conference was organised and led by Dr Melis Özdel, then the newly appointed Director of the UCL Centre for Commercial Law." — ECIP Foreword. | Includes bibliographical references and index.

Identifiers: LCCN 2019052340 (print) | LCCN 2019052341 (ebook) | ISBN 9781849466752 (hardcover) | ISBN 9781509901050 (Epub)

Subjects: LCSH: Maritime law—Congresses.

Classification: LCC K1150.A6 I577 2016 (print) | LCC K1150.A6 (ebook) | DDC 343.09/6—dc23

LC record available at https://lccn.loc.gov/2019052340

LC ebook record available at https://lccn.loc.gov/2019052341

ISBN: HB: 978-1-84946-675-2
ePDF: 978-1-50990-104-3
ePub: 978-1-50990-105-0

Typeset by Compuscript Ltd, Shannon

To find out more about our authors and books visit www.hartpublishing.co.uk. Here you will find extracts, author information, details of forthcoming events and the option to sign up for our newsletters.

FOREWORD

This book presents nine papers delivered at the two-day Conference on Commercial Maritime Law held at University College London in May/June 2016.

The object of the conference was to explore whether there is a body of commercial maritime law that is applied by courts and tribunals around the world and, if there is, the extent to which the common law and the civil law (as applied in continental jurisdictions) have contributed to it.

Against this background, the distinguished speakers addressed a number of carefully identified topics ranging from general principles, such as contract interpretation (Sir Bernard Rix), the responsibilities of actual carriers (Professor Francis Reynolds and Professor Dr Pieter Schampe) and insurance and disclosure (Peter Macdonald-Eggers QC), to specific topics including *res cogitans* (Stephen Cogley QC) and an interesting comparison of the liabilities of the Master '*qualitate tua*' in continental law and of the vessel herself in a common law action *in rem* (Professor Marc Huybrechts).

The conference was organised and led by Dr Melis Özdel, then the newly appointed Director of the UCL Centre for Commercial Law. She herself contributed an analysis of 'The Doctrine of *Res Judicata* in Commercial Maritime Arbitration', which demonstrated the value of securing finality in international arbitration including how important the rule of issue estoppel can be in achieving it.

This book brings these valuable and thought-provoking papers to a broader audience, and it will be widely welcomed. The respective roles of the common law and the civil (continental) law can be a subject of interest and importance in any international tribunal, as I know from personal experience in Dubai. There, the Dubai International Financial Centre (DIFC) and the Dubai World Tribunal have set international precedents in establishing a common law jurisdiction alongside national laws based on a Civil Code. And it is particularly relevant in maritime law, reflecting as that does the needs of seaborne international trade in all jurisdictions, arbitration included.

I was honoured to be asked to give a keynote speech at the conference. In it, I stressed the importance, as I see it, of searching for harmony rather than discord in these endeavours. Happily, that approach was supported in the papers which followed, and I commend them to the many readers who now will have access to them.

Anthony Evans
10 October 2019
London

PREFACE

This book is a collection of papers presented as part of the international maritime law conference at University College London in 2016. Bringing together internationally renowned scholars, the conference stimulated lively debate as well as providing a meaningful contribution to the legal scholarship in various areas of commercial maritime law.

The title of the book, *Commercial Maritime Law* is a reflection of what many legal scholars and practitioners in the field have long desired: a common framework of commercial maritime law. The contributors to this project have sought to unravel the complexities encountered when attempts are made to bridge the gap between common law and civil law in commercial maritime law. They discuss some particular areas in which the common law and civil law are divided, the impact of these differences on the interpretation of maritime contracts and the procedural aspects of the common law and civil law divide in commercial maritime law.

The theme underpinning the discussions in the book has become even more relevant with the UK's scheduled withdrawal from the EU, which will no doubt bring significant changes to the country's legal landscape for future decades. While uncertainty still hangs over Brexit, it is hoped that this book will shed light on some of the key differences between legal traditions in the context of commercial maritime law.

Melis Özdel
24 August 2019
London

TABLE OF CONTENTS

LIST OF CONTRIBUTORS

Stephen Cogley QC, 4 Pump Court, UK

Stephen is a barrister at 4 Pump Court. Stephen is a particularly versatile advocate, having crossed over from pure modern chancery and insolvency to commercial and shipping work. He is often instructed in large disputes that involve both chancery/insolvency and commercial issues. Many of his cases involve international aspects and he frequently works with teams of lawyers from other jurisdictions in cases that typically commence with anti-suit injunctions, freezing injunctions and other forms of interim relief. He is recognised and recommended in these areas. Stephen regularly appears in the Court of Appeal, Commercial Court and Chancery Division as well as undertaking arbitrations. Stephen's international practice includes involvement in a number of oil and gas arbitrations for and against large multinationals and state entities in various jurisdictions.

Recent high-profile cases include acting for Sudan in its oil ownership/pipeline transit fee disputes with South Sudan; the commissioners of oil field pumping stations in a US $1 billion arbitration; Alexander Vik in his dispute with Deutsche Bank; Nob Su in various disputes; various cross-border insolvency disputes arising out of the collapse of KLC in Korea and SANKO in Japan (numerous cases in various jurisdictions) and OW Bunkers; on behalf of P&I insurers and others in respect of the recent Iranian sanctions; the builders of the biggest Cargo vessel ever constructed, which foundered on its maiden voyage; NITC in its recent well-publicised US $1.5 billion insurance/Iranian sanctions/refinancing dispute; office-holders seeking recovery against the insolvent's indemnity insurers; shareholders in a multi-million 944 Petition involving allegations of fraud and breach of fiduciary duty; and solicitor allegedly involved in a major city fraud.

Professor Martin Davies, Tulane University, Tulane Maritime Law Centre, USA

Martin Davies is Admiralty Law Institute Professor of Maritime Law at Tulane University Law School in New Orleans, Director of the Tulane

Maritime Law Center, and Professorial Fellow at Melbourne Law School, Australia.

He holds the degrees of MA and BCL from Oxford University, England, and an LLM from Harvard Law School. Before joining Tulane, he was Harrison Moore Professor of Law at The University of Melbourne in Australia and before that he taught at Monash University, The University of Western Australia and Nottingham University. He has also been a visiting professor at universities in Italy and Singapore.

He is author (or co-author) of books on maritime law, international trade law, conflict of laws, and the law of torts. He has also published many journal articles on these topics. He also has extensive practical experience as a consultant in maritime matters and general international litigation and arbitration, in Australia, Singapore and the US. He has advised on cargo claims, arrest and admiralty matters, drafting bills of lading, sea waybills and charterparties, collisions and limitation of liability, oil pollution, salvage, marine insurance, maritime arbitrations and international sale of goods.

Emeritus Professor Francis Reynolds, Oxford University

Francis Reynolds DCL, QC (Hon) is an Emeritus Professor at the University of Oxford; a barrister and Honorary Bencher of the Inner Temple and a Fellow of the British Academy, a Titulary Member of the CMI and Honorary Professor in the International Maritime Law Institute of the IMO, Malta. He is one of the authors of *Carver on Bills of Lading*.

Emeritus Professor Marc Huybrechts, University of Antwerp, Belgium

Marc A Huybrechts is Emeritus Professor of Transport Law at the University of Leuven and at the Antwerp University, and visiting Professor at Dalian Maritime University. He is an advocate at the Bar of Antwerp and Emeritus Auxiliary Justice at the Antwerp Appeals Court. He is member of the Law Commission on the reform of Belgian Maritime Law. Until 2015 he was editor of the section 'Transport law' in the *International Encyclopedia of Laws*.

Peter MacDonald Eggers QC, 7 King's Bench Walk, UK

Peter MacDonald Eggers QC is a barrister practising at 7 King's Bench Walk, specialising in commercial law, including insurance and reinsurance, shipping, energy, commodities, international trade and arbitration.

Peter is co-author of *Good Faith and Insurance Contracts*, author of *Deceit: The Lie of the Law*, and a Contributing Editor of *Chitty on Contracts*. He is a Visiting Professor at University College, London.

Peter has appeared in numerous commercial cases, including recently in *The Cape Bari (Limitation Convention), Suez Fortune Investments Ltd v Talbot Underwriting Ltd* (CTL and sue and labour), *Rathbone Brothers plc v Novae Corporate Underwriting* (subrogation), *The Princess of the Stars* (reinsurance and typhoon warranty), *Sea Glory Maritime Co v Al Sagr National Insurance Co* (good faith and ISM), *Arash Shipping v Groupama* (Iranian sanctions and fleet policy), *Masefield v Amlin* (ATL and piracy), *The WD Fairway* (CTL and abandonment), and *Limit v AXA* (good faith and reinsurance).

Dr Melis Özdel, UCL, UK

Melis Özdel is a lecturer in Law at University College London and Director of the UCL Centre for Commercial Law. She has taught academic and professional courses and has published in various areas of maritime and international trade law. She is the author of *Bills of Lading Incorporating Charterparties* (2015, Hart Publishing), which is a seminal contribution to existing literature on the subject. Since its publication, she has received numerous invitations from renowned international organisations and has spoken at their conferences.

Melis is also a member of the Chartered Institute of Arbitrators, Turkey Bar Association and a supporting member of the London Maritime Arbitrators Association. She has a vast experience in multitude of sectors, including shipping, international trade and commodities, international arbitration, and construction.

Sir Bernard Rix, 20 Essex Street, International Judge of the Singapore Commercial Court

Sir Bernard Rix is Professor of International Commercial Law at Queen Mary University of London. He retired as Lord Justice of Appeal in 2013 after 20 years in the Commercial Court and the Court of Appeal. He is an arbitrator and mediator and has been appointed to the Cayman Islands Court of Appeal and Singapore International Commercial Court.

He was educated at New College Oxford, of which he is an honorary fellow, and at Harvard Law School, where he was a Kennedy Scholar. He is a member of the Advisory Council of BIICL (British Institute of

International and Comparative Law), former Chairman of the Advisory Council of CCLS and former director of the London Philharmonic Orchestra.

At Queen Mary, he lectures on insurance, shipping, arbitration and commercial law, and is convening a new module next year entitled Transnational Problems in Commercial Contracts.

Professor Dr Dieter Schwampe, Partner, Dabelstein & Passehl Rechtsanwalte, Hamburg

Dr Dieter Schwampe, born 1957, studied Jurisprudence and Japanology at the Universities of Constance, Bonn and Hamburg, and obtained his first state exam in 1981. From 1981 to 1982 he was an Assistant at the Institute for Private International and Foreign Law at Hamburg University. During that year he also completed his law doctorate with a thesis on Charterers' Liability Insurance. Dieter Schwampe qualified as a German lawyer in 1985 and started his career in the Hamburg law firm Dabelstein & Passehl in 1985. He became a partner in 1988 and served as Managing Partner of his firm from 2001 to 2013.

Dieter Schwampe is a member of the Hamburg Bar Association, the German Lawyers Association, the US Maritime Law Association (MLAUS) and the International Bar Association (IBA). He is President of the German Maritime Law Association (DVIS) and Board Member of the Hamburg Association of Insurance Science. He is also an Executive Council Member of Comité Maritime International (CMI) and a member in CMI's International Working Groups on Marine Insurance (of which he was Chairman from 2009 to 2013) and CMI's International Working Group on Unmanned Ships: He also is Vice-Chairman of the Working Party on Marine Insurance of Association International de Droit des Assurance (AIDA) and a member of the Legal an Liability Committee of the International Union of Marine Insurance (IUMI). As a member of the German Maritime Arbitration Association (GMAA) he is an active arbitrator and as also served on international panels of other arbitration associations. Since 2013 he is Professor of Law at Hamburg University, where he teaches shipping law, transport law and marine insurance law. He is regularly invited to speak on national and international seminars and conferences, and is the author of numerous books and articles on various aspects of shipping and marine insurance law.

Dieter Schwampe's special areas of practice are insurance law as well as shipping law. In insurance law he is a specialist in hull as well as P&I insurance, cargo insurance, re-insurance and commercial specialties. Beside company and supervisory law of insurance companies he also intensively works in the insurance broker's liability area. In shipping law he specialises in bills of lading, charter parties, collisions, salvage and general average.

Lawrence Teh, Partner, Dentons Rodyk Davidson, LLP, Singapore

Lawrence Teh is a partner in Dentons Rodyk & Davidson LLP's Litigation & Arbitration Practice Group. Lawrence advises clients and acts as an advocate in all areas of commercial law and appears regularly as leading counsel in the Singapore courts, in arbitration and in other forms of dispute resolution. He is also appointed regularly as an arbitrator in international disputes. He has particular experience in international trade and commodities, maritime and aviation, banking and financial services, onshore and offshore construction, mergers acquisitions joint ventures and other investments, and insurance in related fields.

Lawrence is currently the Chairman of the Alternative Dispute Resolution (ADR) Committee at The Law Society of Singapore. He is a Fellow of the Chartered Institute of Arbitrators, a Fellow of the Singapore Institute of Arbitrators, and a panel arbitrator at the Singapore International Arbitration Centre. He chaired the committee that drafted the Law Society Arbitration Rules and is a panel arbitrator of the Law Society Arbitration Scheme. Recently, he was appointed the Administrator of the Comite Maritime International (CMI) in 2013, and Chairman of the Promotion Committee of the Singapore Chamber of Maritime Arbitration (SCMA). He is also a Council Member of the Legal Practice Division in the International Bar Association (IBA).

TABLE OF CASES

UK

China

Greece

Ireland

South Africa

The Netherlands

EU

Hong Kong

Belgium

Australia

Canada

United States

India

Singapore

Hong Kong

TABLE OF LEGISLATION

UK

Germany

EU

US

Australia

Canada

South Africa

Greece

Turkey

New Zealand

China

Singapore

1

Cross-border Insolvency and Admiralty: A Middle Path of Reciprocal Comity

PROFESSOR MARTIN DAVIES*

I. Introduction

The global financial crisis of 2008 produced a quick[1] and disastrous decline in the global shipping business,[2] leading to the insolvency of several major shipping lines, mostly in the form of Chapter-11-like 'rehabilitation' or reorganisation proceedings, in which the shipping line sought to trade out of its financial difficulties.[3]

* Admiralty Law Institute Professor of Maritime Law, Tulane University Law School, Director, Tulane Maritime Law Center.

[1] cf S Chambers, 'Dry Bulk Bonanza', 2007 3 *Seatrade* 20; with G Miller, 'Dry Bulk Turns to Chapter 15'(2009) 6523 *Fairplay* 11.

[2] For years, the shipping trade press has contained a litany of woe about the continuing slump in the global market. Given the number of trade publications, there are literally too many articles to count, but a small but representative selection with illustrative titles is A Lonsdale, 'Too Many Ships, Too Little Cargo' (2009) 6513 *Fairplay* 18; G Miller, 'Second Wave of Restructuring Looms' (2010) 6609 *Fairplay* 20; I Middleton, 'Financing Crunch' (2012) 4 *Seatrade* 13; J Dolphin, 'Dr. Strangelove, or How I Learned to Stop Worrying and Love the Restructuring Process' (2012) 28 *Marine Money* 12; J Tenev, 'Triage in the Trough – Advantaged Alternatives in International Marine Insolvencies' (2012) 28 *Marine Money* 12; G Miller, 'Escaping the Debt Trap' (2014) 6782 *Fairplay* 8.

[3] For example, in July 2012, the Sanko Steamship Co, established in 1934, petitioned for reorganisation under the Japanese Corporate Reorganization Act. See *Evridiki Navigation Inc v The Sanko Steamship Co*, 880 F Supp 2d 666, 668, 2012 AMC 1817, 1818–19 (D.Del, 2012). Sanko was at that time one of Japan's (and the world's) largest shipping companies with a fleet (owned and chartered) of 156 ships. See R Wright and E Tsui, 'Sanko bankruptcy blow for bulk shipping', *Financial Times*, 8 July 2012. Sanko survived and continues to operate with a much-diminished fleet of 14 ships. See http://www.sankoline.co.jp/en/fleet_list.

The post-2008 wave of shipowner insolvencies brought to light some pressing questions for the law relating to cross-border insolvency. By its very nature, much of the shipping business is global in scale, with the result that a shipowner may have mobile assets (its ships) dispersed all around the world when it opens insolvency proceedings in its base of operations.[4] An insolvency with globally spread assets is not that unusual but, for good or ill, ships are different from other assets,[5] in that there is an ancient and well-established body of law giving rights to creditors in ways quite different from those that apply in relation to their land-based counterparts.[6] When a shipowner becomes insolvent, or when it appears that it soon may be so, creditors often move to arrest its ships or attach its other assets wherever in the world they can be found, using admiralty procedures designed to protect the interests of local claimants. When that occurs, a head-on collision arises between insolvency law and admiralty law, raising interesting conceptual questions for both. This remains a very topical question, as there are still very few signs of recovery in the global shipping market.[7]

Admiralty law would allow the creditor to proceed against the shipowner's assets wherever they were seized, notwithstanding the existence of insolvency proceedings in the debtor's home country. Indeed, one of the principal purposes of the traditional admiralty procedures of arrest and attachment is to allow local creditors to get satisfaction of their claims, notwithstanding the insolvency of a distant foreign shipowner. In contrast, in insolvency law, the 'golden thread' of universalism calls for courts in

[4] Some foreign ship operators have tried to open Chapter 11 proceedings in the US, despite sometimes tenuous connections between their business and the US, in an attempt to take advantage of the extraterritorial effect of the worldwide automatic stay under 11 USC § 362(a). This chapter does not deal with that situation. See A DeNatale and C Mechling, 'Shipping Companies Find a Safe Harbor in US Bankruptcy Courts', *New York Law Journal*, 4 March 2013.

[5] See the following well-known exchange between two British judges, both specialists in maritime law: (Lord) M Mustill, 'Ships are different – or are they?' [1993] *Lloyd's Maritime & Commercial Law Quartely* 490; (now Mr Justice) D Steel, 'Ships are different – the case for limitation of liability' [1995] *Lloyd's Maritime & Commercial Law Quarterly* 17.

[6] For example, maritime law gives priority to involuntary creditors such as tort claimants over voluntary creditors such as mortgagees. Although this may seem confrontingly alien to securities and insolvency lawyers, some have argued that the logic of the maritime law scheme of priorities should be applied on land, rather than vice versa. See K van de Biezenbos, 'A Sea Change in Creditor Priorities' (2015) 48 *University of Michigan Journal of Law Reform* 595.

[7] J Hanscom, 'That sinking feeling' (2016) 1 *Seatrade* 11.

other countries to cooperate with the courts in the country of the debtor's insolvency to ensure that all of its assets are distributed to its creditors under a single, orderly, system of distribution.[8] If the debtor's assets have been seized by admiralty judicial process in another country, the principle of universalism calls for them to be released, and for the admiralty creditors to participate in the debtor's insolvency proceedings.

At first sight, the underlying imperatives of these two bodies of law appear to be irreconcilable. It seems that one or other must prevail at the expense of the other. If admiralty prevails, the admiralty proceedings in the country of arrest or attachment will proceed as usual, notwithstanding the existence of insolvency proceedings in the debtor's home country.[9] If insolvency prevails, the admiralty proceedings must be discontinued so as to ensure that all creditors participate equally in the insolvency proceedings.[10] Predictably, maritime lawyers prefer the first alternative. This is, after all, why admiralty procedures have existed for hundreds of years. Equally predictably, insolvency lawyers prefer the second alternative. To them, the right to proceed against the debtor's assets in admiralty amounts to little more than an illegitimate form of preference for a particular class of creditors. This would seem to be a zero-sum game. Whichever body of law wins, someone will regard the outcome as illegitimate or inappropriate.

The goal of this chapter is to suggest a third way, a middle path that achieves the main goal of universalism, recognising the primacy of the insolvency proceedings, while also preserving the right of admiralty claimants to secure their claims by proceeding against the debtor's assets wherever in the world they may be found. This middle path depends upon the notion of reciprocal comity, by which each country – that of the admiralty arrest or attachment and that of the insolvency proceedings – respects the legitimacy of the other's proceedings and laws.[11] Respect should

[8] The phrase 'golden thread' in relation to universalism was coined by Lord Hoffmann in *Re HIH Casualty & General Insurance Ltd* [2008] 1 WLR 852 (HL), 861–62.

[9] See, eg, *Holt Cargo Systems Inc v ABC Containerline NV* [2001] 3 SCR 90 (SC Can) (admiralty proceedings in Canada allowed to proceed, notwithstanding the existence of insolvency proceedings in Belgium).

[10] See, eg, *Evridiki Navigation Inc v The Sanko Steamship Co*, 880 F Supp 2d 666 (D Del, 2012) (admiralty proceedings in the US terminated because of the existence of insolvency proceedings in Japan).

[11] See generally E Janger, 'Reciprocal Comity' (2011) 46 *Texas International Law Journal* 441.

be mutual. If respect is not reciprocated, it is no more than enforced acquiescence or self-abnegation.

The UNCITRAL Model Law on Cross-Border Insolvency[12] implements the concept of universalism by requiring enacting countries to stay any proceedings against a debtor upon recognition of the existence of insolvency proceedings in the debtor's centre of main interests (COMI).[13] The EU's Insolvency Regulation[14] (which has been replaced and superseded by the Recast EU Insolvency Regulation)[15] implements a modified form of universalism, giving primacy to insolvency proceedings in the debtor's COMI and the law of the country where they are opened (the *lex concursus*), but preserving pre-existing rights *in rem* granted by the laws of other EU Member States.[16]

Comity demands that a country where the debtor's assets have been arrested or attached using admiralty procedures must recognise the primacy of insolvency proceedings in the debtor's COMI. *Reciprocal* comity demands that the country of the insolvency proceedings should recognise and respect the legitimacy of the security granted by the admiralty procedures in the country of arrest or attachment. Both the Model Law and the Insolvency Regulation (and Recast Regulation) can accommodate a reciprocal comity approach of the kind recommended here. This chapter explains how, focusing mainly on the Model Law, which, although not yet widely adopted, has been enacted in several important maritime

[12] UNCITRAL Model Law on Cross-Border Insolvency with Guide to Enactment and Interpretation (UNCITRAL Secretariat, 2014) (hereafter 'Model Law'). Chapter 15 of the US Bankruptcy Code (11 USC §§ 1501–32) is modeled on the Model Law.

[13] Model Law, Art 20(1). There is a considerable body of law about what constitutes the debtor's COMI, when it should be determined, and questions of 'COMI migration' as companies try to position themselves for a possible impending insolvency. This chapter does not address any of those issues, but rather takes a prior determination of the debtor's COMI as read. For further consideration of these issues, see, eg, M Arnold, 'Truth or Illusion? COMI Migration and Forum Shopping under the EU Insolvency Regulations' (2013) 14 *Business Law International* 245; J Hallock, Note, 'Time Out: The Problematic Temporality of COMI Analysis in Chapter 15 Bankruptcy Cases in the Second Circuit' (2015) *Columbia Business Law Review* 1074.

[14] Council Regulation (EC) 1346/2000 on Insolvency Proceedings (EU Insolvency Regulation).

[15] Regulation (EU) 2015/848 of the European Parliament and Council of 20 May 2015 on Insolvency Proceedings (Recast), which took effect on 26 June 2017 (EU Recast Insolvency Regulation).

[16] EU Insolvency Regulation, Arts 4, 5; EU Recast Insolvency Regulation, Arts 7, 8.

jurisdictions, including Australia, Canada, Greece, Japan, Korea, South Africa, the UK and the US.[17]

The appropriate relationship between the law of the country of arrest or attachment and the law of the opening of insolvency proceedings depends in part upon the order in which proceedings are commenced. The next section of this chapter explores the different possible permutations.

II. Three Permutations

One of the most troublesome aspects of the relationship between insolvency proceedings and admiralty proceedings in different countries is the fact that the nature of that relationship changes according to the order in which the various proceedings are brought. That is true not only as a matter of priority and precedence, but also, as a practical matter, in relation to the assets of the debtor themselves. In particular, as will shortly be shown, the extent of the debtor's insurance cover for pre-existing liabilities will depend upon the order in which proceedings are brought.

There are three significant moments in the kind of case under consideration here: the commencement of admiralty arrest or attachment proceedings (A); the opening of insolvency proceedings in the debtor's COMI (I); and recognition of the insolvency proceedings as a foreign main proceeding (FMP) in a country that has enacted the Model Law (R). These three events can occur in three possible sequences: A-I-R, I-R-A and I-A-R.[18] The three permutations raise different implications about the relationship of reciprocal comity between the country of arrest/attachment and the country of the FMP. As a practical consequence, it follows that there cannot be a single, 'one size fits all' solution to the legal issues raised in these cases. The appropriate international solution must depend upon the sequence of events.

[17] UNCITRAL Model Law on Cross-Border Insolvency (1997), available at http://www.uncitral.org/uncitral/en/uncitral_texts/insolvency/1997Model_status.html.

[18] There are six possible combinations of the three variables A, I and R: A-I-R, A-R-I, I-R-A, I-A-R, R-I-A and R-A-I. Because recognition of an FMP cannot possibly precede the opening of insolvency proceedings in the COMI, R cannot precede I, which removes the theoretical combinations A-R-I, R-I-A and R-A-I.

A. A-I-R: Admiralty Proceedings before Insolvency Proceedings

This permutation is the one that most pointedly raises the supposed competition between insolvency and admiralty. Admiralty claimants may have proceeded against the debtor's vessel(s) before its insolvency either because they have learned of the possibility of an impending insolvency or in the ordinary course of things, unaware of the possibility that the operator of the vessel(s) against which they are proceeding is in sufficiently dire straits that it may soon be forced into insolvency in its COMI. The admiralty claimant's knowledge, intention or motive is irrelevant, however. All that matters for present purposes is that the admiralty claimant has proceeded to enforce what admiralty law has always regarded as a secured claim before insolvency proceedings were opened. Should the subsequent opening of insolvency proceedings bring an end to the pre-existing admiralty proceedings, thereby quite possibly extinguishing the security that those admiralty proceedings give to the claimants? Or should the admiralty claimants' 'first strike' against one of the main assets of the debtor be allowed to stand, possibly giving them what amounts to a preference over other creditors?

The UNCITRAL Model Law deliberately left that question up to enacting states, thereby eschewing the possibility of an internationally uniform answer. Article 20(2) of the Model Law modifies the effect of the mandatory stay called for by Article 20(1) by providing:

> The scope, and the modification or termination, of the stay and suspension referred to in paragraph 1 of the present article are subject to [*refer to any provisions of law of the enacting State relating to insolvency that apply to exceptions, limitations, modifications or termination in respect of the stay and suspension referred to in paragraph 1 of the present article*].

UNCITRAL's 'Guide to Enactment and Interpretation' states that the purpose of Article 20(2) is to limit the effect of the mandatory Article 20(1) stay by reference to any exceptions or limitations that may exist under the law of the enacting country, such as local laws allowing the continuation of pre-existing claims by secured creditors.[19] The 'Guide to Enactment' says

[19] UNCITRAL Model Law on Cross-Border Insolvency with Guide to Enactment and Interpretation (UNCITRAL Secretariat, 2014) p 85, para 183.

that an insolvent debtor enjoying the benefit of Article 20 must accept the imposition of restrictions by the enacting country, even if they are different, and possibly more stringent, than they would be under the law of the FMP.[20] That is consistent with a reciprocal comity approach because it requires both the enacting country (the country of arrest/attachment) and the country of the FMP to acknowledge and respect the laws of the other. The country of arrest/attachment must respect the existence of the FMP in another country by staying the existing admiralty proceedings in its courts, but the country of the FMP (and the debtor invoking insolvency protection) must respect the fact that the country of arrest/attachment may choose to preserve the priority of claims secured before the insolvency proceedings were opened.

The EU achieves a similar result by leaving the effect that subsequently opened insolvency proceedings might have on pending proceedings as a question to be determined by the law of the country of the pending proceedings.[21]

Thus, Article 20(2) of the Model Law means that a country enacting the Model Law could provide that the mandatory Article 20(1) stay does not apply to a pre-existing action by any secured claimant,[22] including one who has proceeded in admiralty to seize a ship by arrest or attachment. Predictably, different countries that have enacted the Model Law have 'filled in the blank' in Article 20(2) in different ways.

Although some enacting countries have provisions allowing secured claimants to continue to proceed against an individual debtor's assets notwithstanding a subsequent bankruptcy filing,[23] some, such as Japan[24] and (perhaps) South Africa,[25] make exactly the opposite provision in relation

[20] ibid p 83, para 178.

[21] EU Insolvency Regulation, Art 15, EU Recast Insolvency Regulation, Art 18 (including pending arbitral proceedings).

[22] See also UNCITRAL Model Law on Cross-Border Insolvency: The Judicial Perspective (UNCITRAL Secretariat, 2014) p 56, para 165.

[23] See, eg, Insolvency Act 1986 (UK), s 285(4).

[24] Act of Recognition of and Assistance for Foreign Insolvency Proceedings (No 129 of 2000), Arts 27–29.

[25] Cross-Border Insolvency Act 2000 (SA), s 20(2) makes the mandatory Art 20(1) stay subject to the requirements imposed by Companies Act 1973 (SA), s 359, which suspended all pre-existing proceedings against a company once a winding-up order was made unless prompt notice was given to the liquidator. However, Companies Act 1973 (SA) was repealed by Companies Act 2008 (SA) without consequential amendment of Cross-Border Insolvency Act 2000 (SA), s 20(2), which leaves the position unclear.

to corporate debtors, providing no 'safe harbour' for pre-existing claims by secured creditors, but forcing all of them to participate in the subsequently declared insolvency.

The UK provides that a pre-existing admiralty claimant is not subject to the Article 20(1) stay if a claim involving a corporate defendant has been 'completed', meaning that there has been a judicial seizure *and sale* before the insolvency proceedings are opened.[26] The result of such a provision is that the admiralty claimant can continue to proceed against the proceeds of a judicial sale notwithstanding the opening of insolvency proceedings, but if the admiralty proceedings have not reached the point of judicial sale when insolvency proceedings are opened, the claimant cannot continue to proceed in admiralty but must participate in the insolvency proceedings.

Some enacting countries, such as New Zealand and Kenya, have 'filled in the blank' in Article 20(2) by giving the court an open-ended discretion to order, upon application by any creditor (including, presumably, a pre-existing admiralty claimant), that the Article 20(1) stay should not apply upon any conditions that the court thinks fit.[27]

Australia[28] and Canada[29] have adopted (or apparently adopted)[30] an interesting intermediate position, which does not exempt pre-existing

[26] Cross-Border Insolvency Regulations 2006 (UK), Art 20(3)(a) provides that 'in the case of a debtor other than an individual', the Art 20(1) stay does not affect any right 'to take any steps to enforce security over the debtor's property' if that right would have been exercisable against the debtor company if it had been the subject of a winding-up order under the Insolvency Act 1986 (UK). Insolvency Act 1986 (UK), s 183(1) provides that where a creditor has issued execution against the goods of a company and that company is subsequently wound up, the claimant cannot retain the benefit of the execution unless it has been 'completed' before commencement of the winding up, which means (s 183(3)(a)) 'completed by seizure and sale'. (The Cross-Border Insolvency Regulations 2006 (UK) were made by the Lord Chancellor and the Scottish ministers pursuant to powers conferred by the Insolvency Act 2000 (UK), s 14.)

[27] See, eg, Insolvency (Cross-Border) Act 2006 (NZ), Sch 1, Art 20(2); Insolvency Act 2015 (Ken), s 720, Sch 5, para 22(2).

[28] Corporations Act 2001 (Cth), s 440B provides that secured parties cannot enforce their secured claims while the company is in administration. Corporations Act 2001 (Cth), s 471C provides that the mandatory stay of proceedings under s 471B when a company is being wound up in insolvency does not affect a secured creditor's right to realise or otherwise deal with its security interest.

[29] Companies' Creditors Arrangement Act 1985 (Can), s 11.02(1)(a); Bankruptcy and Insolvency Act 1985 (Can), s 271(3) make the stay subject to the exceptions that would apply in Canadian domestic proceedings. Bankruptcy and Insolvency Act 1985 (Can), ss 69(2)(a), 69.1(2) and 69.3(2) allow proceedings by secured creditors to continue; *Federal Business Development Bank v Quebec* [1988] 1 SCR 1061.

[30] The Australian completion of Art 20(2) has been described as 'beguilingly ambiguous' (see *Kim v Daebo International Shipping Co Ltd* (2015) 232 FCR 275, 277, [7], per Rares J; *Hur v Samsun Logix Corp* (2015) 109 ACSR 137, 141, [21] per Rares J) because it refers simply

secured claims from the mandatory Article 20(1) stay if the insolvent debtor is in administration, but allows them to continue if the insolvent company is in liquidation. That would mean that the proceedings would be stayed if the insolvency proceedings in the FMP were to be some form of rehabilitation, so that the corporate debtor still had some prospect of surviving its insolvency and so still needed 'breathing space', but not if the company were in liquidation without any prospect of survival.

The US did not 'fill in the blank' in Article 20(2) at all, perhaps because it did not enact Article 20 in the form suggested by the Model Law. Chapter 15 of the Bankruptcy Code contains no provision modifying the effect of the mandatory stay upon recognition of an FMP. Indeed, far from referring to a local provision preserving the effect of pre-existing proceedings in relation to secured claims, the Chapter 15 provision mandating a stay upon recognition of an FMP cross-refers to a local provision that specifically applies the mandatory stay to (among other things) 'any act to create, perfect, or enforce against property of the debtor any lien to the extent that such lien secures a claim that arose before the commencement of [the insolvency proceedings].'[31] Thus, the US is to be grouped with Japan and (perhaps) South Africa, as a country providing no 'safe harbour' for pre-existing claims by secured creditors.[32]

However the enacting country 'fills in the blank' in Article 20(2), it is important in the A-I-R permutation to determine which pre-existing admiralty claims count as secured claims, and which do not. It seems beyond doubt that maritime lien claims should be regarded as secured claims. The traditional view of an action to enforce a maritime lien is that it is the perfection of an inchoate right that the claimant has over the liened vessel from the moment the claim arises.[33] The process is often described as 'foreclosure', which highlights the idea that the claimant has a kind of property right or charge over the liened ship, analogous to a mortgage or *hypothec*.[34] Common law countries disagree about what kinds of claim,

to Corporations Act 2001 (Cth), Ch 5: see Cross-Border Insolvency Act 2008 (Cth), s 16(b). Corporations Act 2001 (Cth), Ch 5, has a variety of different stay provisions that affect the position of secured creditors differently at different points in the process of insolvency.

[31] 11 USC § 1520(a)(1); 11 USC § 362(a)(5).

[32] See above nn 25–29.

[33] *Harmer v Bell (The Bold Buccleugh)* (1851) 7 Moo PC 267, 284, 13 Eng Rep 884, 890.

[34] In *The Nestor*, 18 F Cas 9, 13 (CCD Me 1831), Story J described the effect of a maritime lien as a 'tacit hypothecation'.

and how many, give rise to a maritime lien, but they do not disagree about the secured effect of such claims when they do arise.[35]

More difficult is the question whether a non-lien claim enforced by the admiralty procedure of arrest or attachment constitutes a secured claim for these purposes. Admiralty claims that can be enforced *in rem* by arrest of a ship are sometimes described as being secured by a 'statutory lien' because they are conferred by statute and not by the general maritime law, although the claimant's 'lien' attaches only at the time of commencement of proceedings *in rem* and not at the time the claim arose, as a maritime lien does.[36] There is English authority for the proposition that a statutory right to proceed *in rem* does make the claimant a secured creditor for purposes of subsequently opened insolvency proceedings.[37] Recent cases in Australia also support the proposition that an admiralty claimant who has proceeded *in rem* is a secured claimant for purposes of subsequently opened insolvency proceedings.[38] Thus, in those enacting countries that have 'filled in the blank' in Article 20(2) by allowing pre-existing secured claims to continue, notwithstanding recognition of an FMP, both maritime lien and 'statutory lien' claims should not be subject to the mandatory Article 20(1) stay.

If the country of arrest or attachment does not make an Article 20(2) exception to the Article 20(1) mandatory stay for pre-existing secured claims, it must stay any admiralty proceedings (with the possible exception of claims based upon maritime liens, a point that is considered in further detail below in the context of I-R-A) and release any security that has been given in relation to the admiralty claim. Unfortunately, that is likely to have the net effect of making all claimant creditors worse off. If the admiralty proceedings predate the insolvency and recognition (ie, if A comes before I and R), the security is likely to take the form of a letter of undertaking (or guarantee)[39] by the shipowner's liability insurer, which is usually a

[35] The history of the disagreement between the American and English views of maritime liens is considered in M Davies, 'In Defense of Unpopular Virtues: Personification and Ratification' (2000) 75 *Tulane Law Review* 337, 341–50.

[36] *C & CJ Northcote v The Owners of the Henrich Bjorn: The Henrich Bjorn* (1886) 11 App Cas 270, 277.

[37] *Re Aro Co Ltd* [1980] Ch 196.

[38] *Programmed Total Marine Services Pty Ltd v Ship Hako Endeavour* (2014) 229 FCR 563, 569, [22], per Allsop CJ; *Kim v Daebo International Shipping Co Ltd* (2015) 232 FCR 275, 277, [8], per Rares J; *Yakushiji v Daiichi Chuo Kisen Kaisha* [2015] FCA 1170, [20], per Allsop CJ.

[39] Although the Club letter is, in essence, a guarantee, in practice it is usually called a letter of undertaking or LOU: see, eg, *Gabarick v Laurin Maritime (America) Inc*, 54 F.Supp.3d 602, 2014 AMC 2668 (ED La 2014).

mutual Protection and Indemnity Association (a P&I Club). The P&I Club letter of undertaking typically includes an undertaking to pay the plaintiff's claim if the court adjudges the defendant (the debtor) to be liable to pay it.[40] The P&I Club letter is given in consideration of the claimant either releasing the ship in question from arrest or refraining from arresting it,[41] in which case the Club letter substitutes for the ship as the *res* against which the *in rem* admiralty proceedings are brought.[42]

Importantly, the P&I Club letter of undertaking typically takes the form of an agreement between the Club and the claimant,[43] and so it cannot be regarded as an asset of the insolvent debtor shipowner.[44] Although the Club's undertaking to satisfy claims against the shipowner is obviously an asset in one sense, in that it relieves the shipowner of an obligation that it would otherwise have, it is not a fungible, transferable asset that can be realised by anyone other than the admiralty claimant. Among other consequences, this means that the Club undertaking is not an asset that the court could entrust to the foreign representative to be brought into the FMP, under Article 21(1)(e) of the Model Law.[45] Thus, if the (former) admiralty claimant participates in the FMP after the admiralty proceedings in the country of arrest/attachment have been stayed, it thereby increases the number of claims against the insolvent debtor without any corresponding increase in the assets available to satisfy those claims. The admiralty claimant is worse off because it loses the security it previously had for payment of its claim, and the other creditors are worse off because their likely recovery is diminished by the participation of another creditor claiming against the remaining assets of the insolvent debtor. The Club could not be forced to increase the assets of the insolvent debtor in the FMP by transferring its undertaking to satisfy any claims to the country of the FMP, because the

[40] A sample Club letter of undertaking can be seen at: http://www.itic-insure.com/support/publications/article/letter-of-guarantee-2980.

[41] ibid. The ship's P&I Club would not give the usual undertaking if the shipowner is in any kind of insolvency proceedings at the time of the admiralty claimant's arrest or attachment. See the consideration of I-R-A and I-A-R below.

[42] See, eg, *Mackensworth v SS American Merchant*, 28 F 3d 246, 252 (2d Cir 1994) ('In accordance with generally accepted practice, this Letter of Undertaking became the substitute *res* for the value of [plaintiff's] claim'); *Petroleos Mexicanos Refinacion v M/T King A*, 554 F 3d 99, 104, 2009 AMC 67, 74 (3d Cir 2009).

[43] See above, n 40.

[44] E Røsæg, 'Shipowner's Limitation of Liability and Bankruptcy' in *Festschrift für Dieter Martiny zum 70 Geburstag* (Tübingen, Mohr Sieback, 2014) 1201.

[45] See, in the US, 11 USC § 1521(a)(5).

Club's undertaking is given to prevent arrest or attachment of the debtor's assets (usually, but not always, a ship) in the country where arrest or attachment has occurred or has been threatened, an event that can no longer occur if that country has stayed proceedings against the debtor.[46]

Accordingly, it would be unwise for a liquidator/administrator/trustee-in-bankruptcy to seek release of a previously-given Club letter of undertaking when applying for recognition of the debtor's insolvency proceedings as an FMP. Recognition should preclude subsequent action against the debtor's assets by admiralty claimants (that would be the I-R-A permutation, considered below), but it should have no impact on pre-existing admiralty claims secured by a letter of undertaking. When acting as foreign representative of the debtor, the liquidator/administrator/trustee-in-bankruptcy should allow any proceedings secured by a Club letter to continue in the country of arrest or attachment, if he or she is acting in the best interests of all claimants.

B. I-R-A: Insolvency and Recognition Proceedings before Admiralty Proceedings

At first sight, this permutation seems to have the most obvious solution. Any admiralty claimant who arrests or attaches a ship after an order recognising an FMP in the debtor's COMI has already been made in the country of arrest seems clearly to be acting in contravention of the court's recognition order. That is plainly true, with the possible exception of maritime lien claims, which are regarded as being claims against the personified ship itself, rather than claims against the shipowner.

Just as Article 20(2) of the Model Law allows enacting countries to 'fill in the blank' about the continuation of existing claims after recognition of an FMP, notwithstanding the general Article 20(1) stay, so also Article 20(4) allows countries to 'fill in the blank' to allow specified classes of claim to be brought after recognition of an FMP. It provides:

> Paragraph 1 of the present article does not affect the right to request the commencement of a proceeding under [*identify laws of the enacting State relating to insolvency*] or the right to file claims in such a proceeding.

[46] In any event, Club rules typically contain an 'ipso facto' termination of cover in the event of the shipowner's insolvency: see below.

The significance of the nature of a maritime lien claim in this context was considered at some length in *Yu v STX Pan Ocean Co Ltd (South Korea)*, a decision of the Federal Court of Australia.[47] In *Yu*, Buchanan J held that a stay of proceedings under Article 20(1) of the Model Law should not preclude a claimant from subsequently bringing an action *in rem* to enforce a maritime lien, because a maritime lien creditor has a secured interest against the ship itself dating from the moment of the event from which the lien arose, rather than merely an *in personam* right against the ship's owner.[48] Thus, any maritime lien claim against one of the debtor's ships should be allowed to proceed, notwithstanding any order recognising an FMP in relation to that debtor.[49] Accordingly, the *Yu* court held that when an Article 20(1) stay has been ordered upon recognition of an FMP, any warrant for arrest of a ship owned or chartered by the foreign debtor should be considered by a judge of the court, rather than by the Admiralty Registrar, so that the judge can determine whether the interest sought to be vindicated by the action *in rem* is a maritime lien.[50] Since *Yu*, orders of this kind have routinely been made by Australian courts when recognising FMPs of ship operators.[51]

The same maritime lien issue arose, but was not decided, in the United States in *In re Daewoo Logistics Corp*,[52] in which a stevedoring company made a Rule C arrest[53] of a ship chartered, but not owned, by a time charterer (Daewoo) that was in rehabilitation proceedings in its COMI, Korea. The stevedoring company's claim was based on an allegation that it had a maritime lien over the ship for necessaries provided to the ship in the US.

[47] (2013) 223 FCR 189.

[48] ibid at 202–03, [40]–[41]. Cross-Border Insolvency Act 2008 (Cth), s 16 provides that for purposes of Art 20(2), the Art 20(1) stay is subject to the operation of the Corporations Act 2001 (Cth), Ch 5, which includes s 471C, which provides that the mandatory stay in insolvency proceedings does not affect 'a secured creditor's right to realise or otherwise deal with the security interest'. Section 16 does not, in its terms, apply s 471C to Art 20(4) as well as to Art 20(2), as Buchanan J in *Yu* held that it does (see 223 FCR 189, 202–3, [41]), but that appears to be a drafting omission, as the corresponding 'blank' in Art 20(4) would otherwise be left blank.

[49] ibid.

[50] *Yu* (2013) 223 FCR 189, 203, [48], per Buchanan J.

[51] See, eg, *Kim v Daebo International Shipping Co Ltd* (2015) 232 FCR 275; *Hur v Samsun Logix Corp* (2015) 109 ACSR 137; *Yakushiji v Daiichi Chuo Kisen Kaisha* [2015] FCA 1170.

[52] 461 BR 175, 2011 AMC 2617 (Bankr SDNY 2011).

[53] Fed R Civ P Adm Supp C(1)(a) allows an action *in rem* to be brought to enforce a maritime lien. Rule C(3) provides that a warrant for arrest of the ship shall be issued after the complaint has been reviewed by the court.

The ship was released from arrest upon the giving of substitute security. Before the arrest occurred, the US Bankruptcy Court for the Southern District of New York had recognised the Korean rehabilitation proceedings as an FMP, and the insolvent debtor (the time charterer) moved for an order holding the admiralty claimant in violation of the recognition order. The Bankruptcy Court held that the mandatory stays imposed as part of the recognition order terminated at the close of the foreign debtor's rehabilitation, which had occurred before the arrest. That rendered the *Yu*-like question moot, as there were other reasons for concluding that the arresting admiralty claimant had not violated the recognition order, and should be allowed to proceed to enforce its maritime lien. Nevertheless, the *Daewoo* facts provide a nice illustration of one aspect of the relationship between recognition of an FMP and a maritime lien claim. The *Yu* order that has become commonplace in Australia refers to ships 'owned or chartered' by the foreign debtor in a recognised FMP. An enthusiastic supporter of the doctrine of personification would gladly accept the proposition that the personified ship is not the same legal person as the owner that is in insolvency proceedings in its COMI, but even a personification sceptic might find it acceptable to allow a maritime lien claim to continue against a ship time-chartered, but not owned, by the foreign debtor.[54] The plaintiff in *Daewoo* asserted a maritime lien over a ship that was not one of the foreign debtor's assets. There is no obvious reason why such a claim should be paralysed because of the existence of insolvency proceedings involving a time charterer, which has only the commercial disposition of the chartered ship, without any possessory right to it.[55]

In contrast, in *In re Daebo International Shipping Co Ltd*,[56] a stevedoring company and other creditors made Rule B attachments[57] of a ship 'leased' by a foreign debtor whose Korean rehabilitation proceedings had

[54] The time charterer of a ship does not have any property right in the chartered ship; indeed, it does not even have a right to possession, but merely the right to direct the ship's commercial disposition. See, eg, *Cheikh Boutros Selim El-Khoury v Ceylon Shipping Lines Ltd (The Madeleine)* [1967] 2 Lloyd's Rep 224, 238, per Roskill J ('It is, of course, axiomatic that in a time charter … delivery does not import any transfer of possession'); *Forrester v Ocean Marine Indem Co*, 11 F 3d 1213, 1215 (5th Cir 1993)('In a time charter, the vessel owner retains possession and control of the vessel …').

[55] ibid.

[56] 543 BR 47 (Bankr SDNY 2015).

[57] Fed R Civ P Adm Supp B allows attachment of any tangible or intangible property of a defendant who is not 'found within the district' where the attachment is to take place, if the plaintiff's claim falls with the court's admiralty jurisdiction.

been recognised as an FMP by the US Bankruptcy Court for the Southern District of New York. The 'lease' was not a typical demise charterparty, but a sale-and-leaseback arrangement that the foreign debtor had previously entered into with one of its creditors as a means of repaying a debt owed to that creditor.[58] Thus, there were two key differences from the *Daewoo* proceedings just described: (1) it was at least arguable that the ship was one of the foreign debtor's assets;[59] and (2) the admiralty process of seizure was not a purported foreclosure of a maritime lien under Rule C, but attachment of property under Rule B pursuant to an *in personam* claim against the foreign debtor. The Bankruptcy Court quite properly vacated the Rule B attachments, holding that if the ship was one of the foreign debtor's assets, the recognition order precluded seizure of it, and if the ship was not one of the foreign debtor's assets, it could not be attached as property of the defendant under Rule B.

The contrast between *Daewoo* and *Daebo* throws a peculiarly American light on the *Yu* distinction, helping to illustrate where it is controversial and where not. If the foreign debtor is only time charterer of the ships in 'its' fleet, then the order recognising the FMP in the I-R-A permutation should not preclude arrest or attachment of any ships in that fleet, which are clearly not assets of the foreign debtor, which has only the commercial disposition of the ships in question. If the foreign debtor actually owns the ships arrested after the recognition order, the court's response should depend upon the court's attitude to maritime liens and the doctrine of personification, which means that in countries that do not subscribe to the doctrine of personification,[60] the ship should be released from arrest/attachment after a recognition order has been made.

Even from the point of view of a personification sceptic, there seem to be sound reasons for allowing arrest proceedings pursuant to a true maritime lien to continue. All common law countries agree that a maritime lien survives sale of the liened ship, other than a judicial sale.[61] If the foreign

[58] *In re Daebo*, 543 BR at 50.

[59] The ship was listed as one of the foreign debtor's 'tangible assets' in the Korean rehabilitation proceedings; see *In re Daebo*, 543 BR at 50. The claimants argued, without success, that the 'lease' was a sham transaction designed to defraud creditors.

[60] The UK is the leading example of a country that rejects the doctrine of personification, see Davies, 'In Defense of Unpopular Virtues' (2000).

[61] The classic case is *Harmer v Bell (The Bold Buccleugh)* (1851) 7 Moo PC 267, 284; 13 Eng Rep 884, 890. See also, eg, *The Rock Island Bridge*, 73 US (6 Wal) 213, 215 (1867) ('A maritime lien … travels with the thing, wherever that goes, and into whosesoever hands it may pass').

debtor were to buy a ship subject to maritime liens as a result of the previous owner's debts, those pre-existing maritime lien claimants could still proceed against the ship in question. This buttresses the view that, although the ship can quite properly be regarded from one point of view simply as one of the assets of the foreign debtor to be dealt with in the insolvency, it is not absurd to regard it as an independent legal person capable of satisfying its own debts, which may or may not be the same as those of its owner.

C. I-A-R: Admiralty Proceedings During Insolvency Proceedings

In practice, this may perhaps be the most common permutation. Once admiralty creditors learn of insolvency proceedings having been opened by the insolvent shipowner debtor in its COMI, they are usually not slow to proceed in admiralty wherever they can find assets belonging to the debtor, in an attempt to secure their claims without needing to participate in the foreign insolvency. Admiralty claimants in countries that have enacted the Model Law must try to act before an order recognising the shipowner-debtor's insolvency proceedings as an FMP has been made, in order to try to stay ahead of the game, and to get their secured (or arguably secured) claims into court before any prospect of the mandatory Article 20(1) stay being made upon recognition of the FMP – in other words, before they are in I-R-A territory.

If an admiralty claimant arrests or attaches a ship after its owner has opened insolvency proceedings in its COMI, there is every prospect that the arrest or attachment will actually take place, without being pre-empted by the provision of security by the ship's P&I Club (or other liability insurer).[62] This is a key difference from the A-I-R situation, in which the shipowner's P&I Club can be expected to give security for the admiralty claims, given that the shipowner remains (at least technically) solvent at the time when the claims are brought. I-A-R is different. P&I Club Rules typically provide that the opening of insolvency proceedings by the shipowner, even rehabilitation proceedings, automatically terminates the shipowner's cover under the mutual insurance scheme

[62] See above, nn 40–41 and accompanying text.

that is the essence of such associations.[63] Such provisions are often called 'cesser' clauses, although (obviously) they differ from the cesser clauses that typically appear in the very different context of voyage charterparties.[64] In some countries this type of clause is referred to as an 'ipso facto' clause because it purports to take effect automatically upon the shipowner's insolvency (or possibly even before). Rule 29 of the UK P&I Club Rules is typical of this kind of provision:[65]

> (A) An Owner shall forthwith cease to be insured by the Association in respect of any and all ships entered by him or on his behalf upon the happening of any of the following events:
>
> …
>
> ii. Where the Owner is a corporation, a) upon the passing of any resolution for its voluntary winding up (other than voluntary winding up for the purposes of company or group reorganisation), b) upon an order being made for its compulsory winding up, c) upon its dissolution, d) upon a receiver or manager being appointed of all or part of its business or undertaking, e) upon its commencing proceedings under any bankruptcy or insolvency laws to seek protection from its creditors or to reorganise its affairs.

The country of arrest or attachment may or may not recognise the 'ipso facto' effect of the Club's purportedly automatic cancellation of the insurance cover provided to a now-insolvent shipowner.

Some countries, such as the UK, accept that 'cesser' or 'ipso facto' clauses of this kind are effective on the basis that the insurer has the ability to stipulate the terms upon which it will provide cover. In *Belmont Park Investments Pty Ltd v BNY Corporate Trustee Services Ltd*,[66] the UK Supreme Court held that the venerable English 'anti-deprivation rule',[67]

[63] The reason for such a provision is that any doubt about the shipowner's insolvency calls into question its ability to act as a co-insurer, as well as an assured, which is a fundamental aspect of the mutuality concept that underlies P&I insurance.

[64] Cesser clauses in voyage charterparties purport to relieve the charterer of any liability once the cargo has been loaded provided that the shipowner has an effective lien over the cargo for freight, deadfreight and demurrage. See eg, *Overseas Transportation Co v Mineralimportexport (The Sinoe)* [1971] 1 Lloyd's Rep 514, 516 *aff'd* [1972] 1 Lloyd's Rep 201 (CA).

[65] The 2016 version of the UK Club Rules is available at http://www.ukpandi.com/fileadmin/uploads/uk-pi/Latest_Publications/2016_Publications/RULES_ONLY.pdf.

[66] [2012] 1 AC 383.

[67] See, eg, *Ex parte Mackay, Ex parte Brown, In re Jeavons* (1873) LR 8 Ch App 643; *Money Markets International Stockbrokers Ltd v London Stock Exchange Ltd* [2002] 1 WLR 1150.

which strikes down any provision in a contract vesting property of a debtor in someone else in the event of the debtor's bankruptcy, does not automatically invalidate provisions in executory contracts that take effect upon insolvency. In *Re Pan Ocean Co Ltd*,[68] it was accepted by both parties that an 'ipso facto' termination of a long-term contract of affreightment upon the event of the shipowner's insolvency was valid under English law, the governing law of the contract, notwithstanding the fact that it would have been invalid under Korean law, the law of the shipowner's insolvency. Morgan, J in *Pan Ocean* explained as follows why that outcome was consistent with *Belmont Park*:[69]

> The contractual provisions which were under review in [*Belmont Park*] were triggered by the relevant company filing for Chapter 11 protection in the US Bankruptcy Court. Judge Peck sitting in the US Bankruptcy Court for the Southern District of New York made a declaration that the contractual provisions in question were ineffective because they were in breach of the US Bankruptcy Code. See *Re Lehman Bros Holdings Inc.*, 422 BR 407. Nonetheless, the contractual provisions were governed by English law and the English courts held that they were effective under English law.

In the light of such cases, it seems clear that the 'ipso facto' effect of 'cesser' clauses in P&I Club Rules would most probably be regarded as valid and effective as a matter of English law, even if they were to be regarded as ineffective by the law of the bankrupt shipowner's COMI.

Other countries, such as the US, regard the 'ipso facto' effect of clauses of this kind as invalid, as the *Pan Ocean* court's reference to the *Lehman Brothers* case makes clear.[70] In *In re Probulk, Inc*,[71] the US Bankruptcy Court for the Southern District of New York held emphatically that 'ipso facto' clauses in P&I Club Rules were rendered invalid by the US Bankruptcy Code, with the result that the insurance rights of insolvent shipowners continued after their petition for bankruptcy, notwithstanding the provisions of the Club Rules. The court said:[72]

> The Clubs' argument … rests on a so-called 'cesser' clause in their contracts, providing that insurance automatically terminates in the event that a member

[68] [2014] *Business Law Review* 1041.
[69] ibid at [17].
[70] See generally, A Coles-Bjerre, 'Ipso Facto: The Pattern of Assumable Contracts in Bankruptcy' (2010) 40 *New Mexico Law Review* 77.
[71] 407 BR 56 (Bankr SDNY 2009).
[72] ibid at 60–61.

> of the Club (the insured) passes 'a resolution for a voluntary winding up.' They claim that this clause results in a termination of coverage even before a bankruptcy or insolvency filing, apparently recognising (without conceding) that the US Bankruptcy Code may invalidate certain forfeitures that result from the act of filing a petition under Title 11. The Bankruptcy Code is not so easily evaded. There is no question that in the circumstances at bar their insurance rights constituted property of the debtors … Section 541(c)(1)(B) of the Bankruptcy Code[73] provides, with exceptions not applicable here, that an interest of the debtor in property becomes property of the estate notwithstanding any provision in an agreement … or applicable non-bankruptcy law … that is conditioned on the insolvency or financial condition of the debtor … There is thus no question that the debtors' insurance rights continued notwithstanding the Clubs' attempt to deem them terminated as a consequence of the resolutions of the boards of directors of the debtors authorizing a bankruptcy filing and the prospective appointment of a trustee or custodian.

If the country of arrest or attachment takes the same view as the US, the P&I Club may be restrained by court order from cancelling coverage, and ordered to provide security according to the terms of the ship's entry with the Club. That is what happened in *In re Probulk, Inc.* If that does occur, the situation will be the same as under A-I-R, as the security given by the Club is 'property of the debtor' only in the country of arrest or attachment, and cannot be transferred to the FMP.[74] For that reason, it would be in the interests of all creditors for their representative to pursue enforcement of the insurance contract in the country of arrest or attachment, rather than trying to repatriate all assets to the FMP, as the A-I-R situation shows.

Among common law countries, the only other countries that expressly nullify ipso facto clauses are Barbados, Canada and New Zealand (in limited cases).[75] Among civil law countries, ipso facto clauses are nullified (at least in some cases) in Belgium, Finland, France, Norway, Poland, Portugal, Sweden and Spain.[76]

On the other hand, if the country of arrest or attachment acknowledges the 'ipso facto' effect of the Club's cancellation of cover immediately upon the shipowner's opening of the insolvency proceedings or even before, as the UK does, it is likely that the ship will actually be seized pursuant

[73] 11 USC § 541(c)(1)(B).

[74] See above, nn 43–46 and accompanying text.

[75] PR Wood, *Principles of International Insolvency*, 2nd edn (London, Sweet & Maxwell, 2007), para 16-030.

[76] ibid.

to judicial process in the country where the admiralty claimants proceed, unless the insolvent shipowner can somehow find some other security (such as a bond or bank guarantee) to provide in order to avert the judicial seizure. In those circumstances, the country where the ship has been seized must decide whether to release the ship once the recognition order is made, or to allow the admiralty claims to proceed on the basis that they are secured claims that were made before the order recognising the FMP was made. As we have already seen in relation to the A-I-R permutation, some countries allow pre-existing secured claims to survive the recognition of an FMP under the Model Law, but others do not.

Thus, the I-A-R permutation is likely to produce a 'race to the courthouse' in those countries that allow pre-existing secured claims to continue notwithstanding recognition of the FMP. Once insolvency proceedings are opened, creditors would be encouraged (if they needed any encouragement) to secure their claims by arrest or attachment wherever they found one of the debtor's ships. Conversely, the foreign representative might move quickly to seek recognition pre-emptively in as many Model Law countries as possible, so as to put the proceedings into I-R-A mode rather than I-A-R mode. Some Model Law countries, such as Japan, have made legislative provision to deal with that possibility, providing that if there are insolvency proceedings that may constitute an FMP and recognition proceedings are pending, any judicial seizure may be put on hold until the recognition occurs.[77] That approach may even be taken where there is no specific statutory authorization to do so, on grounds of judicial economy. For example, in *Evridiki Navigation Inc v Sanko SS Co*,[78] the US District Court for the District of Maryland ordered release of a ship that had been seized by admiralty claimants even before the making of an order recognising the shipowner's insolvency proceedings as an FMP, because 'it appears inevitable that those claims [ie, the admiralty claims] will never be adjudicated in this Court.'[79]

If the admiralty claimant wins the 'race to the courthouse' by arresting or attaching the debtor's ship before an order recognising a foreign FMP

[77] Act of Recognition of and Assistance for Foreign Insolvency Proceedings (No 129 of 2000), Art 25(2) ('Where a petition for recognition of foreign insolvency proceedings is filed, the court may issue a stay order under the provisions of the preceding paragraph even before issuing an order on the petition.').

[78] 880 F Supp 2d 666, 2012 AMC 1817 (D Md 2012).

[79] ibid at 674.

has been made, and if that claim is allowed to continue, notwithstanding the later recognition order, the country of arrest/attachment would retain custody of the ship, at least initially. In those circumstances, it might well be best for the court in the arresting country to exercise its discretion under the Model Law, Article 21(1)(e),[80] to entrust the seized ship to the foreign representative so that it can be treated as an asset for the benefit of all creditors, not merely those who seized it by judicial process. Article 21(2) provides that such an order can only be made where it is 'in the interest of the creditors' to do so.[81] Here, 'the creditors' appears to mean local creditors, not all creditors. Although the Guide to Enactment of the UNCITRAL Model Law says that Article 21(2) is designed to protect 'local interests', meaning the interests of 'local creditors',[82] it also says, in relation to Article 22, that it is not advisable to take only the interests of local creditors into account when considering the exercise of discretionary relief under Article 21.[83] Thus, for example, the US enactment of Article 21 requires the court to be satisfied that 'the interests of creditors in the United States are sufficiently protected',[84] but the US enactment of Article 22 provides that discretionary relief under Article 21 may be given 'only if the interests of the creditors and other interested entities, including the debtor, are sufficiently protected'.[85] In *SNP Boat Service, SA v Hotel le Saint James*,[86] the US Bankruptcy Court for the Southern District of Florida harmonised the meaning of those phrases in the following way (emphases in the original):[87]

> Thus, according to the Model Law, a bankruptcy court *must* be satisfied that *local creditors*' interests are 'sufficiently protected' before allowing a foreign representative to distribute property in a foreign proceeding, and though not an express requirement, is *not precluded* from satisfying itself that *foreign creditors*' interests are "sufficiently protected" before allowing a foreign representative to distribute property in a foreign proceeding.

This interpretation points in the direction of a 'reciprocal comity' solution, taking into account the interests of both the country of arrest/attachment

[80] See above, n 45.
[81] See, eg, 11 USC § 1521(b), the enactment of this Model Law provision in the US.
[82] UNCITRAL Guide to Enactment (n 19), para 192.
[83] ibid at para 198.
[84] 11 USC § 1521(b).
[85] 11 USC § 1522(a).
[86] 407 BR 56 (Bankr SDNY 2009).
[87] 483 BR 776, 784 (Bankr SD Fla 2012).

and the country of the FMP. The most obvious way in which the country of arrest/attachment can satisfy itself that the interests of local creditors are protected is to take steps to ensure that the FMP country should continue to recognise the secured status of the pre-existing admiralty claims given by the arresting/attaching country after the asset has been entrusted to the creditors' representative.

For example, in *In re Atlas Shipping A/S*,[88] a Danish shipowner was declared bankrupt by a court in Denmark, the shipowner's COMI. Several creditors then used the admiralty procedure of Rule B attachment in the United States to attach funds of the Danish shipowner in New York banks.[89] The case thus stood in the I-A-R posture, because the plaintiff's seizure of the debtor's funds in New York occurred before recognition of the Danish bankruptcy proceedings as an FMP. After the US Bankruptcy Court for the Southern District of New York recognised the Danish proceedings as an FMP under Chapter 15 of the US Bankruptcy Code,[90] the Danish foreign representative asked for an order vacating the Rule B attachments and entrusting the attached funds to her under the US enactment of Article 21 of the Model Law,[91] so that she could remove those funds from the US and make them subject to administration by the bankruptcy court in Denmark. The court turned the funds over to the Danish foreign representative, noting:[92]

> The foreign representative acknowledged … that if the relief is granted, it is without prejudice to creditors' rights, if any, to assert in the Danish bankruptcy court their rights to the previously garnished funds. This is sufficient protection to the creditors here.

The court acknowledged, however, that: 'It will then be up to the [Danish] court to determine what benefit, if any, [these creditors] should enjoy from having obtained' the Rule B attachments in the US.[93]

Reciprocal comity would require the country of the FMP to grant the admiralty claimants the same secured status in the bankruptcy proceedings that they obtained in the country of arrest/attachment. The country of

[88] 404 BR 726, 2009 AMC 1150 (Bankr SDNY 2009).
[89] See above, n 58.
[90] 11 USC § 1515.
[91] 11 USC § 1521.
[92] 404 BR 726, 742 (Bankr SDNY 2009).
[93] ibid at 747.

arrest/attachment would act with comity by respecting the primacy of the insolvency proceedings (the FMP) in the country of the debtor's COMI, but the country of the FMP would respect the secured status legitimately conferred by the admiralty law of the country of arrest/attachment.

In order for the FMP country to take that view, at least in relation to maritime liens, it would have to take the position that the conferral of maritime liens is a matter of substance, not procedure, so that recognition of foreign maritime liens is governed by the law governing the underlying dispute (the *lex causae*), not the law of the forum (the *lex fori*). Courts in Canada,[94] Germany (at least in cases not entirely within the EU),[95] Australia,[96] and, possibly, China,[97] take the view that recognition of foreign maritime liens should be determined by the *lex causae* – ie, by the relevant foreign law. Courts in the UK,[98] Singapore[99] and Croatia[100] take the view that the security for a claim, even a claim governed by foreign law, is a matter of procedure to be determined by the *lex fori.* If the country of the FMP insolvency proceedings adopts the latter position, the country of arrest should not release the arrest or attached property to the debtor's foreign representative without an undertaking by that representative to give the admiralty claimants the same secured status in the FMP as they would have if the admiralty proceedings were allowed to continue in the country of arrest/attachment.

Even if the country of the FMP recognises maritime liens from other countries as substantive rights giving the claimants secured status in the insolvency proceedings, it must make a further determination about whether to give those secured claims the same priority that they would

[94] *Todd Shipyards Corp v Altema Compania Maritima SA (The Ioannis Daskelelis)* [1974] SCR 1248; *Marlex Petroleum Inc v Ship Har Rai* [1987] 1 SCR 47; *Holt Cargo Systems Inc v ABC Containerline NV* [2001] 3 SCR 907.

[95] *Einführungsgesetz zum Bürgerlichen Gesetzbuche* (EGBGB), Art 45(2).

[96] *Reiter Petroleum Inc v Ship Sam Hawk* [2015] FCA 1005.

[97] Law of the People's Republic of China on the Laws Applicable to Foreign-related Civil Relations (2010), Art 37 provides that in the absence of any choice by the parties, rights *in rem* in movable property are governed by 'the law of the place where the property is located when the legal fact occurs', which appears to be the law of the place of arrest or attachment.

[98] *Bankers Trust International Ltd v Todd Shipyards Corp (The Halcyon Isle)* [1981] AC 221.

[99] *The Andres Bonifacio* [1993] 3 SLR(R) 71; *Precious Shipping Public Co Ltd v OW Bunker Far East (Singapore) Pte Ltd* [2015] 4 SLR 1229.

[100] Reply of the Croatian Maritime Law Association to the Comité Maritime International's International Working Group on Cross-Border Insolvency Questionnaire, Question 15, to be found at http://www.comitemaritime.org/Cross-Border-Insolvency/0,27129,112932,00.html.

enjoy under the law of the arrest/attachment. As a practical matter, it seems unavoidable to conclude that matters of priority, as opposed to recognition of secured status, must be determined by the *lex fori* of the FMP.[101] To give foreign secured claims the same priority that they enjoy under the law that confers their secured status might lead to insoluble conundrums, if each of several recognized *leges causae* gives a different priority to secured claims of particular kinds. Reciprocal comity requires the country of the FMP to recognise the legitimacy of the secured status conferred upon the admiralty claims by the law of the country of arrest/attachment. It does not, and arguably cannot, require the country of the FMP to give the same priority among secured claims that the country of arrest/attachment would do.

For example, if admiralty proceedings are brought by a necessaries supplier in Country A, which would give such a claim priority over the claim of a mortgagee,[102] and a claim is brought by the ship's mortgagee in Country B, which would give the mortgagee's claim priority over the claim of a necessaries supplier,[103] Country FMP cannot apply the priority rules of both *leges causae* even if it recognises the liens conferred by the laws of Countries A and B, because those two laws indicate directly opposite results, leading the FMP court into an impasse that could only be resolved by applying its own law (the *lex fori*).[104] Admittedly, this suggestion provides no solution for the situation where the *lex fori* of the FMP does not have priority rules for the two claims in question, perhaps because it would not regard either type of claim as secured, but some version of a *lex fori* seems unavoidable.

In terms of judicial economy, it would make sense for the court in the arresting country to make a ruling about the secured status of the claimant's claim (and, perhaps, its priority) when ordering that the arrested

[101] See M Davies and K Lewins, 'Foreign maritime liens: should they be recognised in Australian courts?' (2002) 76 *Australian Law Journal* 775.

[102] For example, US law gives a maritime lien for necessaries provided in the US priority over a preferred mortgage is subordinate to a maritime lien: see 46 USC §31326(b)(2).

[103] For example, English law gives a mortgagee's claim priority over the claim of a necessaries supplier. See DC Jackson, *Enforcement of Maritime Claims*, 4th edn (London, Informa, 2013), [23.155].

[104] This is the practice in the US, where the ranking of all maritime liens is determined by applying the law of the forum (*lex fori*), even though recognition of foreign liens is generally regarded as a matter of substance, as in *Loginter SA v M/V Nobility*, 177 F Supp 2d 411 (D Md, 2001). See *Potash Co of Canada Ltd v M/V Raleigh*, 361 F Supp 120 (DC Canal Zone 1973); *Rayon y Celanese Peruana SA v M/V PHGH*, 471 F Supp 1363 (D Ala 1979); *Rainbow Line, Inc v M/V Tequila*, 341 F Supp 459 (SDNY, 1972), *aff'd* 480 F 2d 1024 (2nd Cir 1973).

ship (or other attached property) be released to the foreign representative under Article 21 of the Model Law. If the court of the FMP is prepared to recognise the secured status of the admiralty claimants' claims (either by applying the *lex causae* to the recognition of foreign maritime liens, or because of an undertaking by the foreign representative), it would nevertheless still be helpful for the court in the country of arrest/attachment to describe the nature of the security associated with the claim and (possibly) its priority. Such a ruling could be made part of the arresting/attaching court's order entrusting the arrested ship or other attached property to the foreign representative under Article 21 of the Model Law. In the absence of such a ruling, the court of the FMP would have to make its own decision about the foreign law of the *lex causae*, which seems unnecessary given that a court familiar with that law must make a prior order in order for the asset to be released so that it can form part of the asset distribution in the FMP.

When both the country of the FMP and the country of arrest/attachment are within the EU, the applicable law is dictated by the Insolvency Regulation (and, with effect from 26 June 2017, the Recast Insolvency Regulation), which provide that the law applicable to insolvency proceedings is the law of the country where the proceedings were opened (the *lex concursus*),[105] except in the case of rights *in rem*, which are not affected by the opening of insolvency proceedings, and so are governed by the law of the country conferring them (the *lex causae*).[106] The English text of Article 5(2) of the Regulation (Article 8(2) of the Recast Regulation) provides that rights *in rem*:

> [S]hall, in particular, mean:
>
> (a) the right to dispose of assets or have them disposed of and to obtain satisfaction from the proceeds of or income from those assets, in particular by virtue of a lien or a mortgage;
> (b) the exclusive right to have a claim met, in particular a right guaranteed by a lien in respect of the claim or by assignment of the claim by way of a guarantee;
> (c) the right to demand assets from, and/or to require restitution by, anyone having possession or use of them contrary to the wishes of the party so entitled;
> (d) a right *in rem* to the beneficial use of assets.

[105] Insolvency Regulation, Art 4; Recast Insolvency Regulation, Art 7.
[106] Insolvency Regulation, Art 5; Recast Insolvency Regulation, Art 8.

Article 5(2)/8(2) has different shades of meaning in the 23 other official languages of the EU, with the result that it is difficult to be certain whether a claim pursued by arrest or attachment can constitute a right *in rem* for purposes of the Regulation, despite the ostensible uniformity of the provisions in the Regulation.[107] Thus, there may even be some doubt about whether a claim secured by a maritime lien is a right *in rem* for purposes of Article 5(2)/8(2).[108] It seems unlikely, however, that arrest or attachment of a ship to secure non-lien claims will be regarded as a right *in rem* for these purposes, and so such claims will fall to be determined by the *lex concursus* in an FMP within the EU in an intra-EU case, depriving the admiralty claimants of any priority they might have obtained by arresting or attaching the debtor's ship before insolvency proceedings were opened.[109] If that is the case, as it seems to be, the 'reciprocal comity' approach advocated in this article has no prospect of success in relation to cases entirely within the EU.

III. Conclusion

Comity should not be a one-way street. If the courts of the country of arrest/attachment defer to the superior jurisdictional claims of the court of the FMP, as comity and the 'golden thread' of universalism demand that they should, they should be entitled to expect a reciprocal degree of respect from the courts of the FMP, which should recognise claims of security legitimately granted by the laws of the country of arrest/attachment.

In the A-I-R permutation, the country of arrest/attachment should respect the existence of the FMP in another country by staying the existing proceedings in its courts, but the country of the FMP (and the debtor invoking insolvency protection in that country) should respect the fact that the country of arrest/attachment may choose to preserve the priority of claims secured (legitimately, by its law) before the insolvency proceedings were opened. In the I-R-A permutation, if the country of arrest/attachment

[107] G Berlingieri, 'Defaulting Shipowners and the Regulation of their Insolvency Status', available at http://www.comitemaritime.org/Uploads/Cross%20Border/Defaulting%20shipowners%20and%20the%20regulation%20of%20their%20insolvency%20status,%20by%20Giorgio%20Berlingieri.doc.

[108] ibid.

[109] ibid.

recognises maritime liens as effective against the personified ship itself, the country of the FMP should respect that fact. In the I-A-R permutation, the courts of the country of arrest/attachment should concede jurisdictional primacy to the courts of the FMP, but should be entitled to demand, in return, that those courts grant reciprocal respect to the secured status granted by arrest or attachment in the country where admiralty proceedings were brought.

The middle way of reciprocal comity requires mutual respect, not enforced acquiescence or self-abnegation on the part of either country. It can be achieved without amending any of the existing international instruments relating to cross-border insolvency, such as the UNCITRAL Model Law or the EU's Recast Insolvency Regulation. All that is needed is for courts to understand the imperatives of both insolvency law and admiralty law, which are not necessarily as incompatible as they may seem at first.

2

Singapore: Common Law Relevance in a Civil Law Asia

LAWRENCE TEH*

I. Introduction

Over the past few years, Asia's economy has grown in leaps and bounds. There is also greater economic integration amongst the countries in Asia. With the increase in economic activities and cross-border trades, there will be a corresponding increase in transnational commercial disputes.

As Singapore strives to position itself as a legal hub within Asia, it must ensure that its legal system remains relevant and attractive as a dispute resolution forum. In its quest to remain attractive and relevant, Singapore has to address the high opportunity costs that arise out of the differences in substantive and procedural laws within the region. These opportunity costs include the need to invest further resources to navigate unfamiliar foreign legal systems, reliance on unfamiliar foreign legal counsels and the potential difficulty in enforcing foreign judgments.[1]

This chapter studies how Singapore, as a common law country, has sought to remain relevant and attractive as a dispute resolution forum in Asia, through 'the convergence of laws and jurisprudence'.

* Partner, Dentons Rodyk & Davidson LLP.

[1] S Menon CJ, 'Shaping the Future of Dispute Resolution Improving Access to Justice', Global Pound Conference Series 2016, Singapore, 17 March 2016, para 13, available at www.supremecourt.gov.sg/news/speeches.

II. Asia in Perspective

Asia's economy is growing at an astonishing rate. Since 2009, foreign direct investments (FDI) into Asia have grown by nearly 30 per cent.[2] In 2013, Asia's gross domestic product (GDP) grew faster than the rest of the world, by more than six per cent.[3] Asia also accounted for more than one-third of global trade and FDI in the same year.[4] This growth is not driven solely by China and India alone. The Association of Southeast Asian Nations (ASEAN) is the third largest economic bloc in Asia and the seventh largest in the world.[5] Between 1993 and 2013, ASEAN's trade has increased six-fold.[6] In 2013, ASEAN economies achieved a combined growth of five per cent, while the estimated global economic growth was less than three per cent.

This economic growth in Asia is expected to continue with greater economic integration within Asia and with its key trading partners. China has laid down plans to develop a 'New Silk Road' (otherwise known as 'One Belt One Road Initiative'), which would connect countries in Asia, North Africa and East Africa. The New Silk Road also aims to link the East Asian Economic Zone with the European Economic Zone.[7] Alongside the New Silk Road, China has also established the Asian Infrastructure Investment Bank (AIIB) to enhance economic integration.[8] On 31 December 2015, ASEAN established the ASEAN Economic Community (AEC). The aim of the AEC is to unify ASEAN's economies into a 'single market and production base so as to facilitate the seamless movement of goods, services, investment, capital and skilled labour within ASEAN'.[9] On 4 February 2016, the Trans-Pacific Partnership Agreement (TPP)

[2] K Shanmugam (Minister for Law), 'Opening Speech', In-House Counsel World Summit 2014, Singapore, 3 June 2014, para 7, available at www.mlaw.gov.sg/content/minlaw/en/news/speeches.html.

[3] K Shanmugam (Minister for Law and Foreign Affairs), 'Speech', International Bar Association 4th Asia Pacific Regional Forum Conference, Singapore, 19 March 2015, para 8, available at www.mlaw.gov.sg/content/minlaw/en/news/speeches.html.

[4] United Nations Conference on Trade and Development Press Release on 24 June 2014, available at http://unctad.org/en/pages/PressRelease.aspx.

[5] ibid para 13.

[6] ibid para 16.

[7] Menon, 'Shaping the Future of Dispute Resolution' (2016) para 7.

[8] Menon (n 1) para 9.

[9] Menon (n 1) para 6.

was finalised and agreed upon. The TPP does not merely remove tariffs, but will affect intellectual property rights, technical barriers to trade and competition policies.[10] A Regional Comprehensive Economic Partnership (RCEP) is also expected to be concluded soon between ASEAN and its free trade partners. The RCEP aims to broaden and deepen ASEAN's engagement with Australia, China, India, Japan, Korea and New Zealand, and to create a 16-party free-trade bloc in the Asia-Pacific region (comprising over 45 per cent of the world's population and one-third of the world's current annual GDP).[11]

While the Asian economy is booming, the heterogeneity of laws in Asia stands as a considerable barrier to doing business in Asia.[12] This heterogeneity of laws in Asia is largely caused by the region's history as colonies of various colonial masters, inheriting the legal tradition and substantive law from the colonial masters. As a result of this lack of common colonial roots and legal tradition, it is hard to harmonise the commercial laws in Asia in the same manner in which the EU has harmonised commercial laws in Europe.[13]

III. Staying Relevant in Asia

In order to benefit from the growing Asian economy, Singapore has sought to develop a robust and efficient legal system and to take advantage of its convenient location to establish itself as a key neutral venue for resolution of transnational commercial disputes.[14] Singapore has tried to cater for and satisfy all the needs of today's transnational commercial disputes

[10] Menon (n 1) para 10.

[11] S Menon, CJ, 'Keynote Address', Doing Business Across Asia – Legal Convergence in an Asian Century, Singapore, 21 January 2016, para 24, available at www.supremecourt.gov.sg/news/speeches; S Chong, JA, 'The Judicial Insolvency Network: A Ready Response in an Imperfect World', paper presented at the World Enforcement Conference, 22 January 2019, para 7, available at www.supremecourt.gov.sg/docs.

[12] Menon, 'Keynote Address' (2016) paras 6 and 7.

[13] S Menon CJ, 'Keynote Address: Transnational Commercial Law – Realities, Challenges and A Call for Meaningful Convergence', 26th LAWASIA Conference and the 15th Biennial Conference of Chief Justices of Asia and the Pacific, Singapore, 28 October 2013, para 40, available at www.supremecourt.gov.sg/news/speeches.

[14] S Menon CJ, 'Building Sustainable Mediation Programmes – A Singapore Perspective' [2015] *Asian Journal of Mediation* 1, para 64.

by lowering the opportunity costs for parties seeking dispute resolution in Singapore. This has been done primarily in two ways: legal convergence and jurisprudence convergence.

A. Legal Convergence

The Honourable Chief Justice of Singapore, Sundaresh Menon, has suggested that legal convergence can be achieved in three ways:[15] convergence of laws on recognition and enforcement of foreign judgments or arbitration awards; convergence of commercial dispute resolution processes; and convergence of substantive business laws.

i. Convergence of Laws on Recognition and Enforcement of Foreign Judgments or Arbitration Awards

Convergence of laws on recognition and enforcement of foreign judgments or arbitration awards can be easily achieved. This objective relates mainly to the procedural laws of the enforcing country and does not require a reconciliation of different substantive laws in order to achieve convergence.[16] However, enforcement of a foreign judgment or arbitration award is still one of biggest problems faced in transnational commerce and dispute resolution today. In this regard, Singapore has taken steps to assist in the enforcement of foreign judgments or arbitration awards in Singapore. Concomitantly, Singapore has also increased the enforceability of judgments and arbitration awards made in Singapore in foreign courts through various conventions and treaties.

Singapore is a signatory of the New York Convention on Recognition and Enforcement of Foreign Arbitral Awards ('New York Convention'). As a signatory state of the New York Convention, a reciprocal system of recognition and enforcement of foreign and Singaporean arbitration awards is in place between Singapore and other signatory states.[17] Beyond the New York Convention, Singapore has also adopted the United Nations

[15] 'Keynote Address' (n 11) paras 10–14.

[16] Menon (n 11) para 11.

[17] Article II of the New York Convention on Recognition and Enforcement of Foreign Arbitral Awards.

Commission on International Trade Law (UNCITRAL) Model Law on International Commercial Arbitration ('Model Law') through the International Arbitration Act.[18] The International Arbitration Act also provides for the recognition and enforcement foreign arbitration awards as if they were awards made in Singapore.[19]

More recently, the Hague Convention on Choice of Court Agreement[20] ('Hague Convention') was agreed upon, to which Singapore is a signatory.[21] The Hague Convention aims to ease the process of recognising and enforcing foreign judgments. Prior to the Hague Convention, foreign judgments were enforced in Singapore either through the Reciprocal Enforcement of Foreign Judgment Act[22] (REFJA) or the Reciprocal Enforcement of Commonwealth Judgment Act[23] (RECJA). Although these Acts provided means for foreign judgments to be recognised, there were limitations to the type of foreign judgments which may be given recognition. First, only judgments from countries whose courts recognise and enforce Singapore judgments[24] and judgments from the UK[25] can be enforced. Second, these judgments must be for the payment of a sum of money as compensation or damages to the injured party ('money judgments').[26]

As a result of the Hague Convention, recognition and enforcement of foreign judgments by Singapore courts is now less restrictive. Being a signatory state to the Hague Convention, judgments made in Singapore would likewise be enforced in other signatory states.[27] In line with its obligations under the Hague Convention, Singapore Parliament recently passed the Choice of Court Agreements Act 2016.[28] Once the Choice of Court

[18] Section 3 of International Arbitration Act (Cap 143A, Rev Ed 2002).

[19] Section 29 of International Arbitration Act (Cap 143A, Rev Ed 2002).

[20] Convention on Choice of Court Agreements done at The Hague on 30 June 2005.

[21] Singapore became a signatory to the Hague Convention on 25 March 2015.

[22] Reciprocal Enforcement of Foreign Judgment Act (Cap 265, Rev Ed 2001).

[23] Reciprocal Enforcement of Commonwealth Judgment Act (Cap 264, Rev Ed 1985).

[24] Section 3 of Reciprocal Enforcement of Foreign Judgment Act (Cap 265, Rev Ed 2001); Section 5 of Reciprocal Enforcement of Commonwealth Judgment Act (Cap 264, Rev Ed 1985).

[25] Section 3 of Reciprocal Enforcement of Commonwealth Judgment Act (Cap 264, Rev Ed 1985).

[26] Section 2 of Reciprocal Enforcement of Foreign Judgment Act (Cap 265, Rev Ed 2001); Section 2 of Reciprocal Enforcement of Commonwealth Judgment Act (Cap 264, Rev Ed 1985).

[27] Above n 19, Art 8.

[28] Bill 14 of 2016, an Act to give effect to the Convention on Choice of Court Agreements done at the Hague on 30 June 2005 and for connected purposes, and to make related

Agreements Act 2016 comes into force, Singapore courts will recognise and enforce all foreign judgments, regardless of whether the foreign court afforded reciprocity in its treatment of Singapore judgments.[29] In addition, foreign judgments that are recognised and enforceable in Singapore's courts are no longer restricted to only money judgments, also including any final decision on the merits, consent judgments or a judgment given by default.[30]

Initiatives have also been taken to achieve convergence with countries that have not ratified the Hague Convention. One recent example of this is the entry into a Memorandum of Guidance on Recognition and Enforcement of Money Judgments in Commercial cases in August 2018 between the Supreme Court of Singapore and the Supreme People's Court of the People's Republic of China. Although this memorandum is not binding, it provides guidelines on how a Singapore Court judgment may be recognised and enforced in the courts of the People's Republic of China, and vice versa.[31]

A draft International Convention on Foreign Judicial Sale of Ships and their Recognition ('Draft Convention') is also currently in the pipelines. The Draft Convention is the brainchild of Professor Henry Li of China and a work product of the Comité Maritime International (CMI). The main difficulty faced in a judicial sale of ships lies predominantly in the registration of the ship by the purchaser at its chosen port of registry. In order for a purchaser of a ship pursuant to a judicial sale to register the ship in another port of registry, the purchaser will first have to obtain a certificate of deletion in the original port of registry. However, some jurisdictions do not recognise foreign judicial sale of ships as capable of giving clean title to the purchaser. As such, they may refuse to issue a certificate of deletion to the purchaser.[32] This would inevitably prevent the purchaser from

amendments to certain other Acts, 2nd Session, 13th Parliament, 2016, (as passed by Parliament on 14 May 2016 and assented to by the President).

[29] ibid, cl 13.

[30] ibid, cl 2.

[31] Memorandum of Guidance dated 31 August 2018 between the Supreme People's Court of the People's Republic of China and the Supreme Court of Singapore on recognition and enforcement of money judgments in commecial cases, available at www.supremecourt.gov.sg/docs.

[32] See *The Acrux* [1962] 1 Lloyd's Rep 405; *The Norsland*, 1972 CarswellNat 18, FC 430; *The Paz*, 1984 (3) SA 261 (N); *The Galaxias* [1988] LMLN No 240 at 2; *The Great Eagle*, 1994 (1) SA 65 (C); *The Katerina*, 2004 [KG04/912P], LJN:BB 4789, Schip & Schade 2007, 108; *The Union* [2005] Jin Hai Fa Shang Chu Zi No 401 – Judgment of the Tianjin Maritime

registering the ship in the chosen port of registry. Further, some jurisdictions require a legal opinion on the effect of a judicial sale to satisfy the registry that the purchaser of a ship from a judicial sale has a clean title to the ship before it would issue a certificate of deletion.[33] The Draft Convention thus aims to provide uniformity of the laws on recognising foreign judicial sale of ships and to enforce the principle that a purchaser of a ship from a judicial sale obtains clean title from the court. CMI has adopted the Draft Convention and is currently awaiting the International Maritime Organisation's (IMO) decision on whether the Draft Convention is to be adopted as an international treaty. Singapore has yet to indicate if it would support this Draft Convention. However, given Singapore's goal of becoming a legal hub in the region, it is important that it supports and ratifies the Draft Convention.

With all these measures in place, Singapore has enhanced the enforceability of judgments or arbitration awards obtained in Singapore in other foreign courts. This will help make Singapore more attractive as a dispute resolution forum for cross-border disputes in general.[34]

ii. Convergence of Commercial Dispute Resolution Processes

The traditional courtroom litigation is no longer the first port of call for disputes that have an international twist to them. This is partly because transnational commercial disputes are unlike the typical run-of-the-mill disputes.

Transnational commercial disputes usually involve parties that come from different cultures and legal systems and have different approaches to dispute resolution. Thus, litigation cannot be the only default option, and Singapore would need a flexible and option-laden model where parties are well placed to choose the ideal mode of dispute resolution. Recognising this, Singapore has sought to equip its legal system with a diversified range of dispute resolution options. The focus is on the provision 'appropriate

Court; *The Ahmet Bey*, 2009 Civil Action No 07-3518, United States District Court, E.D. Pennsylvannia; *The Sam Dragon* [2012] JEHC 240.

[33] Members of the Maritime Law Association of Singapore have encountered situations where the registrar required a legal opinion on the effects of a judicial sale ordered by Singapore courts to be satisfied whether the purchaser received clean title from the sale (such as Greece).

[34] Parliamentary Debates Singapore: Official Report, vol 94 at col 1158 at 2:55pm (14 April 2016).

dispute resolution' as opposed to alternative dispute resolution.[35] The ideal system would be one that is customised to each individual case, keeping in mind the subject matter, the parties and the desired outcomes.[36]

In 1991, Singapore started the Singapore International Arbitration Centre (SIAC). Arbitration is a useful alternative to courtroom litigation as it provides for flexibility in the procedure and parties can decide on the procedural rules that govern the arbitration. For instance, parties can adopt the International Bar Association (IBA) Rules on the Taking of Evidence in International Arbitration, which is a combination of civil law and common law rules on evidence. Parties are also free to choose their representation and are not required to necessarily be represented by lawyers. Finally, parties are also free to choose foreign law or non-national law (eg mercantile law) as the governing law of their dispute. One of the reasons why Singapore is the third most preferred venue for arbitration in the world today[37] is due to the achievements of the SIAC.

In 2015, the Singapore International Mediation Centre (SIMC) was formed. Singapore recognised that, in Asia, bringing a party to court to litigate a dispute is not the conventional response to a dispute. Harmony and amicable resolution are highly valued in the dispute resolution process and is attractive for parties who desire to continue business relationships.[38] In many Asian cultures, disputes are usually resolved with the help of a respected member of the society. Thus, the aim of SIMC is to provide a less costly and less adversarial method of resolving disputes, and to promote the harmonious settlement of disputes. To further strengthen the mediation framework and to develop Singapore into a centre for international commercial mediation, the Ministry of Law is also in the midst of drafting a Mediation Bill. The key features of this proposed Mediation Bill include: (i) the recording of mediated settlement agreements as an order of court; (ii) confidentiality of mediation proceedings; (iii) stay of court proceedings whilst parties enter mediation; and (iv) participation of foreign mediators and foreign-qualified counsel in mediation sessions.

[35] Menon (n 1) paras 22 and 23.

[36] Menon (n 1) para 25.

[37] S Menon, CJ, 'The Special Role and Responsibility of Arbitral Institutions in Charting the Future of International Arbitration', keynote address, SIAC Congress 2018, 17 May 2018, para 49, available at www.supremecourt.gov.sg/news/speeches.

[38] Second Minister of State for Law, Indranee Rajah, Second Reading of the Mediation Bill 2016, Singapore parliament, 9 January 2019, para 6, available at www.gov.sg/~/sgpcmedia/media_releases/minlaw/speech.

In 2015, the Singapore International Commercial Court (SICC) was also formed. The SICC is a division of the High Court of Singapore, and it was established to hear commercial disputes that have little or no connection to Singapore.[39] The SICC is also Singapore's first specialist commercial court. Other specialist commercial courts include the London Commercial Court, Delaware Court of Chancery and the Commercial Court of Victoria. Specialist commercial courts benefit from the existing structure of court proceedings, and yet have different procedural rules that are customised and tailored to the needs of transnational dispute resolution. For example, the bench in a specialist commercial court can consist of international judges with vast experience in dealing with issues of foreign law and different legal systems. Parties can also engage foreign legal counsel to provide representation and make submissions on foreign law as opposed to proving foreign law as a question of fact, as is traditional under the common law system.[40] Specialist commercial courts like the SICC have been described as marrying the advantages of arbitration and litigation while avoiding their drawbacks.[41]

Most dispute resolution clauses today require parties to mediate first before resorting to arbitration or litigation. With the SIAC, the SIMC, the SICC and traditional courtroom litigation, Singapore has ensured that it has the capabilities, as a dispute resolution forum, to provide for the needs of the parties. Parties can first attempt to mediate at the SIMC. If the mediation fails, they can then transition to arbitration with the SIAC. Concomitantly, if arbitration proceedings are already ongoing, the SIAC-SIMC Arb-Med-Arb Protocol ('AMA Protocol') allows a stay of arbitration proceedings administered by the SIAC in favour of mediation conducted by the SIMC. If mediation is successful, parties can then record their settlement agreement before the arbitral tribunal as an enforceable consent award.[42] Having a forum which has the capabilities to address all aspects of the dispute resolution process helps smoothe the transition process from one method to the other.

[39] Menon, 'Building Sustainable Mediation Programmes' [2015] para 73.

[40] *Lazard Bros & Co v Midland Bank Ltd* [1933] AC 289; Rule 25 of *Dicey, Morris and Collins on The Conflict of Laws*, 15th edn (London, Sweet and Maxwell, 2012) 318.

[41] S Chong, JA, 'Judicial Reform: Reshaping the Civil Justice System in Singapore', speeach at the Judicial Conference of the Supreme Courts of the G20, 10 October 2018, para 22.

[42] AMA Protocol, available at http://simc.com.sg/siac-simc-arb-med-arb-protocol.

iii. Convergence of Substantive Law

Singapore has also sought to reduce the negative effects of Asia's diverse regulatory environment by bridging the gap between the laws of different countries and to 'iron out the unnecessary and undesirable differences'.[43]

Singapore courts have not shied away from consulting other judicial courts for guidance on difficult questions of foreign law. In *Westacre Investments Inc v The State-Owned Company Yugoimport SDPR*,[44] the Court of Appeal was faced with the question of whether an English judgment was enforceable in England, such that the Singapore court could enforce the English judgment under the RECJA. The expert opinions submitted by the parties disagreed completely, and the Court of Appeal was faced with a difficult task of determining the English legal position as regards enforcement of the English judgment. Instead of making a determination on the question, the Court of Appeal directed the appellant to seek an English court's determination of whether the English judgment was enforceable in England[45] and deferred to the decision of the English court.[46]

Building on this initiative of the Court of Appeal, the Supreme Court of Singapore has entered into various memoranda of understanding with other courts to refer questions of foreign law. In 2010, the Supreme Court of Singapore and the Supreme Court of New South Wales entered into such a memorandum of understanding.[47] Under the memorandum, if there was a question of New South Wales law, the Courts of Singapore would consider directing parties to take steps to have the question determined by the Courts of New South Wales and vice versa.[48] The Supreme Court of Singapore also entered into similar memoranda of understanding with the Dubai International Financial Centre Courts[49] and the courts of New York.[50]

[43] Menon (n 11) para 15.

[44] *Westacre Investments Inc v The State-Owned Company Yugoimport SDPR (also known as Jugoimport-SDPR)* [2009] 2 SLR(R) 166.

[45] ibid para 10.

[46] ibid para 17.

[47] Memorandum of Understanding between the Supreme Court of Singapore and the Supreme Court of New South Wales on references of questions of law dated 14 September 2010.

[48] ibid Art 1.

[49] Memorandum of Understanding between the Supreme Court of Singapore & Dubai International Financial Centre Courts on References of Questions of Law dated 19 January 2015.

[50] Menon (n 11) para 14.

Singapore has also entered into memoranda of understanding with other countries to foster greater cooperation and collaboration. In 2008, Singapore entered into a memorandum of understanding with Vietnam, with the aim of working towards enhancing greater understanding of each country's laws, legal systems and legal institutions.[51] In 2014, Singapore entered into a memorandum of understanding with Myanmar to cooperate to, amongst others, promote international and cross-border practices and develop commercial law, banking law, financial and investments, and trade in goods and services.[52]

More recently, the ASEAN Chief Justices Meeting ('ACJM') was established in Singapore on 23 August 2013. It aims to be a regular forum for Chief Justices in ASEAN judiciaries to engage in dialogue and to promote close relations and build mutual understanding among the ASEAN judiciaries. After the ACJM was renamed as the Council of ASEAN Chief Justices ('CACJ') in 2016, the ASEAN Judiciaries Portal ('AJP') was launched in 2018.[53] The AJP serves as an online platform which provides information about the judiciaries and legal environments of the ASEAN member states. It also contains an intranet where its members can have internal discussions and consultations, such as to facilitate greater judicial cooperation amongst the ASEAN judiciaries.[54]

Another important avenue for convergence of substantive law is the initiatives of organisations like the UNCITRAL and the American Law Institute (ALI), who have developed numerous conventions and codes, such as the Convention on Contracts for International Sale of Goods (CISG) and the Uniform Commercial Code (UCC), to name a few. Taking cue from UNCITRAL and ALI, as well as the success of the Organisation for Harmonisation of Business Law in Africa (OHADA),[55] Singapore launched the Asian Business Law Institute (ABLI). The ABLI is

[51] Ministry of Law, 'Singapore and Vietnam sign agreement on legal and judicial cooperation', available at www.mlaw.gov.sg/news/press-releases/singapore-and-vietnam-sign-agreement-on-legal-and-judicial-cooperation.html.

[52] Ministry of Law, 'Factsheet for the Memorandum of Understanding between The Ministry of Law of the Republic of Singapore and The Supreme Court of the Union of the Republic of Myanmar on the Singapore-Myanmar Integrated Legal Exchange', available at www.mlaw.gov.sg/content/dam/minlaw/corp/News/Sg%20Myanmar%20MOU%20factsheet.pdf.

[53] Website of the Council of ASEAN Chief Justices, available at https://cacj-ajp.org.

[54] S Menon, Speech at the launch of the ASEAN Judiciaries Portal, Singapore, 27 July 2018, available at www.supremecourt.gov.sg/Data/Editor/Documents.

[55] Menon (n 11) para 8.

dedicated to collecting, studying, testing and implementing ideas on legal convergence. With a focus on Asia,[56] ABLI's objective is to put forward practical solutions that will appeal to policy-makers, legal practitioners and businesses,[57] and to promote meaningful convergence.[58] ABLI will achieve this by conducting original research into business law and policies of Asia, identifying common grounds and points of departure between different jurisdictions.[59] Apart from the research work, ABLI will also reach out to the relevant stakeholders and establish a strong feedback channel to ensure continued relevance in the work that ABLI undertakes.[60]

Singapore has also sought to align its own domestic laws with international practices. It has ratified and implemented numerous conventions, such as the CISG and the Hague Rules as amended by the Brussels Protocol 1968.[61] Currently, Singapore is in the midst of giving its insolvency regime a makeover to bring it closer to the UNCITRAL Model Law on Cross-Border Insolvency (Insolvency Model Law). The Insolvency Law Review Committee (Committee) had recommended that the Insolvency Model Law should be adopted without any reservations or qualifications to limit the applicability of the Insolvency Model Law on reciprocity.[62] The Committee recognised that this must be the approach adopted to achieve the purpose of having 'a clear, predictable and comprehensive legal framework for managing all cross-border insolvencies'.[63] Further, to impose restrictions on the applicability of the Insolvency Model Law would mean that not all cross-border insolvency cases would fall under the Insolvency Model Law. Such cases would have to rely on the common law, which the Committee observed as being uncertain and controversial.[64] A significant step towards a coordinated approach between

[56] ibid para 20.

[57] ibid para 28.

[58] ibid para 29.

[59] ibid para 30.

[60] ibid para 32.

[61] Rectified and implemented into Singapore's legislation in Sale of Goods (United Nations Convention) Act (Cap 283A, 1996 Rev Ed) and Carriage of Goods by Sea Act (Cap 33, 1998 Rev Ed) respectively.

[62] Insolvency Law Review Committee, 'Report of the Insolvency Law Committee', p 238, para 35, available at www.mlaw.gov.sg/content/dam/minlaw/ipto/assets/documents/Report%20of%20the%20Insolvency%20Law%20Review%20Committee.pdf.

[63] ibid p 237, para 34.

[64] ibid.

insolvency courts is the establishment of the Judicial Insolvency Network in October 2016. The Judicial Insolvency Network is a platform for sustained and continuous engagement between insolvency judges.[65] It has culminated in the issuance of a set of 'Guidelines for Communication and Cooperation between Courts in Cross-Border Insolvency Matters', which sets out key features to be reflected in a protocol or order of court for communication and cooperation among courts, and insolvency representatives and other parties in cross-border insolvency proceedings.[66] In Singapore, these guidelines would supplement all legislation, rules and procedure concerning insolvency.[67]

B. Jurisprudence Convergence

As a former British colony, like many others, Singapore's legal system is inherited from the British. Her legal system is based in the common law, where the law is developed incrementally by the courts, complemented by legislation. In that regard, English common law still plays a very large part in the development of Singapore law, and English authorities are still regarded as highly persuasive precedent to Singapore courts. However, the ability of the courts to incrementally develop the law in a common law tradition has also allowed Singapore courts to depart from the English position and change the law to be closer and more in line with the laws and practices of other Asian civil law countries.

i. HSBC v Toshin – *A Departure from English Law*

HSBC Institutional Trust Services (Singapore) Ltd (trustee of Starhill Global Real Estate Investment Trust) v Toshin Development Singapore Pte Ltd[68] (*HSBC v Toshin*) is a good example of how the Court of Appeal of Singapore has departed from the established position under English law, in favour of a law which is more congruent with the practice in Asia.

[65] Website of the Judicial Insolvency Network, available at www.jin-global.org/about-us.html.

[66] Chong, 'The Judicial Insolvency Network' (2019), para 20.

[67] Supreme Court of Singapore, Registrar's Circular No 1 of 2017, dated 1 February 2017.

[68] *HSBC Institutional Trust Services (Singapore) Ltd (trustee of Starhill Global Real Estate Investment Trust) v Toshin Development Singapore Pte Ltd* [2012] 4 SLR 738.

In *HSBC v Toshin*, the appellant and respondent were parties to a lease agreement. The lease agreement provided a mechanism to determine rent that was payable for each new rental term (rent review mechanism). In particular, the rent review mechanism provided that:

> Prior to the commencement of each Rental Term (other than the first), the Lessor and the Lessee shall in good faith endeavour to agree on the prevailing market rental value of the Demised Premises (excluding service charge payable and disregarding the value of all fixtures and fitting installed by the Lessee) for [the] purpose of determining the New Annual Rent for the relevant Rental Term.[69]

One of key issues for the Court's determination was whether a term of the contract requiring parties to in 'good faith endeavour to agree' was valid in law, and if the Court is of the opinion that such a term is valid, the legal content of such a term.[70]

The respondent, citing the English authority *Walford v Miles*,[71] argued that a duty to negotiate in good faith is inherently repugnant to the adversarial position of the parties in a negotiation. In *Walford v Miles*, Lord Ackner considered that:

> The reason why an agreement to negotiate, like an agreement to agree, is unenforceable, is simply because it lacks the necessary certainty. The same does not apply to an agreement to use best endeavours. This uncertainty is demonstrated in the instant case by the provision which it is said has to be implied in the agreement for the determination of the negotiations. How can a court be expected to decide whether, subjectively, a proper reason existed for the termination of negotiations? The answer suggested depends upon whether the negotiations have been determined 'in good faith.' However, the concept of a duty to carry on negotiations in good faith is inherently repugnant to the adversarial of the parties when involved in negotiations. Each party to the negotiation is entitled to pursue his (or her) own interest, so long as he avoids making misrepresentation. To advance that interest he must be entitled, if he thinks it appropriate, to threaten to withdraw from further negotiations or to withdraw in fact, in hope that the opposite party may seek to reopen the negotiations by offering improved terms.[72]

[69] ibid [6].
[70] ibid [1].
[71] *Walford v Miles* [1992] 2 AC 128.
[72] ibid 138.

Earlier Singapore cases were also consistent with *Walford v Miles*. *Ng Giap Hon v Westcomb Securities Pte Ltd*[73] considered there was no general implied duty of good faith under the common law.[74] Further, *Sundercan Ltd v Salzman Anthony David*,[75] following *Walford v Miles*, also held that a mechanism in place to determine the payment schedule by negotiation was akin to an agreement to negotiate is unenforceable.[76]

However, the Court of Appeal in *HSBC v Toshin* declined to follow *Walford v Miles*. The Court of Appeal first distinguished *Walford v Miles* on the basis that *Walford v Miles* was a case involving pre-contractual negotiations while *HSBC v Toshin* was a case involving an express term in a contract. The Court of Appeal was of the view that a valid distinction can be drawn between the two scenarios. In the former, parties have greater latitude and are free to walk away from the negotiation at any time, for whatever reason. In the latter, however, the parties have committed themselves to the agreement and are bound by the overarching contract.[77] This view is also supported by the English Court of Appeal decision in *Petromec Inc, Petro-Deep, Societa Armamento Navi Appoggio SpA v Petroleo Brasileiro SA*[78] (*Petromec v Petroleo*), which held that the decision of *Walford v Miles* did not have the effect of invalidating an express term requiring parties to negotiate in good faith.[79]

Further, the Court of Appeal in *HSBC v Toshin* saw no reason why an express agreement to negotiate in good faith should not be upheld.[80] The Court of Appeal took note of Associate Professor Philip J McConnaughay's observations,[81] namely that a term requiring parties to negotiate in good faith is a core term in many Asian contracts and captures the essence of contractual obligations in the Asian tradition. Unlike the Western view that terms requiring negotiation in good faith impose no real obligations, from an Asian tradition perspective, such a term is no less substantive in content

[73] *Ng Giap Hon v Westcomb Securities Pte Ltd* [2009] 3 SLR(R) 518.
[74] ibid [60].
[75] *Sundercan Ltd v Salzman Anthony David* [2010] SGHC 92.
[76] ibid [25].
[77] Above n 68 at [37].
[78] *Petromec Inc, Petro-Deep, Societa Armamento Navi Appoggio SpA v Petroleo Brasileiro SA* [2006] 1 Lloyd's Rep 121.
[79] ibid [121].
[80] Above n 68 at [40].
[81] ibid.

than a term relating to price, payment and delivery. Such a term embodies and expresses the traditional Asian belief that a contract is 'tentative rather than final, unfolding rather than static, a source of guidance rather than determinative, and subordinate to other values'.[82] Viewed in this light, terms requiring good faith negotiations are 'consistent with [Singapore's] cultural value of promoting consensus' and 'it is in the wider public interest in Singapore as well to promote such an approach towards resolving differences'.[83]

ii. Sembcorp Marine v PPL Holdings – *Roadmap to Harmonisation*

While Singapore seeks to achieve harmonisation and convergence in the law, and to adapt and change its laws and practices so as to align itself for the sake of consistency with other Asian civil law countries, Singapore courts adopt a very cautious approach, careful to ensure that any new law or practice does not offend the existing established laws and procedures of Singapore.

In *Sembcorp Marine v PPL Holdings*,[84] the Singapore Court of Appeal had the opportunity to reconsider the laws on interpretation of contractual terms and the admissibility of extrinsic evidence. The prevailing law in England, as enunciated by Lord Hoffmann in *Investors Compensation Scheme Ltd v West Bromwich Building Society*[85] (*ICS v West Bromwich*), is that 'absolutely anything which would affect the way in which the language of the document would have been understood by a reasonable man' is admissible, excluding previous negotiations of parties and any declaration of subjective intent by the parties.[86] This approach is very similar to the civil law approach to admissibility of extrinsic evidence, which allows contracts to be proven by any means and the approach contained in transnational conventions (such as the CISG).[87]

[82] Associate Professor PJ McConnaughay 'Rethinking the Role of Law and Contracts in East–West Commercial Relationships' (2000–2001) 41 *Virginia Journal of International Law* 427, 448–49.

[83] Above n 68 at [40].

[84] *Sembcorp Marine Ltd v PPL Holding* [2013] 4 SLR 193.

[85] *Investors Compensation Scheme Ltd v West Bromwich Building Society* [1998] 1 WLR 896.

[86] ibid at 912–13 cited in *Sembcorp Marine Ltd v PPL Holding* [2013] 4 SLR 193 at [35].

[87] Above n 74 at [37].

The Court of Appeal in *Sembcorp Marine Ltd v PPL Holding* recognised the importance of harmonisation and convergence in commercial law. However, the Court of Appeal also stressed the need to assess the harmonisation and convergence in the round, taking into account the laws of Singapore and the litigation process in general.[88] The Court of Appeal pointed to Singapore's adversarial litigation system and discovery process as features that will militate against the acceptance of the approach to allow any evidence to be adduced as extrinsic evidence. Under Singapore's adversarial litigation system, parties are free to admit any evidence which they think is useful or helpful to their case.[89] If the courts adopted too relaxed an attitude towards the admission of evidence, this could lead to a flood of evidence being adduced by the parties, leaving the judge to sift through excessive amounts of evidence.[90] This is neither time- nor cost-efficient.

The Court of Appeal's discussion on the admissibility of extrinsic evidence in *Sembcorp Marine v PPL Holdings* shows that the Singapore Courts are open-minded[91] and willing to examine other approaches and potential efficacy for possible incorporation into Singapore's law.[92] It sets out a roadmap for the manner in which Singapore courts could adopt laws and practices from foreign jurisdictions without upsetting the foundations of its own system.[93] The courts should begin by setting out the parameters of the discussion. On one end, there is the law and/or practice of a foreign jurisdiction that Singapore could consider adopting. On the other end, there is the established law of Singapore. With this parameter defined, the court could then decide where on the spectrum Singapore can potentially move towards.[94] The court would then go on to consider: (i) whether the foreign law and/or practice can be traced back to a common law doctrine; (ii) whether the existing legislations of Singapore prevent the adoption of the foreign law and/or practice; and (iii) whether

[88] ibid [38].
[89] ibid [66].
[90] ibid [66].
[91] See BC Bitas, 'A Practical Lesson from Singapore and its Relevance to Transnational Convergence' (2014) 26 *The Singapore Academy of Law Journal* 50, para 17.
[92] ibid para 18.
[93] ibid para 21.
[94] ibid para 23.

the foreign law and/or practice would be consistent with Singapore's common law adversarial practice.[95]

The recent case of *Vinmar v PTT*[96] serves as a good illustration of how the Singapore Court of Appeal is open to depart from its previous decisions to ensure that Singapore law keeps up with commercial realities and developments in the approach taken by other jurisdictions. In *Vinmar v PTT*, the Singapore Court of Appeal had to deal with the question of whether the merits of a dispute should be evaluated at all in deciding an application for stay of proceedings on the basis of an exclusive jurisdiction clause. Although there were at least four of its previous decisions[97] which engaged in an examination of the merits, the Singapore Court of Appeal recognised that there was a 'turning of the tide' in judicial attitudes in England[98] and Hong Kong,[99] where the relevance of merits was increasingly doubted. Accordingly, the Singapore Court of Appeal decided, 'for reasons of principle, policy and coherence', to make a restatement of the law such that the merits of a defence are now irrelevant in the determination of any application for a stay of proceedings on the basis of an exclusive jurisdiction clause.[100]

Based on the results of an empirical study of Singapore cases between 1965 and 2008, it has been found that although English cases continue to be a point of first reference, the Singapore courts do not blindly follow English law without consulting other jurisdictions.[101] In this regard, the Singapore courts have been said to be 'building a Singaporean jurisprudence through the careful selection and amalgamation of the best practices and norms from a wide range of jurisdictions'.[102]

[95] ibid para 25.

[96] *Vinmar Overseas (Singapore) Pte Ltd v PTT International Trading Pte Ltd* [2018] SGCA 65.

[97] *The Jian He* [1999] 3 SLR(R) 432; *The Hung Vuong* [2000] 2 SLR(R) 11; *Golden Shore Transportation Pte Ltd v UCO Bank* [2004] 1 SLR(R) 6; *The Hyundai Fortune* [2004] 4 SLR(R) 548.

[98] *Donohue v Armco and ors* [2002] 1 Lloyd's Rep 425; *Euromark Ltd v Smash Enterprises Pty Ltd* [2013] EWHC 1627; *CH Offshore Ltd v PDV Marina SA and ors* [2015] EWHC 595.

[99] *Hyundai Engineering & Construction Co Ltd v UBAF (Hong Kong) Ltd* [2013] HKCU 2237; *Deltatre Spa v Hong Kong Sports Industrial Development Ltd* [2018] HKCU 2939.

[100] Above n 96 at [113].

[101] See G Yihan, 'An Empirical Study on the Development of Singapore Law' (2011) 23 SacLJ 176, 220.

[102] ibid 221.

iii. Importance of Openness

Keeping the legal system open and accessible to the public is another important way to promote convergence. Openness and accessibility involves making judgments available to the public. While most laws in Asia are codified by statute, a great part of the laws is still developed by judges and arbitrators in the way they interpret the written laws of the country.

As more disputes are being referred to arbitration, we could potentially find ourselves in a situation where, apart from statutes, we no longer have any other sources of law to rely on. One of the key features of arbitration is confidentiality. As a result, most arbitration awards and decisions rendered are not published.[103] These decisions are important because one needs to understand the law before one can identify the differences and study how meaningful convergence can be achieved. It is also helps the courts and arbitral tribunals to be consistent in their reasons and decisions.

One proposal is for arbitration decisions to be published with the necessary anonymisation to protect the identities of the parties.[104] The courts have adopted this approach for decades, particularly for family disputes and cases that involve minors. By anonymising the judgment, the courts can provide confidentiality and protection to the parties, and yet allow the rest of the country to benefit from its decision and reasoning process and to understand what is required of an individual under the laws of the country.

IV. Instances of Convergence in Asia

Beyond Singapore, there is also a similar push towards both legal and jurisprudence convergence in Asia in respect of maritime law.

At the start of this year, Zhou Qiang, President of China's Supreme People's Court, stated China's intention of creating an international maritime

[103] The vast majority of arbitral awards are not published. See E Zlatanska, 'To Publish, or Not to Publish Arbitral Awads: That is the Question …' (2015) 81 *Arbitration* 25, 25. However, there are some arbitration institutions that are willing to publish awards made under them (eg the International Chamber of Commerce (ICC), the SIAC, etc).

[104] An example of this would be the *Singapore Arbitral Award*, a journal which publishes redacted arbitral awards decided under the SIAC Rules.

judicial centre at the National People's Congress. To clarify, China's intention is not to create a new court that specialises in maritime disputes, but to strengthen and bolster the influence and prestige of the Chinese maritime courts at the international level.[105] China recognises that the current period is the best opportunity to develop its maritime courts.[106] With the New Silk Road initiative, the Chinese maritime courts will play a very important role in developing its maritime law, in support of the initiative.[107]

The China's Supreme People's Court recognises that for its maritime courts to become the international maritime judicial centre, China must learn and understand international maritime laws and practices and must actively participate in the creation of new international laws and regulations.[108] In that regard, one can foresee a legal convergence of the substantive maritime law in China in the near future, whether it is by means of China adopting international maritime laws and practices as its own, or as a creator of new international maritime laws and practices through conventions (such as the Draft Convention that is currently before the IMO).

It is also observed that Asian common law courts are starting to look more at each other's judicial decisions as opposed to established English positions.

In *The Alas*,[109] the Hong Kong court had to consider whether the procedure of arrest was still available to a plaintiff once its claim against the defendant had crystallised in a judgment or arbitration award.[110] The Hong Kong court was urged by the defendants to consider the English position in *The Alletta*,[111] that once a plaintiff obtains a judgment *in rem* in respect of its claim, the plaintiff is no longer entitled to arrest the vessel as security for the satisfication of unpaid judgment.[112]

[105] Susan Finder, 'China's Maritime Courts: Defenders of "Judicial Sovereignty"', *The Diplomat*, 5 April 2016, available at http://thediplomat.com/2016/04/chinas-maritime-courts-defenders-of-judicial-sovereignty.

[106] 高法资讯, '贺荣：围绕建设海事司法强国目标 全面加强海事审判工作', available at http://mp.weixin.qq.com/s?__biz=MzA3MjEwNzYzOQ==&mid=402862976&idx=2&sn=5adea370ad73eb25ebfc5923147162a2&scene=5&srcid=0328LMqoFtQZcAZ3cv1Qj3PY#rd.

[107] ibid.

[108] ibid.

[109] *The Alas* [2014] HKCFI 1281.

[110] ibid [9].

[111] *The Alletta* [1974] 1 Lloyd's Rep 40.

[112] Above n 106 at [24].

Prior to *The Alas*, the Singapore court had the opportunity to consider this issue and the English position in *The Alletta*. In *The Daien Maru No 18*,[113] the Singapore court declined to follow the position stated in *The Alletta*.[114] Instead, it held that if a plaintiff who instituted an action *in rem* against a ship could assert as against the world that the ship was a security to his or her claim, then in principle, where such a plaintiff had obtained judgment, he or she could still properly assert that the ship was a security for the judgment and could therefore arrest the ship.[115]

Having reviewed the decision in *The Daien Maru No 18*, the Hong Kong court agreed with the position taken in *The Daien Maru No 18* and declined to follow *The Alletta*.[116] The Hong Kong court concluded that an arrest of a ship is a mere procedure, whose the object is to obtain security to satisfy any judgment that may be obtained.[117] The Hong Kong court also agreed with the judge in *The Daien Maru No 18* that it was 'extremely odd that the right of security by the arrest of a vessel is available to a plaintiff who merely asserts a claim whereas it is lost when he finally obtains a judgment in the action'.[118]

In *Citic Pacific Limited v Secretary for Justice and Commissioner of Police*,[119] the Hong Kong Court of Appeal considered the issue of whether internal confidential documents held by employees of an organisation may be covered by legal advice privilege or whether such privilege only covers direct communications between the organisation's legal department and its external lawyers. At that time, given the English Court of Appeal decision in *Three Rivers*,[120] English law proceeded on a narrow definition of a 'client' such that internal communications between employees were equated with information from third parties and were not protected by legal advice privilege.[121] On the other hand, the approach taken by the

[113] *The Daien Maru No 18* [1983–1984] SLR(R) 787.
[114] ibid at [3]–[10].
[115] ibid at [16].
[116] Above n 106 at [24].
[117] ibid.
[118] ibid.
[119] *Citic Pacific Limited v Secretary for Justice and Commissioner of Police* (unreported, 29/06/2015, CACV 7/2012).
[120] *Three Rivers District Council v Governor and Company of the Bank of England (No 5)* [2003] QB 1556.
[121] Note that there seems to be a departure from this position under English law in light of the recent English Court of Appeal decision in *The Director of the SFO v Eurasian Natural Resources Corporation Limited* [2018] EWCA Civ 2006.

Singapore Court of Appeal in *Skandinaviska Enskilda Banken AB*[122] was that the only relevant issue is whether the communication is made for the purpose of obtaining legal advice. This was also the approach taken in the United States[123] and Australia.[124] The Hong Kong Court of Appeal was of the view that the English approach in *Three Rivers* did not provide effective and meaningful protection for confidentiality in the process of obtaining legal advice in the litigious as well as the non-litigious context and decided to bring itself in line with the approach taken by the United States, Australia and Singapore.[125]

V. Conclusion

Singapore's existence is tied to the unending search to be relevant and attractive in Asia. Just as Singapore offers facilities and connectivity in business that are not easily found elsewhere in Asia, it must also offer legal facilities and connectivity to be relevant in Asia where the majority of jurisdictions are civil law.

Facilities and connectivity lie in championing legal convergence as the key to efficient legal business. They also lie in developing the common law to be sensitive to and to accommodate non-common law principles. They illustrate the strengths of the common law – the adaptability across wide regions, principled rules that are sensitive to circumstances, and a sense of fairness in novel situations.

[122] *Skandinaviska Enskilda Banken AB* v Asia Pacific Breweries (Singapore) Pte Ltd and others [2007] SGCA 9 at [41].

[123] *Upjohn v United States* (1981) 449 US 383, 390.

[124] *Pratt Holdings v Commissioner of Taxation* (2004) 136 FCR 357, 386–87.

[125] Above n 119 at [46], [50], and [63].

3

The Common Law and Civil Law Traditions of Contract Interpretation in the Context of Maritime Law

SIR BERNARD RIX*

I. Introduction

I would like to examine those traditions first in principle and then by reference to two cases which I think allow for interesting insights into the different approaches of the two traditions. One of those cases is a maritime case, which arose out of an arrest in a French port, an agreement for the release of the vessel, the provision of security, and the resolution of the dispute under French law in the English courts. The other is a construction dispute, which went to international arbitration and was subsequently the focus of enforcement proceedings in both the English and the French courts. Although that case arose out of a construction agreement, it could just as well have arisen out of a charterparty.

The two traditions of the common and the civil law should first be considered. I will begin with the common law, and then go on to the civil law. I do not think that there are important differences between the various nations that practise the common law, but I will concentrate on the common law as it is found in England.

* An earlier version of this lecture was published in the *Scandinavian Institute of Maritime* Law Yearbook, SIMPLY 2014/MarIus No 456.

II. The Principles of the Common Law

The principles of the common law may have been formulated over time in slightly different ways, but I do not believe that these differences, although sometimes spoken of as being revolutionary, are in truth fundamental. What does change over time is the spirit of interpretation, and that spirit sometimes waxes more literal and sometimes waxes more purposive. Some generations have been more caught up with the meaning of words, and some generations have been more willing to be guided by the purpose of the contract. That division, between what have been called the 'literal goats' and the 'purposive sheep', is the modern battleground of interpretative dispute.

First, however, I will address the primary rules of interpretation, what might be described as the common law equivalent of the UNIDROIT Principles, which seek to encapsulate the civil law approach to the interpretation of international commercial contracts.[1] The universal purpose of course is to ascertain the common intention of the parties, but that is to be done in England by an *objective rule* of interpretation, rather than by seeking what the parties were intending subjectively. The English view is that, because it is the *common* intention of the parties which counts, it follows that their individual *subjective* intentions are irrelevant. What counts is what they have said or written to one another as expressive of their intentions, and that language is to be interpreted for what it would convey to reasonable people positioned as the contracting parties were at the time of their contract. Thus the primary rule has been expressed in modern jurisprudence as follows:

> Interpretation is the ascertainment of the meaning which the document would convey to a reasonable person having all the background knowledge which would reasonably have been available to the parties in the situation in which they were at the time of the contract.[2]

That is the first of five principles which Lord Hoffmann set out in his judgment in *Investors Compensation Scheme v West Bromwich Building Society*.[3]

[1] UNIDROIT Principles of International Commercial Contracts (2016).

[2] *Investors Compensation Scheme v West Bromwich Building Society* [1998] 1 All ER 98 at 114.

[3] [1998] 1 All ER 98 at 114–15.

That was what he considered to be the primary rule and the rest may be said to be commentary. When Lord Hoffmann formulated his five principles, it was thought by some that this marked a revolution in our interpretative principles. That was in 1998. But now, only last year, in *Arnold v Britton*, the Supreme Court has produced another so-called revolution, and in Lord Neuberger's leading judgment in that case, there is not even mention of the *Investors Compensation Scheme* case.[4]

With that warning, I think it is nevertheless instructive to take it in stages. This involves in effect the history of contract interpretation in England in our own times. If we deconstruct Lord Hoffmann's primary rule we will note:

- The parties and their intentions have been disembodied: the parties are not central; the central person is the reasonable interpreter. That is typical of the common law, which, save where honesty is in question, always seeks to objectify the problem.
- But the reasonable interpreter is no longer, if he ever was, but as he has sometimes been expressed to be, 'the man on the Clapham omnibus'. The reasonable interpreter is the person who is put back into the position of the parties, with their knowledge, at the time of contract.
- The parties' knowledge at the time of contract is often referred to as the 'matrix' of the contract. The matrix is that background of knowledge and aspiration which is *mutual* to the parties. Because of the primary rule of objective interpretation, the court is only interested in what is known mutually to both parties.
- The emphasis is on the time of contract. Therefore the courts are not interested in how the parties may conduct themselves to one another after the contract has been made. Post-contractual conduct is sometimes said to be entirely irrelevant to contractual interpretation. Pre-contractual negotiations are also irrelevant, but under a separate rule, Lord Hoffmann's rule (3), to which I will come shortly.
- As so often in the common law, the rule is softened by the use of the epithet 'reasonable' or the adverb 'reasonably'. You will see both words appear in Lord Hoffmann's primary rule. It again reflects the objective standpoint of the common law. But it permits the courts a degree

[4] *Arnold v Britton* [2015] UKSC 36, [2015] AC 1619.

of manoeuvre in an area which is of course, by definition, otherwise entirely within the autonomy of the parties.

Lord Hoffmann's third rule is one of the most distinct rules of English law and differs from the approach of the civil law. It is an exclusionary rule which prevents recourse to the parties' pre-contractual negotiations. Thus –

> The law excludes from the admissible background the previous negotiations of the parties and their declarations of subjective intent. They are admissible only in an action for rectification. The law makes this distinction for reasons of practical policy …[5]

That exclusionary rule was reconsidered by the Supreme Court recently in *Chartbrook v Persimmon Homes*, but was reaffirmed.[6] In the course of his judgment in *Chartbrook*, Lord Hoffmann contrasted the English rule with the rule in civil law jurisdictions. There he said this:

> Supporters of the admissibility of pre-contractual negotiations draw attention to the fact that Continental legal systems seem to have little difficulty in taking them into account … But these instruments reflect the French philosophy of contractual interpretation, which is altogether different from that of English law. As Professor Catherine Valcke explains in an illuminating article ('On comparing French and English Contract Law: Insights from Social Contract Theory') (16 January 2009), French law regards the intentions of the parties as a pure question of subjective fact, their volonté psychologique, uninfluenced by any rules of law. It follows that any evidence of what they said or did, whether to each other or to third parties, may be relevant to establishing what their intentions actually were … English law, on the other hand, mixes up the ascertainment of intention with the rules of law by depersonalising the contracting parties and asking, not what their intentions actually were, but what a reasonable outside observer would have taken them to be.[7]

Lord Hoffmann went on to explain the English approach of excluding reference to pre-contractual negotiations. In effect, Lord Hoffmann says that, because the *civil* law is interested in subjective intent, it makes sense to look for it in the negotiations for the contract. From the *common* law point of view, however, negotiations are not necessary as a source of the parties'

[5] [1998] 1 All ER 98 at 114.

[6] *Chartbrook Ltd v Persimmon Homes Ltd* [2009] UKHL 38, [2009] AC 1101.

[7] [2009] AC 1101 at [39]. See also C Valcke, 'On Comparing French and English Contract Law: Insights from Social Contract Theory' (2009) 4 *Journal of Comparative Law* 69.

intentions, and then a number of pragmatic reasons combine to produce a rule, which is centuries old, to exclude as generally unhelpful a rummage through all the detritus of negotiations. It is accepted that now and then a nugget of gold might be found, but what Lord Hoffmann called the chance of 'more precise justice in exceptional cases' is outweighed by the practical disadvantages in the general run.

It is only in Lord Hoffmann's fourth and fifth rules that he finally comes to talk of language as a source of meaning or intention. He said: 'The meaning of words is a matter of dictionaries and grammars; the meaning of the document is what the parties using those words against the relevant background would reasonably have been understood to mean.'[8] And then this:

> The 'rule' that words should be given their 'natural and ordinary meaning' reflects the common sense proposition that we do not easily accept that people have made linguistic mistakes, particularly in formal documents. On the other hand, if one would nevertheless conclude from the background that something must have gone wrong with the language, the law does not require judges to attribute to the parties an intention which they plainly could not have had.[9]

It is to be observed that when Lord Hoffmann comes to the parties' language, he refers to 'words' and 'dictionaries'. Of course, language is made up of words, but we all know that the meaning of words depends on their *context*, and that language merely interpreted through a dictionary, with their lists of many different meanings, would be a very unsatisfactory process: as may be witnessed where an unskilled interpreter translates from one language to another by simply relying on a dictionary. I would therefore prefer to defer to the parties' language rather than just to their words.

And that is what the Supreme Court has now done in the recent case of *Arnold v Britton*. This decision has gone back to enthroning language as the principal tool of interpretative principles. The Court was concerned to emphasise that purposive construction and the invocation of commercial common sense have to make way for the language in which the parties have expressed themselves. I give you a sample from Lord Neuberger's judgment:

> [S]ave perhaps in a very unusual case, that meaning is most obviously to be gleaned from the language of the provision. Unlike commercial common sense

[8] [1998] 1 All ER 98 at 115.
[9] ibid.

> and the surrounding circumstances, the parties have control over the language they use in a contract … while commercial common sense is a very important factor to take into account when interpreting a contract, a court should be very slow to reject the natural meaning of a provision as correct simply because it appears to be a very imprudent term for one of the parties to have agreed …[10]

One could debate, but perhaps without profit, where one enters this net of doctrine. I would respectfully suggest that what is important to remember is that:

- The autonomy of parties over their own contract means that one should always start with their own language and with due respect for it; particularly in formal contracts written by lawyers.
- Although language is the tool of all of us, it is the parties' contract against a private background of mutual knowledge and aspirations which has to be taken into account.
- The interpretative function of the courts is to find the parties' common intention from an objective viewpoint.
- It follows that private knowledge and private intentions are of no relevance.
- Pre-contractual negotiations are excluded because they are regarded as generally being an unprofitable source for finding a common intention.
- The intention to be found is that of the date of the contract: therefore what comes after the contract can only be of assistance to the extent that it can throw light on a common intention at the time of contract.
- Where interpretative problems arise, the logic of the contract and its purposes can be highly instructive and may well be determinative.
- In any event it is the contract as a whole, and not just individual words in it, which have to be interpreted. In this respect, as has been said on many occasions, 'Context is everything'.

III. The Civil Law Approach

Let us now consider, perhaps more briefly – as befits my lesser familiarity to it! – the civil law approach, to see where it is similar and where it

[10] *Arnold v Britton* [2015] UKSC 36, [2015] AC 1619, 1628.

differs from the approach of the common law. The great, and magnificently terse and elegant statement of the Code Napoleón, which is more or less repeated in various languages in so many of the fundamental codes of civil law nations all over the world, and which has survived unchanged for over 200 years, is contained in Article 1156. In the English translation of the Code Napoleón which I have in my library at home, Article 1156 is rendered thus: 'In agreements it is necessary to search into the mutual intention of the contracting parties, rather than to stop at the literal sense of the terms.'[11] In the original French it reads: '*On doit dans les conventions rechercher quelle a été la commune intention des parties contractantes, plutôt que de s'arrêter au sens littéral des termes*.' I would just pause for a moment over the wonderful wording of this wonderfully brief statement. It takes only two lines of text to make a number of critically important points:

- It refers to language, but with the warning that the interpreter must not 'stop' (*arrêter*) at the 'literal' sense of the terms.
- It follows, although it is a matter of implicit interpretation rather than express language, that one must at least 'start' with the language, even if one does not 'stop' with its literal sense.
- What one must concentrate on, however, is what the article begins with, which is not the language of the contract itself, but 'the common intention of the parties'.
- That common intention, and I emphasise that, as in the common law, it is of course the *common* intention of the parties which is referred to, is to be 'sought': the French word is 'rechercher'. That suggests an active

[11] At the time of the lecture which this chapter reproduces, the change effected to Article 1156 was still in draft, though see the Draft Ordonnance for the Reform of the Law of Contract, The General Regime of Obligations, and Proof of Obligations February 2015, Translation of the proposed new text by James Cartwright, Bénédicte Fauvarque-Cosson and Simon Whittaker, available at http://www.textes.justice.gouv.fr/art_pix/Draft-Ordonnance-for-the-Reform-of-the-Civil-Codepdf.pdf. The draft became law as of 1 October 2016, but see the addition to the original language of Article 1156 (now contained in Article 1188) of the qualification: 'Where the common intention of the parties cannot be discerned, a contract is to be interpreted in the sense which a reasonable person placed in the same situation would give to it'. The draft was said to contain controversial provisions. It was said to aim at objectifying the French law of contract interpretation, thus making it more fit for commercial parties, but at the same time the French Minister of Justice, Mme Christiane Taubira, had claimed that the reform would make it 'more protective of the most vulnerable people', which sounds as though it also aimed at performing the functions of a consumerist law of contract interpretation.

and compelling process for the search: it is a case of research, a digging out, a careful sorting out: in the sense in which one commonly talks of the 'search for truth'.

- In a very real sense, what Article 1156 tells you is that you must be careful not to be a literalist goat.

That is a good note on which to return to the current tension between a literal and a purposive approach to interpretation. I would respectfully suggest, however, that this is a false dichotomy. There is to my mind no doubt that the interpreter has to take into account *both* the language adopted by the parties, *and* the purposes for which they contract. Sometimes those purposes are usefully stated in the contract itself; sometimes they have to be discovered by a process of analysis of the contract. Often that analysis is the hardest and also the most important part of contractual interpretation. A purposive construction will often enable the court to decide between two or more possible alternatives. But the weight to be ascribed to language and to purpose in any particular case can never be a matter of rule. The fascination of contractual interpretation is that each problem is a world on its own. This is not only because each contract is different, but also because the causes of dispute vary.

Sometimes the contract is deliberately ambiguous, because it is the only way the parties could reach agreement. The parties themselves do not know how it is meant to operate in certain circumstances, even if they have their own, often conflicting ideas, about that. Sometimes the problem arises from a gap in the contract, because not everything has been foreseen, or covered, or even thought as being necessary to state, since it is so obvious. Sometimes, there are errors of draftsmanship, as where definitions are misdrafted, or references misstated. Sometimes there are errors of misunderstanding. Sometimes the contract simply does not provide for some unexpected turn of events, and then the way in which the contract operates in the new circumstances may be awkward. But the solution still has to be found in the contract itself. The courts, under their interpretative function, cannot make a new contract for the parties.

But it is often the case that in such circumstances, where the parties did not anticipate the problem that has arisen, it is almost impossible to speak sensibly of a common intention of the parties save in the most disembodied or, as we say, objective sense. In such circumstances, since contracts are primarily about the allocation of risk, the courts have to make a judgment about where, in the light of the parties' contract as a whole, the risk is intended to fall.

The principles of the common law let me draw this section of the chapter to a close by highlighting two linked points by way of contrasting the common and civil law approaches. First, the common law approach excludes, as you have heard, both pre-contractual negotiations and post-contractual performance as being relevant to the process of contractual interpretation.

In both respects, the civil law differs, for the civil law excludes nothing in its search for the intention of the parties, and, as we know, is even willing to take into account the subjective intentions of individual parties, in its attempt to discover the common intention of the contracting parties.

The second and linked point I would make, however, is that it always has to be remembered that the common law and the civil law also differ in their procedure as well as in their substantive law. When it comes to procedure, the common law favours discovery of documents on a substantial scale, and it also favours live cross-examination of witnesses. The civil law, as I understand it, favours neither.

Now, if the civil law were to pursue the common intention of the parties in pre-contractual negotiations and post-contractual performance by the common law procedure of extensive disclosure of documents and cross-examination of witnesses, then it would never get to the end of the matter! And similarly, if the common law were to adopt the civil law approach to the interpretation of contracts and still retain its procedural liberality, it too would never get to the end of the matter. So the civil law has an extensively speculative substantive law of contract interpretation, but controls it by a more stringent approach to procedural opportunities; while the common law has a narrower approach to the substantive question of contract interpretation in part for the very reason that otherwise it would have to curtail its procedural approach to the search for truth.

Having dealt with these general principles, the two cases I mentioned at the outset should be analysed. The first is *The Spirit of Independence*.[12] It concerned a vessel arrested in France by a shipyard for the cost of repairs done for the account of demise charterers. The yard claimed to have a

[12] *The Spirit of Independence (formerly known as 'Caribia Viva')* [1999] 1 Lloyd's Rep 43.

maritime claim against the charterers under the Arrest Convention, which was directly incorporated into French law.[13] The vessel was released from arrest when the registered owners' P&I Club gave a conditional letter of guarantee. The condition was that the yard had to establish a valid claim against the owners and not merely against the charterers, or else a maritime lien against the vessel itself. The letter was governed by French law, but the parties preferred to debate their disputes in England.

Essentially three preliminary issues arose. Firstly, for the purposes of the Arrest Convention as it was interpreted under French law, were the owners or their vessel answerable for the debt of the charterers? Secondly, for the purposes of adequate security to gain release from arrest, was conditional security permissible? Thirdly, for the purposes of the letter of guarantee, was it in fact conditional on the owners' or the vessel's liability, or did it answer to the charterers' liability? So the case involved a question of the interpretation of the Arrest Convention and in that context a question of the interpretation of the guarantee.

The matter was debated in the Commercial Court, as it happened before me. Distinguished French experts gave evidence on French law. Contrary to what would have happened in France, where there was no binding precedent, only three rather unilluminating decisions in the *Cour de cassation* and a welter of conflicting jurisprudence in the numerous courts of appeal around France, all the cases were presented to me by the French experts, together with a large amount of writings of French jurists which tried to make sense of the conflicting jurisprudence. In France, each court would simply have made up its own mind as to the scope of the Convention, and similarly of the letter of guarantee, without considering the jurisprudence.

On the question of contractual interpretation, I was entertained to submissions based on the negotiations as well as the subjective intentions of the parties. The negotiations in fact showed that the parties attempted on the one side to obtain an unconditional guarantee and on the other side to provide only a conditional guarantee. So the negotiations helped only to show that both interpretations were theoretically in play. Ultimately, however, the question had to be decided on the wording of the guarantee. I held that, however wide the admissible evidence of the parties' intentions, the letter of guarantee permitted the owners to argue that under

[13] International Convention relating to the Arrest of Sea-going Ships (adopted 10 May 1952, entered into force 24 February 1956) 439 UNTS 193.

the Convention they, as distinct from the charterers, were not obliged to give any security.

As for the Convention, it emerged that it had been enacted into English law in different terms from its automatic incorporation in French law, so that the issues which arose in the present case could not arise in England. I considered, as I was invited to do, all the French jurisprudence and all the French commentators. Nevertheless, I do not think a French court would have done that, or been invited to do that. I concluded that an owner of a vessel arrested for its charterer's debt was entitled to make his security conditional on the owner's or his vessel's liability. I decided to that effect both on the basis of the preponderance of the jurisprudence as analysed, but in any event on the equity of the situation, as the French experts said I was entitled to decide in the absence of binding jurisprudence. That equity was revealed by the fact, as was common ground, that the vessel, if left under arrest without security, could not have been taken in execution of the establishment of the charterer's debt.

The other case to mention is the famous case of *Dallah v Government of Pakistan*.[14] Dallah was a Saudi company which had entered into a memorandum of understanding (MOU) with the *Government of Pakistan* to acquire land in Mecca and there construct housing for pilgrims performing Hajj. Pursuant to that MOU, Dallah proceeded to enter into a construction agreement with a trust created by the Government, and that was the contract in question. The Government was not a signatory to the contract. There had been talk of a government guarantee, but none had been obtained.

Unfortunately, the Government ordinance which had created the trust lapsed automatically at the end of three months, unless it was renewed, which it was not, with the result that Dallah lost its contract partner and its contract. On the other hand, the Secretary of the Government's Ministry of Religious Affairs, who had also been the secretary of the trust's board, wrote to Dallah, on the Ministry's notepaper, shortly after the expiry of the trust, to give notice of termination of the contract citing a failure by Dallah to submit timely specifications.

The contract contained an arbitration clause, providing for ICC arbitration in Paris. Dallah claimed against the Ministry, ie against the

[14] *Dallah Real Estate and Tourism Holding Co v Ministry of Religious Affairs of the Government of Pakistan* [2010] UKSC 46, [2011] 1 AC 763.

Government, in arbitration, and the Government asserted that it was not a party to the contract or to the arbitration agreement, and so the distinguished tribunal, which included a retired Law Lord from England, Lord Mustill, rendered an initial award on its jurisdiction. It found that the Government was a party to the contract. It applied 'those transnational principles and usages reflecting the fundamental requirements of justice in international trade and the concept of good faith in business'. The tribunal did so, having decided that it did not need to determine the applicable law of the contract. As for good faith, you will recall that the concept of good faith is an inherent and express part of the civil law – it is to be found, for instance, in Article 4.8 of the UNIDROIT Principles – but that it is not an expressly recognised part of English law.[15] Having established its jurisdiction under the doctrine of *kompetenz kompetenz*, the arbitral tribunal in *Dallah* went on to make a second award, against the Government, for $20 million, and it was that award which was taken to England for enforcement under the New York Convention.

Enter the English courts. The enforcement claim came before the Commercial Court, the Court of Appeal and the Supreme Court. Each court held that the arbitrators had been wrong to find that the Government was a party to the contract and arbitration agreement, and they therefore refused to enforce the second award. In doing so, they applied French law, as mandated by the New York Convention, on the ground that that was the law of the country in which the award had been made. Evidence of French law was given by distinguished experts before the Commercial Court.

In the Supreme Court it was common ground that the applicable French legal principles had been correctly assessed in the lower courts. What remained at issue was how those principles were to be applied. Following its defeat in England, Dallah went to France and asked the French courts to enforce the arbitrators' award instead – and succeeded.

An interesting and informative article[16] has been written by Jacob Grierson and Dr Mireille Taok, an English barrister and a member of the Paris Bar respectively, although both working in American law firms in Paris. In their article they suggest that the difference between the English

[15] Although a case has recently been decided in the Commercial Court in which the doctrine of good faith has been expressly invoked in order to supply an implied term: *Yam Seng v International Trade Corporation Ltd* [2013] EWHC 111 (QB), [2013] 1 All ER (Comm).

[16] J Grierson and Dr M Taok, '*Dallah*: Conflicting Judgments from the UK Supreme Court and the Paris Cour d'appel' in (2011) 28 *Journal of International Arbitration* 4, 407.

and the French courts' approaches to the same French law was that the English courts were more influenced by what had happened in the period leading up to the agreement, in particular the replacement of the Government by the trust and the refusal of the Government to give a guarantee of the trust; whereas the French courts were more influenced by what had happened after the agreement had been made, such as the involvement of the Government, and the inactivity of the trust, in performance of the contract and the sending of a termination letter on the Government's rather than the trust's notepaper. They also speculated that, *sub silentio*, although nothing was said about the doctrine of good faith, it was nevertheless a decisive influence.

If that is so, then this case shows that English and French courts, applying the same law, nevertheless do so in different ways, each influenced by their own traditions.

IV. Conclusion

The authors of the article suggest that whereas the English common law approach pays more attention to the bargain struck by the parties, the French approach – let us call it the civil law approach – will adopt a more holistic approach to search out the just result.

Perhaps the common law tradition will give you more of the bargain and the civil law will give you more of justice. But the business man, the shipping owner and charterer, and the sellers and buyers of goods and the banks which finance them and the insurers who insure them would probably say: More of the bargain *is* more of justice. The bargain is the parties' own allocation of risk. Or to put the matter another way: there may be a more objective and a more subjective view of justice.

And there is another possibility. The arbitration award itself was *not* decided under French law but, as I mentioned, under those 'transnational legal principles and usages reflecting the fundamental requirements of justice in international trade and the concept of good faith in business'. French law prides itself on upholding arbitration awards, at any rate in the absence of serious lack of due process. So perhaps the unspoken aspect of French law which held sway was its willingness to uphold the award. This is an inexhaustible subject, but I will leave it there.

4

Actual Carriers in Civil Law – The German Example

PROF DR DIETER SCHWAMPE*

I. Introduction

Being a German lawyer only, I will not dare and try to cover the subject for civil law in general. Rather I will restrict my discussion to the concept of actual carriers as it is found in German law today. I will start by making some remarks on the scenarios with which we are confronted when we deal with actual carriers. This will be followed by a short introduction on German law prior to the introduction of the concept of actual carriers to the Commercial Code, and then I will discuss briefly the various rules contained in German law on actual carriers.

II. Factual Scenarios Involving Actual Carriers

At the most basic level, contract of carriage is a contract entered into between a consignor and a carrier for the carriage of goods or passengers from the place of taking over the goods or passengers to the place of delivery. Where goods are carried, another person comes into play: the receiver or consignee.[1] In this chapter, I will also concentrate on

* Partner of the law firm ARNECKE SIBETH DABELSTEIN Rechtsanwälte Steuerberater Partnerschaftsgesellschaft mbB, Hamburg.

[1] § 407 German Commercial Code (HGB).

carriage of goods and make reference to carriage of passengers only where this area of law had an influence on the development of German law on the carriage of goods.

Those involved in the daily practice of transport know that there may indeed be cases, in which a transport is performed in the way just described. The contractual carrier arrives at the premises of the consignor, picks up the goods, carries them to the premises of the consignee and delivers them there. In this basic case, there is only one carrier: the contractual carrier, who carries the goods themselves. I will refer to this contract as the original contract of carriage. The parties to it are the original consignor and the original carrier; the beneficiary is the original consignee. If this were all that happens in real life, there would be no need for a concept of actual carriers.

But in many, if not in the majority of cases, life is more complicated. In modern societies with diversified economies and division of services, what in the outset is a business involving only three persons – the consignor, the carrier and the consignee – develops into a complex multi-party operation.[2] It may start by the carrier subcontracting the whole transport to another carrier. Here we have one carrier, who has contracted with the shipper for the transport of the goods, but who does not perform any part of the transport themselves. For the purposes of this chapter I will refer to such carriers as 'non-performing carriers'. There may even be more than one non-performing carrier. A party who actually performs the transport is usually referred to as the actual carrier.

As just mentioned, more than one non-performing carrier may be involved. Equally, more than one actual carrier may also be involved. A typical example would be a long-haul carrier, who has concluded the original contract of carriage with the original consignor, and who subcontracts with a carrier for picking up the goods at the consignor's premises, to bring them to the carrier's own freight yard, where they consolidates these goods with goods from other customers, and carries all goods to their freight yard at destination, where they employ another carrier for deliveries to the various consignees.

[2] H Thume, 'Die Haftung des ausführenden Frachtführers nach § 437 HGB' (2000) *Zeitschrift für Versicherungsrecht, Haftungs- und Schadensrecht* 1071, 1072.

In practice, thus, we are regularly confronted with structures involving a number of non-performing and a number of actual carriers. Involvement of more than one actual carrier usually, but not always, involves trans-shipment of the goods. This already is the case where a pallet is transferred from one truck to the other. Where different transport modes are combined is a more obvious example. We refer to this as combined or multi-modal transport. Here the transfer from one transport means to the next may include complex operations, like those in sea and air terminals, which usually include transport within the terminal and often also a certain time of storage in a terminal.[3] Those carrying out such trans-shipment operations may be carriers, in the sense that they also perform at least part of the transport themselves. But in case of sea and air transshipment, there are usually separate and independent operators, who are only engaged in performing the transshipment.[4] Here the question arises whether they can be described as actual carriers, or whether they are legally something different. As will be discussed below, German law largely treats them as actual carriers.[5]

In the absence of any rules on actual carriers, in case of loss of or damage to the goods carried, the consignor and consignee would have claims in contract against their contractual partner, the contractual carrier, and possibly non-contractual claims in tort – in German terminology we would rather use the term 'delict'.[6] But claims in delict are less attractive for a claimant, not only because of different rules on burden of proof, but also because of the possibilities for exoneration, which exist for vicarious delict liability, but not for vicarious contractual liability.[7] It is obvious that in such cases there are no contractual relations between the consignor and the actual carriers.

Prior to the introduction of the concept of actual carriers to the Commercial Code, attempts had been made to fill the contractual gap

[3] R Herber, '§ 509' in *Münchener Kommentar zum HGB*, 3rd edn (Munich, CH Beck, 2014) 902, 904.

[4] R Herber, 'Die Haftung des Unterfrachtführers gegenüber den Ladungsbeteiligten des Hauptfrachtvertrages' (2013) *Transportrecht* 1.

[5] Herber, '§ 509' (2014) 902, 905, 915.

[6] Printed Matter of the Bundestag 13/8445, draft legislation of the Federal Government – draft Act amending the law of Forwarding, Freight and Storage (trans) 73, 73, 75.

[7] Herber, 'Die Haftung des Unterfrachtführers' (2013) 1, 3.

by allowing the original consignee to pursue contractual claims not only under the original contract of carriage, but also under any sub-contract under which they are a consignee.[8] The idea generally was striking because under German law a contract of carriage is a contract for the benefit of a third party, namely the consignee.[9] However, the idea has two flaws. The first one is that it only works in respect of actual carriers delivering to the original consignee. It does not work where the actual carrier performs only an intermediate leg of the carriage. In this case, it is not the original consignee who takes delivery from an intermediate actual carrier, but someone else – usually a further performing carrier.[10] The second flaw is that the courts simply did not allow it.[11] They recognised the fact that an original consignee may indeed be the consignee also under a sub-contract of carriage, so that generally the law should give them rights also under such a sub-contract. However, the courts did not allow such rights on the basis of § 432 Commercial Code. The existence of § 432 was treated as evidence that the law-maker disapproved such direct claims under sub-contracts since § 432 would not have otherwise been necessary. As a matter of fact, apart from the concept of actual carriers having had infiltrated German law through international conventions anyhow, this jurisprudence was one of the reasons for finally introducing the concept of actual carriers into the Commercial Code.[12] It is somewhat ironic that only after such introduction did the German Federal Court of Justice change decades of jurisprudence by finally allowing claims of original consignees also under sub-contracts of carriage.[13] But it is fair to say that this change of jurisprudence does not solve the situation generally because, as just mentioned, it only helps in respect of actual carrier on the final transport leg, who delivers to the original consignee.

[8] K Rammig, 'Neues vom ausführenden Frachtführer' (2007) *Zeitschrift für Versicherungsrecht, Haftungs- und Schadensrecht* 1190, 1197.

[9] Herber (n 4) 1, 4.

[10] K Rammig, 'Die neuen Vorschriften über den ausführenden Frachtführer' (2013) *Zeitschrift für Transportrecht und Schifffahrtsrecht mit dem Recht des Überseekaufs sowie Versicherungsrecht, Zollrecht und Außenwirtschaftsrecht* 81, 83, 87.

[11] *Transportrecht* 1988, 108 (as cited in R Herber, 'Wer ist ausführender Frachtführer?' (2011) *Transportrecht* 359, 360).

[12] J Knorre, 'Zur Haftung des ausführenden Frachtführers nach § 437 HGB' (1999) *Transportrecht* 100.

[13] BGH Transportrecht 2007, 425 (as cited in Herber (n 3) 902, 911).

III. German Law Prior to the Introduction of the Concept of Actual Carriers

Modern German transport law started with the Commercial Code of 1898. The Code is still in force, but both the sections on general transport as well as on carriage by sea have been reformed – first in 1998 and later in 2013. The real 'door-opener' was the general transport law reform. The maritime law reform mainly took over the concept from the general transport law.[14]

Going back to the original transport law as contained in the Sixth Chapter of the Fourth Book of the Commercial Code, the contractual carrier's liability was dealt with in § 429 of the Commercial Code then in force. It provided for liability of the contractual carrier alone and contained no reference to any carrier other than the contractual carrier. If the contractual carrier employed other persons to fulfil their duties under the contract of carriage, § 431 of the Commercial Code then in force provided that fault of such persons was attributed to the contractual carrier with the consequence that the contractual carrier had to make good loss of or damage to the goods caused by the fault of such persons. In this context, I avoid using the term 'servants', as it might carry the notion of some kind of integration into the business of the contractual carrier.

Obviously, all such persons are embraced as well, but § 431 also covered independent contractors. This raises the question whether an actual carrier was a third party under § 431, for whose fault the contractual carrier was liable. Technically an actual carrier would qualify as such a third party, but the question was not of real relevance, as actual carriers were addressed separately by § 432 of the Commercial Code then in force. § 432 sub-sections 1 and 2 of the Commercial Code then in force read:

(1) If the contractual carrier, for the purposes of performing the transport, hands over the goods to another carrier, he is liable for the performance of the carriage until delivery to the consignee.
(2) By taking over the goods together with the original consignment note, the subsequent carrier enters into the contract of carriage according to the consignment note and assumes an independent obligation to perform the carriage as per the consignment note.

[14] Rammig, 'Die neuen Vorschriften über den ausführenden Verfrachter' (2013) 81.

The law referred in subsection (1) to the 'performance' – '*Ausführung*' – of the carriage. This seems to be a rather modern phrase, which we find later also in the Hamburg Rules, where it is used in Article 1 sub-section (2) for defining the 'actual carrier',[15] and lately in the Rotterdam Rules, where it is used in Article 1 sub-section 6 and 7 in order to define 'performing party' and 'maritime performing party', respectively.[16]

But German law at that time did not refer to an 'actual' carrier, but to a 'subsequent' carrier – a term similar to the 'successive' carrier, which we will find half a century later in Article 34 CMR,[17] of the 'succeeding railway', as referred to in Article 35 § 1 CIM 1980.

As we have seen, § 432 sub-section (2) gave rise to a claim for the entitled party, which in essence was a claim that was identical to the original contractual claim to the extent that this was reflected in the consignment note. There were different views on the dogmatic basis for such claims – whether these were genuine contractual claims, whether they were quasi-contractual claims or whether they were statutory claims with the content of contractual claims.[18] In my view, the best arguments refer it as a statutory extension of contractually liability, but despite the presence of so many learned professors of law I do not intend to go into these dogmatic details.

What is of significance, however, is that such liability of a subsequent carrier was conditional upon two things. They had to take over the goods, and the original consignment note had to be handed over to them. In practice, one rarely sees that an original consignment note is handed over to a subsequent carrier. At least in German practice, this way of providing the cargo interests with a direct contractual, or quasi-contractual, claim against the actual carrier did not really work.[19]

I have already briefly mentioned that the concept of actual carriers had infiltrated German law already earlier through international conventions prior to the two major reforms of the Commercial Code in 1998 and 2013.

[15] United Nations Convention on the carriage of goods by sea from 31 March 1978.

[16] United Nations Convention on Contracts for the International Carriage of Goods Wholly or Partly by Sea from 11 December 2008.

[17] Convention on the Contract for the International Carriage of Goods by Road from 19 May 1956.

[18] See generally, I Koller, '§ 437 HGB' in *Transportrecht: Kommentar zu Spedition, Gütertransport und Lagergeschäft*, 8th edn (Munich, CH Beck, 2013) 432, 432, 435; R Herber, '§ 437' in *Münchener Kommentar zum HGB*, 3rd edn (Munich, CH Beck, 2014) 291, 296.

[19] Printed Matter of the Bundestag 13/8445, 73 (trans).

I will not go too deeply into this, as this is not an area of peculiar German law and concepts, but it is the result of Germany ratifying those conventions. One example is the Guadalajara Convention in the field of air transport, the purpose of which mainly was to introduce the actual carrier concept into international air transport,[20] which was then dominated by the Warsaw Convention and its amendments. Article 2 of the Guadalajara Convention stipulated that if an actual carrier performs the whole or part of carriage which is governed by the Warsaw Convention, both the contracting carrier and the actual carrier shall be subject to the rules of the Warsaw Convention, the contracting carrier for the whole of the carriage, the actual carrier solely for the carriage which he performs.[21]

An interesting feature of the Convention was the way it dealt with the acts or omissions of servants and agents. Not only were the acts or omissions of servants and agents of the actual carrier deemed to be those of the contracting carrier, but the same applied also the other way round. The acts or omissions of servants and agents of the contractual carrier were deemed to be those of the actual carrier.[22] We will later see that this concept was not taken over by the general and maritime transport law reforms. However, German national air transport law at that time was somewhat aligned with the Convention,[23] though with the express limitation that the acts and omissions of the contractual carrier's servants and agents were attributed to the actual carrier only if they were related to the air transport performed by the actual carrier.

Another example is the Athens Convention of 1974 on passenger liability.[24] This was not only ratified by Germany, but its provisions were introduced also to the national German law under § 664 Commercial Code as then in force. This Convention referred to the 'performing' carrier, not to the 'actual' carrier. However, Article 4 stipulated that if the performance of the carriage or part thereof had been entrusted to a performing carrier, the performing carrier shall be subject and entitled to the provisions

[20] Convention supplementary to the Warsaw convention for the unification of certain rules relating to international carriage by air performed by a person other than the contracting carrier, signed in Guadalajara from 18 September 1961.

[21] ibid, Art II.

[22] R Herber, 'Wer ist ausführender Frachtführer?' (2011) 359, 360.

[23] S Schaffert, '§ 437' in CT Ebenroth, K Boujong, D Joost and L Strohn (eds), *Handelsgesetzbuch: HGB Band 2: §§ 343–475h*, 3rd edn (Munich, Verlag Franz Vahlen, 2015) 797, 798.

[24] Athens Convention relating to the Carriage of Passengers and their Luggage by Sea dated 13 December 1974.

of the Convention for the part of the carriage performed by him.[25] The Athens Convention also dealt with the acts and omissions of servants and agents, but different from the Guadalajara Convention it only attributed the acts and omissions of the actual carrier's servants and agents to the contractual carrier, but not the other way round.[26]

As a result of ratification, and partly incorporation of these and other international conventions, in German law, there were all kinds of different rules on actual or performing carriers, but only for international transports and for certain means of transport.

IV. (Current) German Law on Actual Carriers

After years of preparatory work, in 1998, there was a major overhaul of German transport law, which not only affected the general transport law as contained in the Fourth Book of the Commercial Code, but also embraced all the transport modes except maritime transport. Prior to the 1998 Transport Law Reform Act, transport law was split up in separate statutes dealing with different transport modes, such as the Inland Navigation Act for inland shipping, the Motor Traffic Regulation for long-haul road transport, the Air Traffic Act for carriage by air and the National Railway Act for rail transport. § 407 Commercial Code in its current version now applies whenever goods are carried on land, on inland waterways or by aircraft, leaving only maritime transport aside. I should add that we also have particular provisions on multi-modal transport.[27] But as far as relevant here they merely refer to general transport law. Under German law, the liability of a multimodal carrier is the same as that of a general unimodal carrier.

The Commercial Code now also includes a provision on actual carriers. In the English translation provided by the German Transport Law Association, § 437 reads in English as follows:[28]

> (1) Where carriage is performed, in whole or in part, by a third party, then that third party (Actual Carrier) shall be liable, in the same way as if he

[25] ibid, Art IV.
[26] ibid.
[27] See generally, Herber, '§ 437' (2014) 291, 303.
[28] www.transportrecht.org/dokumente/HGB_4_Buch_2013_DGTR_d_en_2016_01_26_RS.pdf.

were the Contractual Carrier, for any damage resulting from the loss of, or damage to, the goods or from delay in delivery during the carriage performed by him. Any agreement with the Consignor or the consignee whereby the Contractual Carrier expands his liability shall affect the Actual Carrier only insofar as the latter has agreed to them in writing.

(2) The Actual Carrier may rely on all objections and defences which the Contractual Carrier is entitled to raise under the contract for the carriage of goods.

(3) The Contractual Carrier and the Actual Carrier shall be jointly and severally liable.

In my view, this translation is not completely accurate. I would say that the German expression '*ausführender Verfrachter*' is better translated to 'performing carrier' rather than 'actual carrier'. From now on I will, therefore, refer to 'performing carrier', instead of 'actual carrier'.

As mentioned, this law does not apply to ocean shipping. Maritime law was reformed 15 years after the general transport law reform. The Maritime Law Reform Act entered into force on 25 April 2013.[29] It also contains a provision on actual carriers. § 509 Commercial Code reads, again as translated by the German Transport Law Association,[30] as follows:

(1) Where carriage is performed, in whole or in part, by a third party who is not the Contractual Carrier, then that third party (Performing Carrier) shall be liable in the same way as if he were the Contractual Carrier, for any damage resulting from the loss of, or damage to, the goods during the carriage performed by him.

(2) Any agreement with the Contractual Shipper or the consignee whereby the Contractual Carrier expands his liability shall affect the Performing Carrier only insofar as the latter has agreed to them in writing.

(3) The Performing Carrier may rely on all objections and defences which the Contractual Carrier is entitled to raise under the contract for the carriage of general cargo.

(4) The Contractual Carrier and the Performing Carrier shall be jointly and severally liable.

You will note that the German Transport Law Association here has chosen the term 'performing carrier' rather than 'actual carrier'. This seems to indicate different original German terms, but in fact both § 437 and § 509

[29] Maritime Law Reform Act dated 20 April 2013.

[30] www.transportrecht.org/dokumente/HGB_5_Buch_Uebersetzung_DGTR_2015_05_11.pdf.

use the same word '*ausführender*', for this reason, I prefer to use the term 'performing carrier' for both provisions.

If you compare the two provisions of §§ 437 and 509, you will note that they are almost, but not completely, identical. One difference is more formal, namely that what used to be a separate sub-section 2 in § 437 has become the second sentence of sub-section 1 in § 509.

Another difference, and this is a significant difference, is that whilst § 437 subjects the performing carrier to liability for loss of or damage to goods and for delay in delivery, the performing carrier in the maritime world is only subjected to liability for loss of or damage to goods. Delay in delivery is not addressed. But this is not the result of an intentional protection for maritime performing carriers. It is simply the consequence of the fact that general carriers under German law are also subject to special transport law liability for delay in delivery, whilst maritime carriers are not.[31] They are also liable, though not under special transport law provisions, but under the default rules of general civil law. It is noteworthy, however, that § 509 does not refer to such general civil law liability. A further substantial difference is that the language used in § 509 is not part of § 437. A performing carrier is only a third party, which is not the contracting carrier.

A. The Identity of the Performing Carrier

Who is a performing carrier? The law requires, both for general and maritime performing carriers, that they are 'third' parties. So, who would be the first and the second party? The Commercial Code does not address this directly, but it does so indirectly by saying that the third party has taken over, in whole or in part 'the carriage'. 'The carriage' in this context is the carriage which the contractual carrier has agreed to perform under the original contract of carriage with its contractual counterpart; in German general transport law terminology it is called the '*Absender*', which may properly be translated to 'consignor'. In the context of maritime law, it is called '*Befrachter*', which means 'contractual shipper'. Therefore, we now know that the performing carrier is a third party, which is neither the contractual carrier nor the consignor or contractual shipper.[32]

[31] Rammig (n 11) 81, 82.
[32] See generally Schaffert, '§ 437' (2015) 797, 800.

The additional language in § 509, which requires that the performing carrier is not the contractual carrier, does not therefore add anything in substance.

However, one person has yet to be addressed: the consignee. In many of the German commentaries on § 437, you will find a somewhat misleading sentence. It says that the performing carrier must not be in a contractual relationship with either the consignor or, what is relevant here, the consignee.[33] I believe this is wrong. A contractual relation with the consignee arises already from a contract of carriage, as it gives the consignee contractual rights against the carrier. Any engagement of a performing carrier, who provides for delivery of the goods to the original consignee, therefore, creates a contractual relationship between the performing carrier and the original consignee.

More important, however, is the question whether an original consignee can be a performing carrier himself. Despite all that has been published on performing carriers, basically one finds no comment as to whether a consignee can be a performing carrier. I believe they can. It is fair to say that a consignee cannot have claims against themselves if they perform part of the carriage themselves and cause damage to the goods whilst they are in their custody. But the consignee is not the only party entitled to damages under a contract of carriage. The consignor can equally be entitled.

Moreover, depending on the circumstances, they may be the party actually suffering the damage if the sale contract provides that the goods are carried at their risk. If the original contractual carrier, or any other sub-carrier, engages with the original consignee by performing part of the contractual transport, in my view they have to be considered as a performing carrier under § 437. There are even better arguments for this under § 509, which only excludes the contractual carrier from being a performing carrier, so that, *argumentum contrarii*, the consignee is not so excluded.

B. Is a Contract Required?

I turn to the next aspect, namely whether a contract – a valid contract – is required. Usually the performing carrier will perform all or part of the

[33] ibid 797, 801.

carriage on the basis of a contract which, again, they usually conclude with another carrier, either the original contractual carrier, or a sub-carrier of such an original carrier. However, the law does not require such a contract. The only relevant aspect is the actual performance. If there is no actual sub-contract with the performing carrier, because the parties, without realising it prior to the performance, did not perfect the contract or did not agree on an essential aspect, or if the contract is void, for example because it is in breach of sanctions, this is irrelevant for the liability of the performing carrier. Even without a valid contract of their own, they become liable together with the contractual carrier.[34]

We do not therefore need a valid contract for the performing carrier. However, do we at least need a valid original contract of carriage at all? And if so, must this contract be subject to German law? Both questions are answered in the affirmative. Without a valid contract of carriage, there would be no basis for making the performing carrier liable as if they were the contractual carrier.[35] The second aspect is trickier. Here views are actually not unanimous. Some say that the contract of carriage may be subject to foreign law as long as the liability of the performing carrier, under conflict of laws rules, is subject to German law.[36] This is certainly not the right moment to discuss conflict of laws issues, which are delicate, because they require determination of whether the performing carrier's liability is a contractual or non-contractual one.

However, regardless of this issue, it would be somewhat weird if German law were to provide that a performing carrier, who would even not necessarily have to be a German performing carrier, would be liable on the basis of German law, when determining their liability under foreign law.[37] First, this could cause conflicts with the law governing the original contract of carriage, if this law also contains provisions, but different provisions, on performing carriers. And second, the provisions on performing carriers are an integral part of the German transport law. There is no indication that the law-maker intended to expose the performing carrier to any greater or lesser liability than that provided for in the Commercial Code. Therefore, liability under § 437 or § 509 requires that the contract of carriage is

[34] Printed Matter of the Bundestag 13/8445 73, 74.

[35] See generally, Koller, '§ 437 HGB' (2013) 432, 432, 435.

[36] Schmidt, '§ 437' in C-W Canaris, M Habersack and C (eds), *Handelsgesetzbuch: HGB Band 12: §§ 407–424; 436–442*, 5th edn (Berlin, De Gruyter, 2013) 204, 209.

[37] Herber (n 19) 291, 295, 296.

subject to German law.[38] Even those legal authorities who deny this finally reach the same result by saying that the performing carrier's liability under foreign law could not exceed that under German law.[39]

C. What is Performed?

What the performing carrier must perform is carriage.[40] This may sound self-explanatory, but it serves an important purpose. What a performing carrier must perform is something that would have made them a carrier, if they had contracted with the original consignor.[41] This excludes any service provided which is not carriage in the sense that it is what a contractual carrier would agree to perform in the contract of carriage. For this reason, neither drivers nor other employees are performing carriers, as they just carry out their employment duties.[42] Neither are the lessors of rental trucks carriers. They just make trucks available, but do not perform carriage services.

D. Liability 'as if he were the Carrier'

And what now is the liability of a performing carrier? The law says that they are liable 'as if he were the contractual carrier'.[43] What they shall be so liable for is loss of or damage to goods and, for general performing carriers, delay in delivery.[44] What it means that the performing carrier is liable as if they were the contractual carrier should first be discussed. What the law creates here is obviously a fiction. It is a requirement under §§ 437 and 509 that the performing carrier has no contract with the original consignor. Once this requirement is fulfilled, the law treats the non-contractual performing carrier as if they had a contract.[45] The first consequence is that the

[38] Herber (n 19) 291, 295; Rammig (n 11) 81, 85.
[39] ibid.
[40] See generally, Herber (n 3) 902, 905, JD Paschke, '§ 437' in H Oetker (ed) *Kommentar zum Handelsgesetzbuch (HGB)*, 4th edn (Munich, C Beck, 2015) 2061, 2063.
[41] Paschke (ibid) 2061, 2063.
[42] Rammig (n 11) 81, 83.
[43] § 437 German Commercial Code (HGB).
[44] See generally Schaffert (n 24) 797, 801, 802.
[45] Herber (n 3) 902, 908.

performing carrier has no greater liabilities than the contractual carrier.[46] If, for example, under the original contract of carriage, the consignor had to load and stow the goods in the vessel and goods are damaged during loading, then the liability of the performing carrier does not include such damage, as their liabilities do not exceed those of the contractual carrier.

Apart from that, the performing carrier does not only have all the liabilities, but also all the rights and defences which the law avails for a contractual carrier.[47] He is liable, thus, for any loss or damage caused whilst the goods were in custody. How to avoid such liability depends on whether they perform general or maritime carriage. In the first case, they have to establish that they could not avoid the loss or damage even by exercising the utmost diligence and that they were unable to prevent the consequences of the loss or damage.[48] If they performs maritime carriage, the requirements are lower. Here they are released insofar as the loss or damage was due to circumstances that could not have been avoided by a prudent sea carrier exercising due care.[49] Apart from this, the performing carrier may also rely on all statutory exclusions from liability as provided for by § 427 for general transport and § 499 for maritime transport.[50]

I now briefly turn to delay in delivery. Nothing special arises here for general transport, as the performing carrier is liable for delay as if they were the contractual carrier.[51] But as mentioned earlier, a similar stipulation is missing in the context of maritime law, simply because the German maritime law does not contain provisions on delay in delivery. Instead, the general rules on default under the German Civil Code apply.[52] Accordingly, an original maritime carrier may be liable for damage for delay under the default rules of civil law. Can the performing maritime carrier be similarly liable? He cannot. Whilst the law stipulates that he is liable 'as if he were the contractual carrier',[53] the law stipulates this only in respect of loss of or damage to the goods.

As mentioned earlier, the Federal Court of Justice allows the original consignee also to raise claims under a sub-contract of carriage if they are

[46] See generally Herber (n 19) 291, 292, 296; Koller (n 19) 433, 434, 440, 441.
[47] ibid.
[48] Herber (n 19) 291, 296 p.
[49] See generally, Herber (n 3) 902, 908.
[50] See generally, Herber (n 19) 291, 298; Herber (n 3) 902, 908.
[51] Schaffert (n 24) 797, 801.
[52] Herber (n 3) 902, 908.
[53] § 437 German Commercial Code (HGB); § 509 German Commercial Code (HGB).

the consignee also under such a sub-contract. This is always the case, if they take delivery under the sub-contract. Consequently, what I would call the final performing carrier is exposed to liability as a performing carrier (and therefore not liable for the delay in delivery) and also as a contractual carrier. Under this sub-contract, they may well be liable for delay in delivery. However, one must always be aware that this is a liability arising from their own contract, not a liability arising from their position as a performing carrier.

E. Availability of Defences

All the above relates to statutory law on the contractual liability of a carrier. But, as we have seen before, there is a requirement for an original contract of carriage to exist and be valid. What about the content of that contract? Are contractual agreements made between the original carrier and the original consignor of any relevance for the performing carrier? The answer is not the typical lawyers answer 'it depends', but an equally indifferent answer: 'yes and no'. Yes, the original contract is of relevance as it provides the rights and defences for the carrier, which go beyond those of the law. § 437 sub-section 2 and § 509 sub-section 3 expressly say that the performing carrier may rely on all objections and defences which the contractual carrier is entitled to raise under the contract for the carriage.[54] The reason for this is that an original consignor, who lessens the burden of their contractual partner, shall not be put into a better position if someone else is performing the carriage. One may be critical in this respect, because the privileges given to the carrier may be privileges they have been given for their own reputation and care. But such argument can be easily countered with the argument that an original consignor, who grants privileges to the original carrier due to their special reputation and care, can avoid other parties benefiting from such privileges by contractually agreeing that the contractual carrier has to perform the carriage themselves and must not sub-contract to other parties.

However, the original contract of carriage is relevant only to the extent that it improves the situation of the performing carrier when comparing it

[54] § 437 German Commercial Code (HGB); § 509 German Commercial Code (HGB).

with the statutory law. Both § 437 and § 509 say that any agreement with the consignor or the consignee whereby the contractual carrier increasing their liability shall affect the performing carrier only insofar as they have agreed to them in writing.[55] In practice, I have never seen this happen.

F. Liability During Own Custody

The performing carrier is liable only for damage 'resulting from the loss of, or damage to, the goods'[56] and in general transport 'or from delay in delivery during the carriage performed by him'.[57] Loss or damage caused and occurred before the beginning and after the end of the custody of the performing carrier do not lead to their liability.[58]

However, there may be situations where, due to circumstances prior to them taking the goods into their custody, the damage occurred during their custody is unavoidable. One example is that the performing carrier takes over the goods so late that even with utmost dispatch it is impossible for them do deliver the goods to the consignee in time. Another example is that a preceding performing carrier has failed to repair the reefer unit of a container, so that even after repairs by the following performing carrier damage occurs to, for example, cooled meat. In these cases, damage occurs during the custody of the carrier, but there is agreement that this does not lead to their liability.[59]

G. Liability for Third Parties

Since the performing carrier is liable 'as if he were the contractual carrier',[60] they are liable for any third party they employ for the performance of their carriage. These are their only employees.[61] But what about the employees of a contractual carrier? Obviously, the contractual carrier would

[55] § 437 German Commercial Code (HGB); § 509 German Commercial Code (HGB).
[56] ibid.
[57] § 437 German Commercial Code (HGB); see generally: Herber (n 3) 902, 908.
[58] See generally, Herber (n 19) 291, 297.
[59] See generally, Herber (n 19) 291, 297; against: Koller (n 19) 433, 440.
[60] § 437 German Commercial Code (HGB); § 509 German Commercial Code (HGB).
[61] See generally Schaffert (n 24) 797, 801.

be liable for their acts and omissions. As the performing carrier shall be liable 'as if he were the contractual carrier', the question arises as to whether they are also liable for the servants of the contractual carrier. The unanimous answer in Germany is 'no'.[62]

H. Limitations of Liability

It is timely to discuss limitations, considering both the quantum and time. As regards quantum, the performing carrier may rely on limitations of liability available to the contractual carrier, such as the statutory limitations. In general transport law, the limit is 8.33 SDR per kilogram,[63] and in maritime law it is 2 SDR per kilogram or 666.67 SDR per package,[64] whichever is higher.

Unlimited liability arises if the performing carrier acted intentionally or recklessly with knowledge that damage would probably result. In general transport law, but not in maritime transport law, limitation is also unavailable if the servants of the performing carrier act intentionally or recklessly.[65] Just as with liability for third parties, intent or recklessness of the contractual carrier alone does not expose the performing carrier to unlimited liability.

As to time limits, claims against the performing carrier are clearly independent from those against the contractual carrier.[66] The statutory time limits start to run with delivery to the consignee.[67] If the performing carrier performs the last leg of the transport the same rules apply. However, if damages arose in the custody of a performing carrier who was not supposed to deliver the goods to the original consignee, the limitation period against them would start earlier than that against the contractual carrier, and it will consequently expire earlier.[68] Some disagree and say that the time starts to run with delivery to the original consignee.[69] I believe this

[62] Schaffert (n 24) 797, 799.
[63] § 431 German Commercial Code (HGB).
[64] § 504 German Commercial Code (HGB).
[65] § 435 German Commercial Code (HGB).
[66] Herber (n 19) 291, 302; Koller (n 19) 433, 446.
[67] Koller (n 19) 433, 446.
[68] Herber (n 19) 291, 302.
[69] See especially, Rammig, 'Die Haftung des ausführenden Frachtführers nach § 437 HGB' (2000).

is wrong. It is correct only for performing carriers in case of multimodal carriage because § 452b sub-section 2 stipulates that the limitation periods start to run upon delivery to the original consignee. There is no such rule for unimodal transport.[70]

As regards suspension of the running of a time limit, it depends on what steps were taken against which party.[71] For example, a claim raised against the contractual carrier suspends the time from running for claims against them, but not the time running for claims against the performing carrier.[72]

V. Conclusion: Special Aspects for Maritime Performing Carriers

The special aspects arising in maritime carriage should finally be discussed. It is noteworthy that the expert commissions that had been installed by the German Ministry of Justice had suggested that the only performing carrier in the case of maritime carriage should be the owner(s) or the bareboat charterer(s) of the carrying vessel(s).[73] The law-maker decided against this. As a result, port terminals carrying out loading, stowage, securing and unloading operations now can incur carrier's liabilities as performing carriers.[74] Also time charterers can incur such liabilities if they are responsible for cargo operations under the time charter party.[75]

A final point to note is related to deck carriage. The maritime law reforms have widened the carrier's liability for deck carriage significantly. Except where the goods are placed in or on a loading device suitable for on-deck carriage, this will mainly be containers, and unless the deck has been properly fitted, goods may be loaded on deck only with the consent of the shipper. More importantly, § 500 now stipulates a no-fault liability for unauthorised deck carriage.[76] This applies also to performing carriers.[77]

[70] See generally, Herber (n 19) 291, 302.
[71] See generally, S Schaffert (n 24) 797, 805.
[72] Koller (n 19) 433, 447.
[73] See generally, Herber (n 3) 902, 904.
[74] Herber (n 3) 902, 915.
[75] K Rammig (n 11) 81, 83.
[76] § 500 German Commercial Code (HGB).
[77] Rammig (n 11) 81, 85.

They will incur liability to the original consignor or consignee even if their own contract of carriage allows them to carry on deck. In such a case, their only remedy will be an indemnity claim against their contractual partner. The law even provides an unlimited no-fault liability for deck-carriage if under deck carriage had been agreed. However, this requires an agreement for under deck carriage, which should be an 'agreement with the contractual shipper or the consignee whereby the contractual carrier expands his liability'.[78] According to § 509 sub-section 2 the performing carrier is bound to it only if he has agreed in writing.

[78] § 509 German Commercial Code (HGB).

5

Actual Carriers in Common Law

PROFESSOR FRANCIS REYNOLDS*

I. Introduction: The Meaning of 'Actual Carrier'

I believe the term 'actual carrier' was first used in aviation law. A simple definition for the maritime context is to be found in the Hamburg Rules:[1]

> Actual carrier means any person to whom the performance of the carriage of the goods, or of part of the carriage, has been entrusted by the carrier, and includes any other person to whom such performance has been entrusted.

I have always found the reference to the 'other person' rather unclear, and the more detailed definition of 'performing party' in the Rotterdam Rules is perhaps more useful:

> Performing party means a person other than the carrier that performs or undertakes to perform any of the carrier's obligation under a contract of carriage with respect to the receipt, loading, handling, stowage, carriage, care, unloading or delivery of the goods, to the extent that such person acts, either directly or indirectly, at the carrier's request or under the carrier's supervision or control.[2]

So I take the term 'actual carrier' to refer to a situation involving a contrast between a 'contracting carrier' and the 'actual carrier', whereby the first refers to a party who, whether or not it operates ships (it may for instance be a non-vessel-owning carrier), enters into a contract to carry goods, in our case by sea; and the second to the party who, whether as an immediate subcontractor or as one operating through one or more layers of

* Professor Francis Reynolds QC, FBA.

[1] Article 1.2.

[2] Article 1.6(a). After that, of course, the Rotterdam Rules for most purposes narrow down to the concept of the 'maritime performing party', which begins another story not within our scope here.

intermediate contracts, actually carries the goods for all or part of the time.[3] Such a party can also be called a 'performing carrier'.

If we assume that the contracting carrier is an independent actor who delegates to others, the main liability of the actual carrier must obviously in principle be a contractual one only to the party, probably the contracting carrier who engaged them. On this analysis, if the shipper (or other claimant, eg receiver), who makes no such contract with the actual carrier, wishes to sue the actual carrier,[4] the action must lie, in common law terms, in tort, in extra-contractual liability for losing,[5] destroying or damaging goods in which the shipper or their successor has or had an appropriate interest.

It is possible to alter this position by establishing a special regime for actual carriers. The first example is again the Hamburg Rules, under which 'All the provisions of this Convention governing the responsibility of the carrier also apply to the responsibility of the actual carrier for the carriage performed by him'[6] and their responsibility is joint and several.[7] The Rotterdam Rules, albeit referring only to a maritime performing party, go further in stating that such a party 'is subject to the obligations and liabilities imposed on the carrier under this Convention and is entitled to the carrier's defences and limits of liability as provided for in this Convention'.[8]

This subjects the actual carrier to the contracting carrier's *obligations* also, and therefore goes one step further than the Hamburg Rules, which only apply to 'responsibility'. The extent to which such a solution or anything similar is applied in civil law countries is a matter dealt with in Professor Schwampe's paper. On the extended wording which includes obligations, one needs to consider what obligations the actual carrier undertakes,[9] and whether its liability is regarded as statutory or contractual,

[3] Sometimes, as in some of the cargo in *The Pioneer Container*, below, after the contracting carrier's voyage is complete.

[4] Reasons for doing so would include desire to arrest the ship and proof of damage.

[5] This might require bailment reasoning; see below.

[6] Article 10.2.

[7] Article 10.4.

[8] Articles 1.7, 19.

[9] There are at least four positive obligations: (i) to carry the goods to destination; (ii) to do so without undue delay, or at the least, within any agreed time; (iii) to exercise care over them while they are in transit; and (iv) to take certain steps on delivery. It is not clear how far the shipper's liability for dangerous goods, which would appear to be strict, is to be taken as modifying the carrier's duties.

which would create implications for the conflict of laws. But nothing like either the Hamburg or the Rotterdam solution has been suggested for common law, the latter of which would require, for the obligations at least, a statutory cause of action. Under common law, the actual carrier gives a contractual undertaking to the contracting carrier, not to the shipper. If the actual carrier is to be sued, the action will lie in tort for losing, destroying or damaging the goods, and the complications which arise will largely be as to the extent to which such a tort claim is affected by the provisions of the main contract of carriage between shipper and contracting carrier (which of course largely means, at present, the Hague or Hague–Visby Rules). The main point to consider for common law is then to what extent the actual carrier can be protected by the stipulations in the main contract of carriage: whereas in at least some civil law countries, as Professor Schwampe points out, the emphasis can be said to be on actually imposing liability on the actual carrier.

II. The Actual Carrier Problem at Common Law

Common law, or at any rate English common law, has been slow to accept third-party rights under contracts. The main theme of this chapter is that the case law in the area of actual carriers (and also stevedores) has been a vehicle for quite remarkable manipulations of reasoning entirely made necessary by this fact. But as I shall also say near the end of this chapter, in England this has now mostly, but not entirely, been made superfluous by legislation of 1999 on third-party contracts.

A. *Adler v Dickson*

The story starts from the fact that a general tort remedy for liability for negligence causing personal injury or loss of or damage to property was in English common law only fully articulated (by case law) in 1932.[10] Before and for some time after that it seems to have been assumed that persons acting under the umbrella of a main contract (employees, agents,

[10] *Donoghue v Stevenson* [1932] AC 562.

subcontractors) were entitled to the protection of that contract – in general a perfectly reasonable view. There was of course only slow development during the Second World War. But it still came as something of a surprise to the profession when in 1954 it was decided that a passenger on the P&O liner *Himalaya*, a Mrs Adler, could sue the master (Captain Dickson) and bosun of the vessel for negligent operation of the gangway at Trieste, causing personal injury. P&O's ticket protected them to the utmost (of course!), but the master and bosun were not party to it.[11]

Passenger matters might be minor commercially, but cargo ship operators use not only many employees, but also many subcontractors and others (who might sometimes be described as agents), and these might now be exposed to actions in tort which could conceivably be independent of the terms on which the main contractor was carrying the goods. The decision therefore caused alarm in maritime commercial circles. Lawyers set to draft a new clause for insertion into bills of lading protecting subcontractors (and others); but before this had been tested the matter was pursued to the highest court in the UK, at that time the House of Lords, in the context of stevedore subcontractors, and it was held in 1962 in *Midland Silicones Ltd v Scruttons Ltd*[12] that they could not rely on the terms of the relevant bill of lading to secure the package or unit limitation or the time bar, the parts of the main contract of carriage principally relevant to subcontractors who do not perform the voyage. For a considerable time after that, attention continued to be focused on stevedores and not on actual carriers, even though the latter were and are equally likely to be subcontractors.

B. A Note on Title to Sue

In most, if not all, legal systems, if a cargo claimant wishes to sue in tort for destruction of or damage to goods, it must normally prove some interest in them. For a common lawyer this would be ownership, possession or perhaps the immediate right to possess. It may sometimes be difficult to know who owned (to use a general term) the relevant cargo at the time

[11] *Adler v Dickson* [1955] 1 QB 158.

[12] [1962] AC 446. There were similar decisions regarding stevedores in the US and Australia around the same time.

it was damaged.[13] And it was decided in the context of cargo claims that merely being on risk in respect of the goods involves a claim for pure economic loss, and that this is not one of the (in common law, somewhat exceptional) cases where such a claim can validly be made.[14] Thus ownership (or something similar) of the goods lost or damaged is crucial. Bringing a tort action may also raise greater problems in that negligence must be proved. Whereas if the actual carrier is regarded as subject to the obligations and liabilities of the contracting carrier, as the Rotterdam Rules provide, the action would be either contractual or statutory (as being Convention-based) rather than tortious.

I now move into the ingenious means that have been employed by common law courts for getting round the doctrine of privity of contract in this context.

C. The Himalaya Clause

The clause drafted to protect subcontractors and the like, which had not come into use at the time of the *Midland Silicones* case referred to above, was soon called the 'Himalaya clause' because of the ship concerned in the original decision, the reasoning in which it was designed to evade: and the term has survived not only to designate clauses of this type, but even into phrases such as 'the Himalaya problem'. It was first tested in England in a case of 1975 on appeal from (as was then possible) New Zealand, *The Eurymedon*.[15]

If one has a strict doctrine of privity of contract it is obviously unlikely that a clause merely purporting to give the benefit of the contract, or of some of it, to a third party is going to have much effect. Most, if not all, shipping lawyers have seen some form of the Himalaya clause, of which there are now many variants, frequently mistranscribed, in bills of lading. From a common lawyer's point of view the elaborate wording appears to be no more than a lengthy attempt to press into service any line of reasoning

[13] This was so in *The Starsin*, discussed below, where there was also a problem as to at which moment the cargo became damaged.

[14] *The Aliakmon* [1986] AC 785. The case also rejects an approach which would regard the tort liability assumed by the actual carrier as simply based on the undertakings in the contract under which it took the goods.

[15] [1975] AC 154.

that some later tribunal might conceivably find relevant, such as agency, creation of an additional party to the contract of carriage and even trust. It is just about possible to utilise some of these in the present context, but in *The Eurymedon* the relevant court, the Privy Council, applied an analysis which, although it owed something to agency reasoning, accepted what was really a different explanation: that the clause created an implied contract between shipper and stevedore under which the stevedore loaded the goods in return for the benefit of the carrier's exclusions and limitations. There were all sorts of difficulties regarding the moment of formation of the supposed contract. (What if the stevedores dropped the goods before they had crossed the ship's rail? Bearing in mind the common law requirement of consideration, what did the stevedores really obtain in return? Presumably the benefit of exclusion and limitation clauses, but what does that mean? A promise not to seek to hold them liable in excess of the limits and, if so, to whom? Does it matter that they were already bound by contract to do what they did? And how can one transmit such reasoning to the stevedores at the port of discharge (who apparently needed a further implied contract because of problems in the statute transmitting the contract to a receiver)? And so forth.) But in a later Australian case, *The New York Star*, the first decision was rather rashly challenged, the famous common law judge Lord Wilberforce (who gave judgment in both cases) saying:

> Although, in each case, there will be room for evidence as to the precise relationship of carrier and stevedore and as to the practice at the relevant port, the decision does not support, and their Lordships would not encourage, a search for fine distinctions which would diminish the general applicability, in the light of established commercial practice, of the principle.[16]

A further problem about the Himalaya clause surfaced later – indeed, quite recently – this time in the context of its application not to stevedores, but to actual carriers. The clause in its standard form has (at least) two parts: one seeks to exempt the carrier from all liability, but the other merely

[16] *The New York Star* [1980] 1 WLR 138. In the High Court of Australia in the same case Barwick CJ had said (in a dissenting judgment): 'Their Lordships' decision in *The Eurymedon* was of great moment in the commercial world, and, if I may say so, an outstanding example of the ability of the law to render effective the practical expectations of those engaged in the transportation of goods. It is not a decision of its nature to be narrowly or pedantically confined.' Lord Hobhouse in *The Starsin*, below, refers at [152] to 'the Barwick contract'.

gives it the benefit of the contractual protections (usually the Hague or Hague–Visby Rules). No one has, so far as I know, adduced a satisfactory explanation for this belt and braces approach. In the context of stevedores it seems to have gone unnoticed. This appears to have been partly because in both *The Eurymedon* and *The New York Star* the time bar had run, so the stevedore was discharged by the operation of the second part of the clause without needing to invoke the first; and partly perhaps because a complete immunity for stevedores was satisfactory to many carriers and may not have worried others.[17] But what was to be done where the complete immunity was claimed by an actual carrier, a subcontractor who, as opposed to a stevedore, actually undertook carriage of goods in respect of a principal contract to the terms of which an international convention was applicable? It might well seem acceptable to give such a party the benefit of the bill of lading regime, but why should it (as opposed to a stevedore) be completely immune from liability?

D. *The Starsin*

The matter came up as late as 2003 in the privity case that gave rise to the most diffuse and complex set of judgments of all, *The Starsin*.[18] This was a direct tort claim against an actual carrier, who initially sought to rely on the first part of the Himalaya clause (that providing for complete non-liability) in the main contract of carriage. One of the five judges in the House of Lords accepted the view that the purpose of this part of the clause was to channel all claims to the contracting carrier only. But the remainder (though with differing reasoning) accepted that the actual carrier could have no more than the protections of the Hague Rules under which the goods were being carried (in accordance with the second part of the clause). To achieve this the implied contract of *The Eurymedon* (whether because it involved participation to a limited extent in the main contract of carriage, or because it was itself a contract of carriage) was held by various means, some less convincing than others, to come under the prohibition of evasion of the Rules in Article III.8.[19] The report contains a striking

[17] Except in Australia, where there may have been disapproval by some.
[18] [2003] UKHL 12, [2004] 1 AC 715.
[19] The most elaborate analysis of the implied contract is given by Lord Hobhouse at [147]ff.

statement by Lord Bingham, the presiding judge, whose reasoning was more general, to the effect that a different conclusion 'would be to elevate form over substance and to invest what is essentially a legal device with a wholly disproportionate legal significance'.[20]

The case also involved another problem relating to actual carriers: the fact that it may not be clear from the bill of lading which of the two potential carriers involved is the carrier in law. In *The Starsin* there was clear indication on the face of the bill of lading that the charterer was intended to be the carrier, but on the reverse was a demise clause[21] under which the owner would be the carrier. A commercial preference for the front of the document rather than the effect of the whole led to the interpretation that the owner was only an actual carrier: but had the result been otherwise he would have been a contracting carrier, and many of the problems would have been avoided. The solution of this serious uncertainty does not concern the regime for actual carriers, but is a matter for regulation of the contents of bills of lading: the Rotterdam Rules contain several pages on the topic.[22]

E. The *Elbe Maru* Clause

Another solution to the problem is an ingenious clause, the effectiveness of which was first accepted in England in the case of *The Elbe Maru*,[23] and forms of which are often also referred to under the title 'Circular Indemnity clause'. The shipper (often referred to as the 'Merchant') in effect promises not to sue sub-contractors. If it does so it may be liable in damages to the owner for the loss caused to the owner by its doing so (if the liabilities are correctly set up); or possibly it agrees to indemnify the owner against loss caused to the owner by its breaching the undertaking. Such a provision sometimes appears not separate, but incorporated into what is otherwise a traditional Himalaya clause. Under some legal systems (including England and Wales) it may be possible to restrain the shipper's action on the basis that the action is one which they promised not to bring. When the clause

[20] [2003] UKHL at [34].
[21] In fact two, one called 'Identity of carrier', inaccurately transcribed.
[22] Articles 35–42.
[23] [1978] 1 Lloyd's Rep 206.

works it has the effect of creating a complete immunity from liability of the subcontractors referred to in it: the intention is to route all claims through the carrier. The obvious problem is that it is only the owner to whom the promise was made who can take whatever steps are available against the shipper or later holder of the bill of lading who disregards the promise made under the clause. There may also be problems as to the application of damages rules and as to the operation of the clause when the bill of lading has been transferred. It may be that in some contexts (eg where the bill is issued by a freight forwarder, or by a member of a consortium) the promise not to sue is easy to enforce if necessary. But if the clause is effective, when applied to an actual carrier (as opposed, for example, to a stevedore), it is open to the same objection as the first part of the Himalaya clause discussed in *The Starsin*: it makes an actual carrier completely immune from liability. It has so far been held that it does not contravene Article III.8 of the Hague and Hague–Visby Rules where the protected subcontractors did not carry the goods: but whether it would otherwise do so was not decided.[24]

F. Hague–Visby Rules Article IV.bis

As is well known, Article IV.bis was adopted at Visby to deal with the problems of actions in tort against carriers and gives the protections of the Rules to servants or agents of the carrier (such as Captain Dickson of the *Himalaya*). It is referred to in the *travaux préparatoires* as being within '*le problème du Himalaya*'. But since it specifically exempts independent contractors from its provisions, it is unlikely that it makes any contribution to the problems of stevedores and actual carriers.

G. A Specialised Common Law Technique: Bailment Reasoning

A different, but substantial, inroad into the problems created by the normal rules of privity of contract can be made by use of bailment reasoning.

[24] *The Marielle Bolten* [2009] EWHC 2552 (Comm), [2010] 1 Lloyd's Rep.648, rightly rejecting some most improbable arguments, and giving a good survey of the problem.

I always call bailment 'the secret weapon of the common law'. The notion stems from a time before the present differentiation of obligations into contract and tort was established, and from a time when some parts of the law proceeded by attaching particular incidents to particular relationships. The reasoning is that if one party (the bailor) transfers a chattel to another person (the bailee) to hold for them, certain appropriate results ensue: 'The duties of a bailee arise out of the voluntary assumption of possession of another's goods'.[25] These duties deal with care of the goods, and will vary in accordance with the purpose of the bailment; and contract terms can be superimposed on the bailment relationship.[26] But the underlying relationship remains present, albeit somewhat underground, in the common law, and can sometimes be invoked with unexpected consequences. I doubt whether there is a clear parallel elsewhere.

H. The Pioneer Container

The first use of such reasoning in the context of actual carriers was established in the case of *The Pioneer Container*,[27] this time on an appeal from Hong Kong, in 1994. This involved multiple proceedings against an actual carrier carrying goods from Taiwan to Hong Kong. In one group of cases, it was carrying goods shipped under Hanjin bills of lading in the US for Hong Kong and transhipped in Taiwan for delivery at Hong Kong; and in the other carrying goods from Taiwan to Hong Kong under a Scandutch bill of lading envisaging transhipment there onto a vessel proceeding to a destination in Europe.[28] The ship was lost in a collision between Taiwan and Hong Kong, and the actual carrier when sued sought to rely on a clause in *its own* bills of lading providing for jurisdiction in Taiwan and the application of the law of Taiwan. These were constituted by a single bill of lading for the trans-shipped Hanjin goods and a single feeder bill for the Scandutch goods proceeding to Hong Kong for trans-shipment.

[25] *East West Corp v DKBS 1912* [2003] EWCA Civ 83, [2003] QB 1509 at [24]. See also substantial discussion in *Yearworth v North Bristol NHS Trust* [2009] EWCA Civ 37, [2010] QB 1.

[26] See *The Starsin* at [135].

[27] [1994] 2 AC 324.

[28] There was a third group of cases involving only goods shipped in Taiwan for Hong Kong.

So the issue was whether the actual carrier between Taiwan and Hong Kong could rely, as against bills of lading holders who had shipped from the US or Taiwan under other bills of lading or derived their interests from parties who had, on the jurisdiction clause in *its own* bills issued only to the principal carriers. The case was therefore not where a third-party actual carrier claimed protection under the principal contract, but one where it was argued that bills of lading-holders were by virtue of the principal contract bound by the terms of *other* bills of lading issued by actual carriers. The link was provided by a clause in the principal bills of lading authorising the contracting carrier to subcontract 'on any terms'. Thus the argument was that a contracting party was *bound* by the terms of another contract, which as a general proposition can be said to be unusual.

The reasoning adopted by the court was that in the first, Hanjin, group the original shippers had bailed their goods to contracting carriers as bailees, and the bailees had been authorised by the subcontracting term to sub-bail the goods to actual carriers and to subject the goods to the actual carrier's terms, which included the jurisdiction clause. With appropriate modification the same reasoning could be applied to the second, Scandutch, group. Therefore both groups were subject to the Taiwan jurisdiction clause.

It should be noted first, that this reasoning only applies to bailees of goods, and so has no relevance to the problems of other sub-contractors such as stevedores (unless they act as bailees). It should be noted also that the clause in the actual carrier's terms sought to be relied on was not one as to regime of liability but simply as to jurisdiction. But if the actual carriers' contract had been a charterparty, which could of course have contained different terms from those in a bill of lading,[29] the reasoning might be applied to reduce the carrier's liability below the bill of lading limits. And by further prolongation, it is said in the later case of *The Starsin* (discussed above), where the actual carrier's contract was a time charterparty, but it incorporated the Hague or Hague–Visby Rules, that the regime of liability established by the Rules could by this method (rather than by Himalaya clause) be introduced into the actual carrier's liability.[30]

[29] As in *The Forum Craftsman* [1985] 1 Lloyd's Rep 291. It could also be so if the bills of lading were not governed by the Hague or Hague–Visby Rules. An argument that such terms were uncontemplated could be deployed.

[30] See Lord Hobhouse at [138]. Subject, of course, to the problem of the incorporation of the Rules into charterparties: see *Adamastos Shipping Co v Anglo-Saxon Petroleum Co* [1959]

I. *The Mahkutai*

The bailment reasoning might also be argued to permit the actual carrier to claim that the sub-bailment to it was on the basis, not of *its own subcontract*, but directly on the terms of the *principal contract of carriage made by the contracting carrier*, thus achieving by a different route the result of protecting the actual carrier by the terms of the main contract. But it is not clear that it would be available for this purpose. A fact situation which might have provided a decision on this point occurred in another case of 1996 on appeal from Hong Kong, *The Mahkutai*,[31] also concerning a jurisdiction clause. Here time charterers issued bills of lading for carriage of plywood in an Indonesian vessel from Jakarta to Shantou in China. The bills of lading contained a power to subcontract, which authorised the role of the owners concerned as actual carrier, and a Himalaya clause. The cargo was damaged and the owners as actual carriers sought to rely on an Indonesian jurisdiction clause, *not* in their own contract, but in the main contract of carriage. Unfortunately for theorists, however, the Himalaya clause, which was directed to the provision for the actual carrier of the benefits of the main contract, on its interpretation was held not to cover a jurisdiction clause.[32] Thus as the parties were assumed to have deliberately excluded the jurisdiction clause from the benefits given to the actual carrier, it was not permissible to achieve a different result by the use of other reasoning.[33] So the interaction of these techniques is not yet clear.[34]

AC 133. Lord Hobhouse also said that such reasoning would place the burden of proof on the bailee to establish the cause of the loss or damage, and it would also make it easier to establish the liability of the carrier for simply losing goods (eg by wrongful delivery).

[31] [1996] AC 650.

[32] On the ground that the clause referred to provisions benefiting the carrier, and a jurisdiction clause did not necessarily do so – and certainly might not benefit an actual carrier: see below.

[33] Despite the fact that the Himalaya clause in question was more or less identical to that in *The Pioneer Container*, in which it was held (see p 344) that such a clause did not bar the bailment reasoning: but it has to be (just about) admitted that the situations are not quite the same (see Lord Goff in *The Mahkutai* at pp 667–68). However, it is clear from *The Rigoletto* [2000] 2 Lloyd's Rep 532 that there can be cases where both lines of reasoning are available: the case chooses the bailment reasoning.

[34] It should be noted that the use of such bailment reasoning can be generally invoked, and is not confined to situations of sub-bailment by a main contractor such as those here. For example, in *East West Corp v DKBS 1912* [2003] EWCA Civ 83, [2003] QB 1509 the reasoning was applied to a shipper who transferred the right under a bill of lading away: it was held to retain rights in bailment against carriers who delivered without bills of lading.

J. Third-party Contract

As Lord Goff said in *The Mahkutai*, 'Though these solutions are generally perceived to be generally effective for their purpose, their technical nature is all too apparent.'[35] So after all these gymnastics, it was satisfactory that in 1999 the law in England and Wales was changed by a statute[36] that permits a third party to enforce a term in a contract if the contract expressly provides that they may, or purports to confer a benefit on them. The latter does not apply if on a proper construction of the contract it appears that the parties did not intend the term to be enforceable by the third party. The third party must be expressly identified in the contract by name, as a member of a class or as answering a particular description, but need not be in existence when the contract is entered into.

Of itself this wording does nothing to help in this context. But the Act goes on to provide that 'Where a term of a contract excludes or limits liability … references in the Act to a third party enforcing the term are to be construed as references to his availing himself of the exclusion or limitation.'[37] This means that in general an actual carrier can avail themselves of defences in the main contract provided that this is intended in its own contract. The intention will usually be manifested by a Himalaya clause in appropriate form.

This development aligns the common law with those legal systems which treat the actual carrier problem as one of a third-party contract. The terms of the legislation, however, clearly require a Himalaya clause or something like it. But its drafting may become simpler because there is no need to invoke the involved agency and collateral contract reasoning hitherto developed from the wording of most versions of the clause. The situation has some similarity with that in the US, where a 2004 decision of the Supreme Court held an inland railway company in the country of destination (the US) was held entitled to take the benefit of a clause in an Australian freight forwarder's bill of lading protecting 'any servant, agent or other person (including an independent contractor) whose services have

[35] [1996] AC 650, 664. So also Lord Bingham in *The Starsin* referred to 'the undoubted artificiality of the reasoning … a deft and commercially inspired response to technical English rules of contract': at [34].

[36] The Contracts (Rights of Third Parties Act 1999).

[37] Section 1(6).

been used in order to perform the contract'.[38] The situation at common law, however, remains one of the use of an action in tort for losing, destroying or damaging goods, and the operation of contractual defences to it. There is no suggestion of any action based on joint and several liability of two parties, which as I have said would require some more extensive reform. Meanwhile the other techniques previously used remain potentially available. It is possible to envisage cases in which they may still require to be invoked.[39]

But two further things must be noted. The first is that while the 1999 Act has special provisions for arbitration clauses, it does not apply to jurisdiction clauses: the Act uses the words 'avails himself of any exclusion or limitation of liability'. A jurisdiction clause is not an exclusion or limitation of liability clause: indeed, it may benefit (or prejudice) both sides to the contract. It was of course in this connection that the litigation and involved reasoning of *The Pioneer Container* and *The Mahkutai* arose and plainly could still arise. The question of agreed jurisdiction is an important one in international commerce, though in some contexts questions of jurisdiction (and arbitration) are of course thought suitable for separate regulation.[40]

The second is that the Act has no effect on the question whether a shipper is bound by the third party's contract where the third party is a bailee (ie, on the *Pioneer Container* reasoning), and this could go outside the realm of jurisdiction clauses.

III. Conclusion: How Things Stand

The common law in England and Wales, and in other common law territories having the 1999 Act, has moved to the treatment of the actual carrier's

[38] *Norfolk Southern Rly Co v James N Kirby Pty Ltd* 543 US 14 (2004). The bill of lading in question was governed by Australian law: there was also a bill of lading issued by Hamburg Sud as first subcontracting carrier containing a slightly different formulation and a lower amount. It was held by use of agency reasoning that the shipper had authorised the goods to be subjected to these terms also. This is difficult to accept: see *Carver on Bills of Lading*, 4th edn (London, Sweeet & Maxwell, 2017), para 7-090. By international standards the decision does not pay proper attention to the relevant issues of the conflict of laws.

[39] For example, some situations where the main contract is varied, rescinded or terminated for breach. See in general *Carver on Bills of Lading* (2017) paras 7-075ff.

[40] For example, Chs 14 and 15 of the Rotterdam Rules: though these are optional for adherence.

liability as in most cases governed by a third-party contract regime. Prior to this there were many ingenious devices and lines of reasoning which could be deployed to give the actual carrier the benefit of the terms of the main contract of carriage, and even after the 1999 Act, there may still be cases (especially in connection with jurisdiction clauses) where, even with the acceptance of third-party contract rights, use of one of the old devices is required. And (of course leaving out the US) there are many other common law territories where there is no such third-party legislation. In some of these it may be necessary to fall back on the rather contorted devices developed in England and Wales during the 1970s and later. But it needs to be said again that there has been no tendency in common law countries to generate reasoning which holds the actual carrier liable on the main contract: the problem is one of defences to a tort action.

6

Suing the Master of a Vessel *Qualitate Qua* in Continental Law and the 'Action *in Rem*' at Common Law: Two Remedies Achieving the Same Result?

PROFESSOR MARC A HUYBRECHTS*

I. Introduction

Serving summons on the Master of a vessel *qualitate qua* (in his capacity as Master) is undoubtedly one of the peculiarities of the continental maritime law.[1] The possibility of suing the master *qualitate qua*, ie as a legal representative of the shipowner, is apparently part of the maritime procedural

* Emeritus Professor of Law, University of Leuven and Antwerp University; Advocate at the Bar of Antwerp.

[1] Is maritime law a separate autonomous branch of the law, or is maritime law a part of general international commercial law? There are two schools of thought: those, such as Professor William Tetley, Frank Wiswall and Georges Ripert, who claim the autonomy of maritime law; and those, such as the French doyen Rene Rodière and the Yale Professors Grant Gilmore and Charles Black, who see maritime law only as a division of international commercial law with some peculiarities. William Tetley calls it 'a complete system of law in all its aspects', see *International Maritime and Admiralty Law*, (Québec, Editions Yvon Blais, 2002) XIV; A Vialard, *Droit Maritime* (Paris, Presses Universitaires de France, 1997) 16; TJ Schoenbaum, *Admiralty and Maritime Law*, 5th edn (St Paul, MN, Thomson/West, 2012) vol 1, 2; G Ripert, *Droit Maritime* (Paris, Editions Rousseau, 1952) Vol II, 249. For a contrary view, see G Gilmore and C Black, *The Law of Admiralty*, 2nd edn (St Paul, MN, Thomson/West, 1975) 46. These authors reject the autonomy of maritime law. See also, P Bonassies and C Scapel, *Droit Maritime* (Paris, LGDJ, 2006) 7–8, where it says (in French): '*Au dix-neuvième siècle la doctrine française (Pardessus et Desjardins) a développé la thèse du particularisme absolu, voir l'autonomie du droit maritime. Cette conception est certainement excessive … Le droit maritime ne peut prétendre à l'autonomie*'.

law, but this possibility is also closely connected with substantive maritime law. Is this option merely procedural in nature, or is there more attached to it?

II. The Position of the Master

The Master of the vessel has always played a key role in shipping and ocean navigation and, as a consequence, in maritime law as well. Historically, the Magister Navis was most of the time probably also the co-owner of the ship which he commanded, and thus he was also a partner in the marine adventure. Many of today's traditional powers of the Master stem from a period where direct communication between the ship and the shipowner was difficult, if not altogether impossible. Therefore, the Master had broad autonomous powers to take the necessary decisions to bring the ship and cargo safely to destination, and the powers of the Master went beyond the normal powers of an agent or an ordinary servant. This resulted also in the perception that the position of the Master was something special, *sui generis*. This is confirmed in several judgments, such as *Lippert & Company v Blaine & Company*, decided in 1871. There, it was said:

> A Master is treated not as an ordinary agent, but as in some sort, and to some extent, clothed with the character of a special employer or owner of the ship, and representing not merely the absolute owner (Dominus Navis), but also the temporary owner or the charterer for voyage (the Exercitor Navis). In short, our law treats him as having a special property in the ship and entitled to the possession of it, and not as having the mere charge of it as a servant.[2]

A. Representation of the Shipowner by the Master in Legal Proceedings: Belgian Law

The study of Belgian maritime law is best started with the scholarly volumes of Constant Smeesters and Gustaaf Winkelmolen in *Droit Maritime*

[2] *Lippert & Company v Blaine & Company* decided by the Supreme Court of the Cape of the Good Hope on 18 November 1871, 25 quoted in J Hare, *Shipping Law and Admiralty Jurisdiction in South Africa* (Cape Town, Juta & Co, 1999) 199 and fn 12. This statement was quoted with approval in BR Bamford, *The Law of Shipping and Carriage in South Africa*, 3rd edn

et Fluvial Belge.[3] Their work is still considered to be the best basic handbook of Belgian maritime law. Our distinguished colleague, Professor Ralph De Wit, Professor of Maritime and Transport Law at the Free University of Brussels, still refers to the book in his lectures as the Bible of the Belgian maritime law. This is what Smeesters and Winkelmolen have to say on the subject:[4]

> *Le capitaine représente l'armement en justice. Le mandat du capitaine a un autre caractère très spécial. Le capitaine représente les armateurs en justice pour tout ce qui est relatif au navire ou à l'expédition. Les actions en justice qui intéressent le navire, peuvent être intentées par le capitaine en son propre nom, alors qu'elles se poursuivent and réalité, pour compte et aux frais de l'Armement. De même, quand on veut l'assigner armement, il suffit d'assigner le capitaine. Ainsi, tous les procès maritimes sont intentés sont au nom du capitaine, sont dirigés contre le capitaine. Bien entendu, le capitaine n'est au procès qu'en sa qualité de mandataire de l'armement, il comparaît « ès qualités. La condamnation prononcée ne pourra pas être exécutée sur ces biens personnels, mais elle pourra être exécutée directement contre le propriétaire et sera exécutée sur le navire même.*

My translation from French is as follows:

> The Master is the legal representative of the owners in legal proceedings. The agency of the Master has a very special character. The Master represents the owners in all legal proceedings for everything that concerns the vessel and her exploitation. Legal actions concerning the vessel can be initiated by the Master in his personal name while in reality they are being pursued on account of the shipowner and at his expense. Likewise, when one wishes to sue the shipowner, it suffices to sue the Master. In this way, all maritime legal proceedings are intended in the name of the Master and are directed against the Master. It is clear that the Master is a party to the legal proceedings in his capacity as an agent for the shipowner. He appears in these proceedings in his 'quality as'. Decisions are not enforced on his personal assets but on the assets of the shipowner.

The decision that is rendered against the Master cannot be enforced against his personal assets, but must be enforced directly against the shipowner,

(Cape Town, Juta & Co, 1983); S Fredericq, 'La représentation en Justice de l'armateur par le Capitaine' (1965) *Revue Critique de Jurisprudence Belge* 408, cited by the Belgian Court of Cassation on 5 April 1963, Revue Critique de Jurisprudence Belge, RCJB 1965, (408) 409–04.

[3] C Smeesters and G Winkelmolen, *Droit Maritime et Droit Fluvial Belge*, 2nd edn (Brussels, Bruylant, 1929) Vol 1, 266.

[4] ibid.

and the decision will be executed against the vessel.[5] What these Belgian authors have said on the issue is almost the same as that already stated in *Grande Ordonnance de la Marine* (1681) prepared by Monsieur Colbert and commented upon by René Josué Valin.[6]

B. The Master in Command at the Time of Service of the Writ

Smeesters and Winkelmolen have explained the position of the Master as the legal representative of the shipowner in a lucid manner and clarified the role of the Master and his powers by referring to very ancient maritime customs. In Belgian case law and legal doctrine, two main issues emerge in relation to the above-mentioned way of starting a lawsuit and, in particular:

- Who is meant by 'the Master' when one wants to sue the shipowner in this fashion?
- Could the application of foreign law impose another solution in the legal proceedings?

The first question is: Which Master is to be sued? Is it the Master who was in command of the vessel at the time the claim arose, or is it the Master who was in command of the ship at the commencement of the action? In 1963, the Belgian Court of Cassation had to deal with this issue and endorsed the traditional case law.[7] The Court ruled that the Master of a ship could represent the shipowner in ongoing legal proceedings if he was the Master in command of the ship at the time when the legal proceedings were issued and served. The possibility to sue the Master *qualitate qua* is no longer available against a former Master who was no longer in command at

[5] ibid Vol 1, 266; I De Weerdt (red.) *Grondbeginselen van het Belgisch Privaatrechtelijke Zeerecht* (Antwerpen, ETL, 1998) 186.

[6] R Josué Valin, *Nouveau Commentaire sur l'Ordonnance de la Marine* (Paris, Chez Jerome Legier, 1760) 568–69 liv II.TITRE VIII, des Propriétaires, Art II.

[7] Court of Cassation, 1st Chamber, 5 April 1963, Pas.1963,I,865-857, *Kapitein Thislandt v NV Pakhuis Meesters en Consoorten*, Revue Critique de Jurisprudence Belge, RCJB (1965) pp 408, 409–12; R Roland and M Huybrechts, 'Maritiem Recht, Overzicht Rechtspraak' (1960–1967) (1968) *Tijdschrift voor Privaat Recht* 459.

the time of service. A summons served on a person who is not competent or who has no capacity to defend the claim is invalid.

Professor Leo Delwaide is of the opinion that the Belgian case law and legal doctrine demonstrate a consensus on the proposition that the Master is the legal representative of the shipowner so that he can act as plaintiff or as a defendant in legal proceedings. The fact that the Master can represent shipowners in legal proceedings is a very rare exception to the traditional French continental procedural rule that no one can engage in a litigation by proxy (*Nul ne plaide par procureur*).[8] The possibility in Belgium to sue the Master as the legal representative of the shipowner is not based on a specific statutory rule, but is based on an ancient maritime law tradition.[9]

III. The Rule is Based on an International Legal Custom

The position of the Master as a legal representative is rooted in private international law. In proceedings before the Antwerp Court of Appeal, it was decided on 30 June 2003 that the Master represented the shipowner in legal proceedings.[10] The earlier decision of the Antwerp Commercial Court in the same litigation was served on the Master as representative of the owner, although it was supposed to be served on the shipowner. Nonetheless, the time to lodge an appeal was triggered by such service and started to run from that moment onwards. A German defendant company, the owner of the MV *Neptune*, appealed the decision of the Commercial Court in Antwerp and claimed that the service of the decision on the Master did not constitute a valid service, as this was contrary to German national/domestic law, particularly to Article 527 of the German Commercial Code.

[8] L Delwaide 'De dagvaarding van de kapitein in het Zeerecht' in *Liber Amicorum Marcel Briers* (Brussels, Gent, Mys & Breesch, 1993) 142.

[9] ibid 147, referring to the decision of the Court of Commerce in Antwerp dated 19 November 1987, published in *European Transport Law* (1988).

[10] See *Partenreederi Ms Neptun v Arquimedes Lazaro Ramirez MV Hapag Lloyd Amazones*, decided by the Court of Appeal Antwerp, fourth Chamber. This appeal case was cited almost in its entirety in the decision of the Court of Cassation referred to in n 11.

However, the Antwerp Appeal Court took the view that the service of the decision by service on the Master of the ship as the representative of the shipowners on 31 December 1997 was valid. Nonetheless, the appeal lodged on 18 February 1998 was not permissible because the time period to lodge an appeal (ie one month after service) had already expired. The reasons given were as follows. In this case, the summons was served on the Master of the vessel *M/V Hapag Lloyd Amazones*. Under international customary law, the Master was considered as the legal representative of the shipowner.[11] The Antwerp justices further stated that:

> Indeed, in traditional maritime law, it is well established that the Master of a ship is to be considered as the legal representative of the shipowner for all matters relating to the use of the ship. Even when the German appellant challenged the view that under German law the Master had no authority to represent the shipowner, this would not preclude the existence of this internationally well-established procedural rule.

Contrary to the contention of the appellant, the possibility to serve a writ onto the Master of a vessel in Belgium, regardless of the nationality of the vessel and the nationality of the owner, is not excluded by Article 34 of the Code of Civil Proceedings. Accordingly, the service on a legal person is deemed to have been done when the copy of the document is handed to the body, to the person or the appointee who is authorised by law, by the Articles of Association or on the basis of a proxy, to represent the legal person in court alone or in conjunction with others.

In this context, the Master should be considered as an appointee with a regular commission and authorised to represent the shipowner in legal proceedings. Consequently, proceedings can be served on the Master according to Article 34 of the Belgian Code on Civil Proceedings. Regarding the ship against which the legal proceedings were brought in June 2003, the Master who was in command of her at the moment of service was considered her legal representative. The decision of the Antwerp Court of Appeal was later tested before the Belgian Court of Cassation.

[11] Court of Cassation in *Partenreederei Ms Neptun v Arquimedes Lazaro Ramirez MV Hapag Lloyd Amazones*, 14 January 2005, Pasicrisie Belge (2005) 89–95 at III Middel (Moyen) aangevochten beslissingen, paras 2 and 3.

A. The Decision of the Court of Cassation

i. The First Ground

The submissions by the defendant suggested that the position of the Master as a legal representative was based on a legal custom under Belgian law and that countries other than Belgium that were active in international shipping had a similar public law or rule. The Court accepted these submissions and said that 'such a public law or rule cannot be seen as an unreasonable unique phenomenon'.[12]

ii. The Second Ground

As a second ground, the Court said:

> [A]lthough legal issues concerning foreign commercial companies or associations are in general governed by foreign law, Belgian procedural law is applicable to the issues of procedure. With reference to service of proceedings on a shipowner, Belgian law will determine under what circumstances service on a master of a vessel is considered to be service on the shipowner. The master of a vessel is supposed to be the legal representative of the shipowner regarding the legal transactions concerning the vessel. Irrespective of the nationality of the shipowner, the master has power to represent the shipowner before the Belgian Courts in all litigation concerning the vessel, and he can bring actions and accept service of proceedings in that capacity.

iii. The Third Ground

As a third ground, the Court further stated:

> The plaintiffs before the Court of Cassation start from the unjust viewpoint that the reference by the appeal judges to an 'internationally accepted custom' refers to the international custom as a source of public international law in the sense of Article 38 of the Statute of the International Court of Justice.[13]

[12] Court of Cassation, first chamber, 14 January 2005, AR 03.0607, Pasicrisie Belge, 2005, I, 89–95 (*Partenreederei MS Neptun GmbH & Co KG / Arquimedes Lazaro R.* Tweede Onderdeel (second part of the answer to the grounds for cassation raised by plaintiffs).

[13] ibid.

In this context, reference should be made to a critical commentary by Professor M Godfroid,[14] who took the view that:

> The solution suggested by the Court of Cassation can be explained by the fact that the legal representation by the Master is to be seen as an exception to the well-established procedural rule *nul le plaide par procureur*, a rule that is being determined by *lex fori*. The rule established in Belgium is that the Master of a vessel has, in his capacity as legal representative of the shipowner, competence to act as a plaintiff or defendant in legal proceedings on behalf of the shipowner in so far as the claim deals with the vessel of which he is in command and for which Belgian Courts may be called upon.

IV. The International Custom According to Section 38 of the Statute of the International Court of Justice

With reference to international customs, the plaintiffs before the Court of Cassation were in error. They asserted that the legal representation of the Master in conformity with Article 38 of the Statute of the International Court of Justice, combined with the Charter of the United Nations, could not qualify as an 'international custom', referring to the requirement that such an international custom, or a generally accepted legal practice or otherwise a well-established practice, must be applied under the premise that such a practice is a legal obligation, the so-called *opinion juris sive necessitates*. The plaintiffs submitted that there was no such international custom according to which the Master can represent the shipowner in legal proceedings with reference to all matters regarding the vessel.

They criticised the appeal judges that they had violated international law, more specifically the legal concept of 'international custom' as defined in Article 38 of the Statute on the International Court of Justice. In response to these submissions, the Cassation judges stated that Article 38 of the Statute of the International Court of Justice deals with the sources of public international law in the sense of the *ius gentium*. This particular case was not, however, concerned with public international law, but with

[14] M Godfroid, '*Vertegenwoordiging van het schip door de kapitein in België*' ('Representation of the vessel by the master in Belgian Law') (2005) *Belgian Commercial Law* 509.

maritime law, which is part of international commercial law and not part of public international law. Consequently, reference to Article 38[15] was not relevant.

V. The Legal Justification of the Legal Representation of the Master

On the decision of the Belgian Court of Cassation, Professor Godfroid reaches the following conclusion in his comment:[16] 'The solution suggested by the Court of Cassation can be explained on the basis that the legal representation of the Master is an exception to the rule "*nul ne plaide par procureur*", which is governed by *lex fori*.'

The view of Professor Godfroid is acceptable for the reasons he mentions, but at the same time his opinion raises some nuances. Professor Godfroid suggests that, according to Belgian law, the Master of a vessel is the representative of the shipowner under Belgian law and that the legal representation is not based on any precise statutory text. The legal representation is purely based on legal custom. His description of 'Belgian law' has to be understood in a broad perspective, covering statutory law, case law and legal custom. It would have been better had Professor Godfroid referred to the legal representation of the Master on the basis of the Belgian law in that broader perspective.

Professor Karen Broeckx characterises the position and the powers of the Master in the framework of a particular type of agency that becomes applicable where the Master makes his agency status known to third parties

[15] See Article 38 of Statute of the International Court of Justice, ch II, 'Competence of the Court', which provides that: '1. The Court, whose function is to decide in accordance with international law such disputes as are submitted to it, shall apply: a. international conventions, whether general or particular, establishing rules, expressly recognized by the contesting states; b. the international custom, as evidence of a general practice, accepted as law; c. the general principles of law, recognized by civilized nations; d. subject to the provisions of Article 59, judicial decisions and the teachings of the most highly qualified publicists of the various nations, as subsidiary means for the determination of rules of law. 2. This provision shall not prejudice the power of the Court to decide a case *ex aequo et bono*, if the parties agree thereto.' The provision can be found at http://www.icj.-cj.org.

[16] M Godfroid, '*Vertegenwoordiging van het schip door de kapitein in België*, noot op Hof van Cassatie', 14 January 2005 (Representation of the Vessel by the Master in Belgium, a comment on the Court of Cassation) TBH 2005/5, 509.

by revealing that he is acting *qualitate qua*. However, it is not required that he reveals the name or identity of the vessel owner.[17] Professor Broeckx is of the opinion that these powers must not be based on a very special civil law contract, namely a contract of 'name borrowing' (*le contrat de prête nom*) precisely because in such a contract the agent must not reveal the name of the person on whose behalf he is acting. This opinion is widely accepted.

Furthermore, Justice De Weerdt[18] expressed the following opinion:

> By legal doctrine and case law, it is accepted that the agent in certain circumstances can act without mentioning the name and identity of his principal provided that he mentions that he acts in his capacity as agent. Such agency is possible when a Master acts as a legal representative of the vessel owner.

In his analysis, Justice De Weerdt makes a distinction between a material/substantive legal party and a formal legal party.[19] The former is a party who holds personal and subjective rights. A formal party to the litigation, namely an agent, in the present context a Master, is a party who has the capacity to represent the interests of the substantive legal party in legal proceedings without having any personal interest.

This opinion is also shared by Professor Delwaide.[20] Professor Delwaide claims that the writ of summons can be served upon the Master in his capacity as legal representative of the shipowner for all legal transactions (contractual or non-contractual) performed by the actual or present Master in his capacity as legal representative in the course of his employment. His opinion is fully in line with those of all the other leading Belgian legal scholars quoted above. As has also been stated by Delwaide, it must be noted that the legal representation of the Master ceases when the

[17] K Broeckx, '*Vertegenwoordiging in recht en naamlening in het geding*' ('Legal Representation and the Contract of Name Lending') (1994–15) *Rechtskundig Weekblad* 248.

[18] L De Weerdt, '*Zeerecht/procedure vertegenwoordiging in rechte*' ('Maritime Law, Procedure Representation in Legal Proceedings') (2003) *Rechtskundig Weekblad* 319.

[19] By a 'material or substantive legal party' in the proceedings we understand a party whose 'financial or material interests' are really at stake in the proceedings, whereas a 'formal legal party' is a party that appears in the proceedings without having a real financial or substantive interest in the proceedings. Such a party will normally appear in cases where only this formal party can introduce an admissible claim in court.

[20] L Delwaide, 'De dagvaarding van de kaptitein in het Zeerecht' in *Liber Amicorum Marcel Briers*, (Antwerp, Gent, Mys & Breesch, 1963) 146.

shipowner is established in a place where the vessel is located. This opinion is also widely accepted.[21]

VI. A Comparative Analysis

The decision of the Court of Cassation discussed above clearly suggests that the concept of 'internationally accepted customary rule' did not refer to the international custom as a source of public international law in the sense of Article 38 of the Statute of the International Court of Justice. Following these discussions, one can raise the question whether this international commercial legal custom can be found in the legal systems of the various maritime nations. A short analysis of various legal regimes leads us to a positive answer.

A. France

The legal representation of the Master as a representative of the shipowner has undoubtedly been recognised. In fact, it stems from what was said in that regard in the *Ordonnance sur La Marine* of 1681.[22] Professor Georges Ripert clearly summarises below the position and powers of the Master as a special legal representative of the owners.[23]

> La nulle en France ne plaide par procureur. Or, par une exception traditionnelle à cette règle, le capitaine plaide en son nom pour le compte de l'armateur. Dans les actions en justice, le capitaine se porte seul demandeur et peut-être assigner seul comme défendeur; le jugement qu'il obtient ou qu'il subit est exécutoire au profit de l'armateur ou contre lui. Le capitaine n'a pas non plus à indiquer qu'il traître au nom du propriétaire du navire. Du moment où il agit pour les besoins du navire, le propriétaire bénéficie des contrats qu'il passe et subit les obligations qu'il contracte.

[21] C Smeesters and G Winkelmolen, *Droit Maritime et Droit Fluvial Belge*, 2nd edn (Brussels, Bruylant, 1929) Vol 1, 189.
[22] See the comment by Réné J Valin in *Nouveau Commentaire* (1760).
[23] R Georges, *Droit Commercial Droit Maritime* (1943) Vol 1 at 706 and 707.

My translation is:

> Nobody in France can entertain a legal action by a proxy. However, by a traditional exception to this rule, the Master of a vessel can appear in court in his own name but on behalf of the shipowner. In legal actions, the Master acts alone as a plaintiff and can be sued as a sole defendant. The decision that he will obtain or the decision that will be rendered against him can be enforced for the benefit of or against the shipowner. The Master need not indicate that he acts on behalf of the owner of the vessel. From the moment that he acts for the needs of the vessel, the shipowner benefits from the contracts that he enters into and he has to face the obligations which the master has contracted.

Professor Pierre Bonassies, Professor Raymond Gouilllod and Professor Antoine Vialard of Bordeaux University have repeated the same message in their textbooks and publications.[24] It has to be stressed that since the introduction of the French Decree of 1969, the legal representation of the Master has been limited in that the representation of the Master in all legal or extra-legal matters is limited to service intended for the shipowner.[25]

B. Germany

In his book, *Das Seehandelsrecht*, Professor Herber also refers to the legal representation by the Master of an oceangoing vessel in procedural matters.[26]

[24] P Bonassies and C Scapel, *Droit Maritime* (Paris, LGDJ, 2006) 294; M Rémond Gouilloud, *Droit Maritime* (Paris, Pedone, 1988) 110; A Vialard, *Droit Maritime* (France, Presses Universitaires de France, 1997) para 174-17; S Patrick 'Action in Rem et Action in Personam' (1997) 1 *Droit Maritime Français* 339. For Scandinavian countries, see T Falkanger, HJ Bull and L Brautaset, *Introduction to Maritime Law* (Oslo, Tano Aschehoug,1998) 243. For Spain, see I Arroyo, *Compendia de Derecho Maritimo* (Madrid, Tecnos, 2005) 117.

[25] French Decree of 1969 provides that: 'Le capitaine dispose enfin d'attribution de représentation judiciaire. En droit classique, il était admis que le capitaine pouvait plaider pour le compte de l'armateur, soit en demande, soit en défense, et la règle est reprise par la disposition de certains textes étrangers (voir article 10.1, al. 2 du Code Malgache). L'article 10 du Décret du 19 juin 1969, quant à lui, dispose seulement que le capitaine peut recevoir tous les actes judiciaires ou extra-judiciaires, adressés à l'armateur. Il semble bien résulter du texte nouveau que si le capitaine peut recevoir les actes judiciaires adressés à l'armateur, il ne peut agir comme demandeur pour le compte de l'armateur. Il en serait toutefois autrement en cas d'urgence pour des mesures conservatoires, eu égard aux dispositions de l'article 8 de la loi du 3 janvier 1969.'

[26] R Herber, *Seehandelsrecht, Systemathische Darstellung* (Berlin, De Gruyter, 1999) 146–55.

C. Belgium

Belgium is preparing a new maritime code and this task has been entrusted to a special legislative commission, known as COMAR. COMAR has enacted the old maritime custom which will now be in section 5.10 of the future new Belgian Maritime Code. The section provides that:

> [A]bsent a contrary statement mentioning the name and seat of the incorporation of the ship owning company or vessel operator, it is irrefutably assumed that the Master who is the addressee in an introductory writ of summons, represents the vessel owner.

VII. The Common Law

Professor John Hare takes the view that the Master enjoys this legal representation capacity also under common law. He states that some of the powers under common law allow a Master to represent the shipowner in legal proceedings, giving the right to institute and defend proceedings in his own name. In support of this statement, he refers to a South African author, BR Bamford, who did fundamental research concerning this issue.[27] According to Bamford, the Master's right to sue in his own name was consistent with the principles of Roman–Dutch law and with the practice of South African courts.

This very short comparative analysis leads us to the conclusion that in various maritime nations, the Master had this exceptional legal capacity to stand in court *qualitate qua* and to represent the shipowner in proceedings. This extraordinary legal capacity is not based on an explicit statutory rule, and it is suggested that such a statutory rule should be enacted, spelling out this legal representation capacity of the Master. Also in France, such a statutory rule has been introduced although the legal capacity of the Master has been seriously restricted.

The practical consequence of this legal representation by the Master is that the creditors who have claims on the vessel can easily sue the

[27] BR Bamford, *Law of Shipping, Carriage in South Africa*, 3rd edn (Cape Town, Juta & Co, 1983).

shipowner, by directing the writ of summons against the Master in his capacity as legal representative *qualitate qua*. This legal capacity of the Master seems to us an essential protective mechanism for the creditors.

VIII. The Action *in Rem*

A. Definition

A totally different situation is prevalent in common law countries, particularly in England and the US. From time immemorial, maritime law, as it was applied in common law countries, offered the possibility to institute an action directly against the vessel, namely an action *in rem*, in which the vessel is the defendant.[28]

In England, this possibility was initially limited to those claims that were protected by a maritime lien but that was later extended by statutory provisions. An action *in rem* can also be brought for many other maritime claims, provided that they are statutorily recognised. For this reason, other maritime claims are frequently referred to as statutory rights *in rem*.[29]

Professor Mandaraka-Sheppard mentions the specific feature of the action *in rem*, stating that:

> The uniqueness of an *in rem* claim under English procedural law lies on its triple function, namely: it assists the claimant (a) to obtain security for the claim; and (b) to invoke jurisdiction of the English court on the merits of the claim; and (c) regarding 'non-truly *in rem*' claims, to have the right in rem crystallised on the property from the time of issue of the *in rem* claim form. In other countries, such as in the United States, the action *in rem* offers even more possibilities. The action *in rem* is closely linked to the personification of the vessel.

B. The Purpose and Use

The English theory is that the action *in rem* is a mere device to get the real defendant (eg the shipowner) into court. Once he has acknowledged the

[28] FD Rose, 'The Action in Rem in English Law' in H Boonk, *English and Continental Maritime Law* (Antwerpen, Maklu, 2003) 45–60.

[29] NJJ Gaskell, C Debattosta and RJ Swatton, *Chorley & Giles on Shipping Law*, 8th edn (London, Pearson, 1987) 6.

service of the writ he submits himself personally to the jurisdiction of the admiralty court and from then on the action continues against him, not only as an action *in rem*, but also as an action *in personam*.[30] In reality, it has to be stressed that the law relating to an action *in rem* has become a fairly complicated issue in England as well as in the US.

One school of thought views the action *in rem* as a totally separate action and a separate legal institution and another school of thought sees action *in rem* as a procedural remedy. Professor Mandaraka-Sheppard comes to the conclusion that in modern times, the procedural view as spelled out by the House of Lords in *The Indian Grace (No 2)* is the prevailing view.[31]

C. The Personification of the Vessel

As discussed above, the traditional action *in rem* is closely linked to the theory of the personification of the vessel.[32] In this context, Goemans states that the modern version of the action *in rem* in the US law can be traced back to early US decisions in the beginning of the nineteenth century, such as *The Nestor*.[33] In these cases, the vessels were the defendants' vessels, and the actions were directed to the vessels.

This raises the question of whether the action *in rem* has a pure common law origin or civil law origin. One school of thought, which is prevailing at present, considers the action *in rem* as a mere procedural instrument, while another sees the action *in rem* as a substantive matter. The substantive theory is particularly supported by Frank Wiswall.[34]

Goemans comes to the conclusion that, under Belgian law, there is no such concept as 'action *in rem*'. There is no possibility for the vessel to entertain an action in court, either as a plaintiff or as a defendant because, under Belgian law, a vessel does not enjoy a status of legal personality.

[30] ibid 7.

[31] A Mandaraka-Sheppard, *Modern Maritime Law* (London, Informa, 2014) Vol I, 107.

[32] See B Goemans, 'De symptomen van de rechtspersoonlijkheid van het schip' (25 May 2007), available at www.droitmaritime.be/Documenten/ZEERECHT%20Nota%20rechtspersoonlijkheid.pdf.

[33] See *The Nestor*, 18 Fed Cas 9 [no 10 126] [CCD Me 1831]. On the personification theory, see also the English judges' decisions in *The Dictator* [1892] PD 304 and *The Bold Buccleugh* [1850] 7 Moo 267, 282. See also P Simon, 'Action in Rem et Action in Personam' (1997) *Droit Maritime Français* 339.

[34] F Wiswall, *Development of Admiralty Jurisdiction since 1800* (Québec, Editions Yvon Blais, 1970).

However, the vessel under Belgian law is open to conservatory arrest or '*la saisie conservatoire*'.

Professor William Tetley is of the opinion that *in rem* actions on the European continent were not really necessary. Consequently, this remedy did not develop because there was always the possibility to sue the owner and at the same time proceed with the attachment or arrest of the vessel under the framework of what is known as *la saisie conservatoire*.[35]

The personification theory has also its detractors, such as Gilmore and Black. Gilmore and Black are absolutely not convinced that the personification of vessels exists.[36] If one indeed accepts the vessel as a legal person, such a legal person should be able to sue. There is such a possibility because of the concept of action *in rem* if we do not see action *in rem* as only a procedural device that is conducive to bringing the real defendant, ie the shipowner, to the court.

Finally, reference should also be made to what Professor Thomas J Schoenbaum has to say about action *in rem*:

> A distinctive feature of admiralty, however, is the availability of a special in rem remedy preserved in supplemental admiralty rule C. An action in rem may be brought (a) to enforce any maritime lien, and (b) whenever a statute in the United States provides for a maritime action in rem or a proceeding analogous thereto.[37]

The author takes the view that an action *in rem* against the vessel can be initiated together with an action *in personam* against whoever is considered to be liable for the claim. The essential condition to exercise the *in rem* action, however, is that the vessel should be found within the jurisdiction so that the vessel can be attached in the jurisdiction where the action will be brought.

It should be recalled that the US is not a party to the 1952 International Convention Relating to the Arrest of Seagoing Ships and that the conditions to start an *in rem* action in the US differs from those applicable in England.[38]

[35] W Tetley, *Maritime Liens and Claims* (Québec, Editions Yvon Blais, 1985) 446 and 485; Tetley, *International Maritime and Admiralty Law* (2002) 406.

[36] G Gilmore and C Black, *The Law of Admiralty*, 2nd edn (St Paul, Thomson/West, 1975) 594.

[37] TJ Schoenbaum, *Admiralty and Maritime Law, Vol 1* (St Paul MN, Thomson/West, 1987) 618.

[38] ibid at 621 where it is stated that 'a prerequisite of in rem jurisdiction is that the property to be arrested must be present in the district where the suit is filed or during pendency of the action'. See also Rose, 'English Law' (2003) 60.

IX. *In Rem* Action in the UK and the Most Recent Case Law

The most important recent UK decision is *The Indian Grace*, the decision of the House of Lords, known as *The Indian Grace (No 2)*.[39] In this decision, the Lords fine-tuned the legal position on the action *in rem* at English common law. The judgment was delivered by Steyn LJ, a Lord Justice of South African origin, a country of mixed jurisdictions based on Roman-Dutch law and the common law.

Professor Mandaraka-Sheppard[40] has clearly spelled out the traditional features of the action *in rem* in English Law, while stating that the *in rem* proceeding is a powerful weapon available to claimants for a number of important matters.[41] She goes on by commenting that prior to *The Indian Grace (No 2)* case, in the absence of acknowledgment of service or submission to jurisdiction, the *in rem* proceeding remained solely *in rem* and no personal jurisdiction over the owner, or the person liable *in personam*, would be created by the service of the writ on the ship. The action would become a combined action *in rem* and *in personam* from the time of the acknowledgment of service.

A. The *Indian Grace (No 2)* Decision

This is a fascinating court decision because Steyn LJ offers us a very detailed analysis of the *in rem* action and its development over the years, while making detailed comments on the various decisions that applied this theory. In conclusion, Steyn LJ argues that the *in rem* theory is in fact based on a fiction, which is certainly in use, but is no longer necessary on account of the Judicature Acts.[42] In this particular case, the defences were based on the *res judicata* argument.

[39] *The Indian Grace (No 2)* [1998]1 Lloyd's Law Rep 1 at 6–7.

[40] A Mandaraka-Sheppard, *Modern Admiralty Law* (London, Informa, 2014) Vol I, 107.

[41] ibid. These matters are as follows: obtaining security for the claim; founding jurisdiction on the merits of the claim, subject to restrictions imposed by the Brussels Regulation; giving effect to maritime lien, an already accrued right on the ship, which dates back to the date of its creation; creating a contingent security right on the ship with regard to a non-truly '*in rem*' claim from the time of the issue of the *in rem* claim; and limiting liability up to the value of the ship arrested.

[42] In *The Indian Grace (No 2)* [1998]1 Lloyd's Law Rep 1 at 10, Lord Justice Steyn said: 'The role of fictions in the development of the law has been likened to the use of scaffolding in the

In *The Maciej Rataj*,[43] the European Court of Justice had previously considered this issue and had clearly stated that an action *in rem* and an action *in personam* are basically actions between the same parties on the same issues. This was an important matter in *The Maciej Rataj*, as the European Court of Justice had to consider whether Article 21 of the Brussels Convention (which is in Schedule 1 to the English Civil Jurisdiction and Judgment Act 1982) was applicable. Article 21 provides:

> Where proceedings involving the same cause of action and between the same parties are brought in the Courts of different contracting states, any Court other than the Court first seized shall of its own motion decline jurisdiction in favour of that Court.

Applying Article 21 of the Brussels Convention, Steyn LJ came to the conclusion that:

> It is now possible to say that for the purposes of section 34, an 'action in rem' is an action against the owners from the moment that the Admiralty Court is seized with jurisdiction. The jurisdiction of the Admiralty Court is invoked by the service of a writ, or where a writ is deemed to be served, as a result of the acknowledgment of the issue of the writ by the defendant before service. From that moment, the owners are parties to the proceedings in rem.[44]

In other words, the conclusion of all this is the shipowners are at the very start parties to the legal proceedings. This again makes it very clear that the real nature of the *in rem* proceeding, which is only a device, is a vehicle by which the shipowners are being sued and brought into the legal proceedings.

B. The Factual Background of *The Indian Grace* Decision

The M/V Indian Grace carried a cargo of munition from Sweden to Cochin, India. During the voyage, a fire broke out in one hold, and part of the

construction of a building. The scaffolding is necessary but after the building has been erected scaffolding serves only to obscure the building. Fortunately, the scaffolding can usually be removed with ease. … The idea that a ship can be a defendant in legal proceedings was always a fiction. But before the Judicature Acts this fiction helped to defend and enlarge Admiralty jurisdiction in the form of an action in rem. With the passing of the Judicature Acts that purpose was effectively spent. … The fiction was discarded.'

[43] See *The Maciej Rataj* [1995]1 Lloyd's Report 302 at [47]–[48].

[44] *The Indian Grace (No 2)* [1998]1 Lloyd's Law Rep 1 at 10.

cargo had to be jettisoned. The remaining cargo was re-stalled and was discharged at final destination on 4 September 1987. The Indian Government started a legal action before Indian courts in 1988 and claimed £7,000 pounds as the value of the cargo that had been jettisoned. On 25 August 1989, prior to the judgment given by the Indian court, a second action was instituted before English courts on behalf of the Indian Government. Thereafter, on 16 December 1989, the Indian court delivered a decision on the first action. On 4 May 1990 the Indian Government arrested *The Indian Endurance*, a vessel belonging to the same owner. The owners appeared in these English arrest proceedings and supplied sufficient guarantee for the claim so that the arrest was lifted and the vessel could continue her voyage. In these English proceedings, the Indian state claimed £2.6 million for the cargo damage.

In English legal proceedings, the main defence was based on the rule of *res judicata*, namely that the same issue had already been litigated between the same parties in India. Before the English court and the English Court of Appeal this argument was raised with reference to section 34 of the Civil Jurisdiction and Judgments Act of 1982.

The High Court judge decided that the *in rem* action was against the ship, whereas the Indian action was an *in personam* action, and that section 34 of the Act was not a bar to the action *in rem*. The Court of Appeal reversed his decision on the grounds that the owner of the vessel was a party to both English and Indian proceedings. This was later confirmed by the House of Lords.

Professor Mandaraka-Sheppard analysed the decision and came to the conclusions that: (i) a service of the *in rem* action also initiates *in personam* action against the person who has a genuine interest to defend the claim, such as the owner or the demise charterer, but it has no bearing on the guarantees that are offered in the framework of an *in rem* action; and (ii) the buyer of a vessel in good faith is not affected by an *in rem* action because he is not the person who is liable for the satisfaction of the claim. In other words, with reference to the enforcement of the maritime lien on the vessel concerned, these proceedings remain strictly *in rem*.[45] A final

[45] Mandaraka-Sheppard, *Modern Maritime Law* (2014) Vol I, 93.

point to make is that she saw the decision as the victory of the procedural theory over the personification theory by the English courts.[46]

X. Conclusion

Both the possibility to sue the master of a vessel as representative of the shipowner, and the action *in rem* under common law are useful tools in favour of creditors against shipowning companies. They both seem to be procedural in nature. These are essential and useful devices, as creditors are regularly confronted by a number of avoidance schemes, exclusions and limitations when they try to collect their claims.

As an example, we could quote the exclusions and limitations provided by the Hague–Visby Rules 1968, the Conventions on Limitation of Liability for Maritime Claims, the International Convention on Civil Liability for Oil Pollution Damage 1992, the Athens Convention relating to the Carriage of Passengers and their Luggage by Sea 1974. On top of all these legal limitations and excuses, owners are never very reluctant to avoid their exposure by all legal means and in some instances by questionable practices.

One can think of the single-ship companies and the practice of quickly organising the sale of the vessel and public auctions in exotic jurisdictions when the shipowning company is faced with large claims. It is not always easy to reach the owner and for that reason these two instruments, the writ of summons directed against the master *qualitative qua* and the action *in rem* might be very valuable and useful tools to help the creditors.

However, these remedies do not necessarily give full satisfaction to the creditors. With reference to the writ of summons to be issued against the master, one still has to be able to find out the identity of the Master who is in command of the vessel at the commencement of the legal action. Furthermore, the writ must be served effectively upon that Master. Suing the Master as a representative together with the *Saisie Conservatoire du Navire* is a valuable tool for the creditors.

[46] ibid 107, where Mandaraka-Sheppard said: 'The effect of the procedural theory, as pronounced by the House of Lords in *The Indian Grace*, is that the real defendant in the rem proceedings is the person interested in the ship who appears in the action to defend the claim.'

With reference to the action *in rem*, some conditions also have to be complied with. The rules have to allow a statutory *in rem* claim or the action must be based on a maritime lien. Moreover, one must be able to arrest the vessel within the jurisdiction where the case will be brought. When the owners do not acknowledge service or where they do not appear in court, the action will be continued as a pure action in rem, ie only against the vessel.[47]

In both truly and none truly *in rem* claims, the value of the ship has always been the limit for the satisfaction of the maritime claims by the creditors. Only when the owners acknowledge service of the writ and appear in court will the claimants possibly be able to execute their claims on all the other assets of the owners. However, one has to take into account of the decision in *The Indian Grace (No 2)* and also the fact that the owners enjoy the Conventions on Limitation of Liability for Maritime Claims treaty limitations.

It seems that these two procedural devices serve the same purpose. Both remedies are procedural in nature and help creditors to collect from owners who otherwise are probably difficult to catch.

[47] Tetley (n 1) 407.

7

The *Res Cogitans*

STEPHEN COGLEY QC*

I. Introduction

On 11 May 2016, the Supreme Court handed down its judgment in relation to the expedited appeal in *PST Energy 7 Shipping LLC & anor*[1] *v OW Bunker Malta Limited & ING.*[2] The fact that the appeal was heard on an expedited basis, and the whole dispute resolution process involving an arbitration, an appeal to the Commercial Court, thereafter to the Court of Appeal, and then the hearing in the Supreme Court, had all occurred within a 10-month period underscores the importance of the case, and the issues that arose in it, to the wider commercial community.

II. The *Res Cogitans*

The Supreme Court decision is essentially split into two halves. The first half, the true ratio of the case, concerned whether a contract in which the parties described themselves as buyer and seller, and the seller supplies goods to the buyer for a price, is to be regarded as a contract of sale as a matter of English Law if both buyer and seller contemplate that the goods – the subject matter of the supply – may have ceased to exist before the point in time at which property is to pass. The significance of the correct

* 4 Pump Court, London.
[1] Owners and managers of *The Res Cogitans*.
[2] [2016] UKSC 23 on appeal from [2015] EWCA Civ 1058.

answer to this question was found in the fact that the seller – OW Malta (OWM) – was insolvent and had not paid its own seller in the chain of contracts. Each contract in the chain – there were others above OWM's seller (OW Bunkers AS – sometimes referred to OW Bunkers Denmark) contained an express retention of title clause: a Romalpa clause. The contract between the buyers – the appellants (owners) OWM – was on OW standard terms of sale. The contract, as well as containing a Romalpa clause also contained an express provision dealing with the capacity in which the buyers (owners), held the goods post-delivery, and prior to property passing. This was described as an express bailment. The goods, the subject matter of the sale, was bunkers, and doubtless in recognition of the fact that to use, and in particular to destroy, goods that are the subject matter of a bailment, is a tortious act – and a breach of contract if the bailment is contractual, there was an express carve out from the restrictions placed upon owners which allowed them to use the bunkers solely for propulsion of the vessel. Thus, whilst prohibited from selling, mixing, pledging or trans-shipping the bunkers during the bailment, which subsisted up until payment of the price, owners were nevertheless allowed to burn the bunkers in order to trade the vessel.

When the OW Group became insolvent without having paid its own supplier of the bunkers, the assignee of its supply receivables,[3] ING, has sought to recover the price from owners.

This happened many times over, with literally hundreds of vessels in various jurisdictions. If the contracts, each of which was subject to English law, were sale contracts, then ING, as assignee, could be in no better position than its assignor – the relevant OW Group company (in this case, OWM). As there was a breach of s 12 of the Sale of Goods Act because OWM never had, and never would have,[4] property then, applying the well-known principles in *Rowland v Divall*,[5] there would be a total failure of consideration and accordingly no obligation to pay the price. This would leave the claims of the suppliers further up the chain – often the physical

[3] There is still a question mark over precisely what is encompassed within the meaning of this phrase in the assignment between, inter alia, the OW Group and its syndicated lenders, the lead bank of which is ING.

[4] So at the very lowest it was in anticipatory repudiatory breach.

[5] [1923] 2 KB 500.

supplier, who would also be claiming the price. The claims advanced by such supplier were either asserting a direct contractual relationship based on the Bunker Delivery Notes, or a tortious claim seeking damages for conversion and/or the value of the bunkers. In many jurisdictions, the physical suppliers' claims gave rise to a maritime lien. The OW terms and conditions contained an express agreement that a US Maritime Lien would apply in favour of OWM. This was clearly a serious problem for parties in the position of the owners of *The Res Cogitans* because it meant that they were facing at least two claims in relation to the bunkers, and multiple arrests. As I have said, this situation was replicated hundreds of times over around the globe.

In some instances, the supplier further up the chain was not the physical supplier, but rather an intermediate supplier – typically a broker. The broker benefited by obtaining a margin. In some jurisdictions parties occupying the position of these brokers in the chain do not have any rights of arrest or maritime liens, which would mean that, unless they could demonstrate a direct contractual relationship with the solvent party at the bottom of the chain – such as the owners in the present case – it had no choice but to claim in OWM's insolvency. So, just pausing, the owners and managers of *The Res Cogitans* were faced with the position where ING as assignee was claiming a debt – said to be the price of the goods – and an intermediate supplier further up the chain was also making the same claim. The owners did not mind paying, but did not wish to pay twice and be arrested in the meantime, and of course the intermediate supplier did not want to find that its only claim was against the insolvent OW entity. Neither did the owners.

Under these circumstances, the owners commenced arbitration under the express provisions of the OW terms and conditions, and sought an expedited hearing of preliminary issues, with a view to obtaining relief declaring that they had no liability to OWM, and accordingly no valid claim had been assigned to ING. In the arbitration, OWM (but in fact ING) argued that it did have a claim under the Sale of Goods Act, or in restitution or for specific performance, and in each instance argued that the contract *was* a sale of goods as a matter of English law. This accords with its stance in other jurisdictions, notably the US and Canada. As an after-thought, it advanced the tentative argument that *if* the owners were correct, and there was no claim for the price as a combination of the earlier decision of the Court of Appeal in *Caterpillar v Holt*[6] and breach of s 12, it would mean the parties in the position of OWM would never have a remedy. The owners repost to this was that even if there was no remedy, this was only because OWM was never able to satisfy its contractual obligations, and so it was hardly unjust that it had no claim.

The arbitrators dealt with the various arguments, and concluded (in effect) that if the Sale of Goods Act applied, there would be no claims under that Act because OWM never had property in the goods, and would never obtain this, but the contract was not one of sale because the essence of a sale is the passing of property, and at the point in time when the property was meant to pass, it was expected that it would not exist. They described this contract as *sui generis*, by which they appeared to mean that the contract was not one of sale – even though it was described as such and contained terms apposite only to a sale – but rather that it was a contract under which the sellers agreed to procure the placing of the bunkers on board the vessel in consideration for a liquidated sum: the price.

The owners and OWM/ING each appealed to the Commercial Court. Males J, hearing the appeal on an urgent basis, concluded that the contract was not one of sale, although it bore many of the indicia and hallmarks of such a contract, but did not truly identify what its precise nature was. He approached the matter as if the contract again was a *sui generis* contract, under which the seller facilitated the provision of the bunkers coupled with a licence to consume. Importantly Males J went on to hold that there was an implied term that the seller had to obtain an effective permission from the true owner in favour of the buyer – here Owners, permitted the buyer to consume the bunkers. As this was an implied condition, as opposed to a warranty, then if that permission was not obtained, there was a breach of condition which discharged the owners from their obligation to pay. In recognition of the fact that the bunkers might not be fully consumed at the point in time at which payment was due (the end of the credit period), he recognised there was a contractual obligation to transfer property in those bunkers that were not consumed, but held that this was not pursuant to a contract of sale, but was some sort of unidentified residual obligation. In recognition of the fact that important and difficult issues of law

[6] [2014] 1 WLR 2365.

arose, which had far-reaching ramifications, Males J gave permission to the owners to appeal to the Court of Appeal, and refused OWM/ING permission. They were seeking permission to appeal because, in effect, apart from in relation to one aspect, he agreed with the arbitrators and rejected OWM's other arguments.

Thus, pausing to take stock, the arbitrators and Males J both concluded that the contract was not one of sale, but was *sui generis*. Males J went further and identified an implied condition in relation to permission to consume.

It is worth noting at this stage that both the arbitrators and the judge were heavily influenced by the fact that it was contemplated that the bunkers may well be consumed in whole or in part before the point in time at which property was meant to pass. They reasoned that existing English Llaw does not recognise the concept of the passing of property in non-existent goods, so it must follow that the parties did not contemplate that property would pass at the point of payment. Thus, the logic runs, the parties were not assuming an obligation to transfer property in exchange for the price. Accordingly, the contract was not a sale of goods within the definition contained in s 2 of the Sale of Goods Act 1979.

The appeal came before the Court of Appeal on an expedited basis. Even though OWM/ING had not been granted permission to appeal, it nevertheless intended to run many of the arguments it had advanced below. It also sought to argue that the earlier decision of the Court of Appeal in *Caterpillar v Holt* was wrong and ought to be overruled. Essentially this case determined that the only circumstances under which a claim for the price could be maintained in relation to a sale contract was by satisfying one or other of the two sub-sections under s 49 of the Sale of Goods Act 1979. In effect, OWM was seeking to argue that it could maintain a claim for the price, even in relation to a contract of sale, outside those stipulated circumstances. The owners, for their part, were arguing essentially one point only: that the contract was a sale of goods within the 1979 Act, and that was the only issue before the Court, but even if it wasn't a sale, the implied condition that Males J had found was not potent enough, and there ought to be an implied term that went further – namely that it was an implied condition and that the seller had, in turn, complied with its own contractual obligations to the party next above it in the chain.

The Court of Appeal only dealt with the sale of goods issue. In its reserved judgment it concluded that because parties at the time the contract was entered into contemplated that most, if not all, the bunkers would be consumed before payment was due – which meant that (almost) inevitably the property would have physically been destroyed – the contract was not one of sale. Differing substantially from Males J and the arbitrators, however, the Court of Appeal concluded that the contract *was* a contract of sale, and within the Sale of Goods Act 1979, in relation to any bunkers that remained unconsumed at the time when payment was due. Furthermore, as a matter of principle, s 12 applied in relation to these bunkers, with the consequence that *if* the unconsumed mass was substantially the whole of the bunkers, there would be a breach of s 12 sufficient to provide an absolute defence in favour of the owners. It is fair to observe that the Court of Appeal assumed that this scenario would be extremely uncommon. In passing, the Court regarded this situation as arising only if the unconsumed amount was substantial because the consideration was not divisible. The sale consisted of one mass: the delivered volume, in relation to which one sum, the price, was payable. Thus a total failure of consideration which arises as a consequence of a breach of s 12 only arises, so the reasoning went, if the amount of unconsumed bunkers in relation to which the breach arose, was of such quantity as to mean that the bargain was effectively worthless. The other issues that arose were not fully considered, although the Court of Appeal rejected any suggestion that the implied condition should be more extensive than that found by Males J.

Again, the matter came on as an expedited urgent appeal in the Supreme Court. To a certain extent the arguments raised mirrored some of those advanced below. The Supreme Court unanimously concluded that the contract was not one of sale. The owners' argument was that the definition of a sale within s 2 of the Act includes not only an outright sale – when property passes at the time the contract is entered into, but also an agreement to sell – where property is to pass in the future. A Romalpa clause is often a feature of an agreement to sell, providing not only that property passes in the future, but only upon payment of the price. Thus, clearly and unambiguously the language used in the contract – the OW terms and conditions – was apposite to a sale, and the goods existed at the point of delivery, were ascertained and appropriated to the contract. At the very least there was an agreement to sell those existing goods at some stage in the future. Accordingly, the agreement was within the Act, and s 12 (as modified to apply to agreements to sell) had to be complied with.

The arguments were obviously more complex than that, but the foregoing represents the essence of the position.

As a sub-text, the owners argued that what might happen to the goods, the subject matter of the agreement to sell thereafter was not relevant. The essential question was one of characterising the contract, at the time entered into from which, then, certain consequences would flow. That characterisation exercise should not take into account, and should not be influenced by, what may or may not happen to the goods after the agreement is entered into. For example the goods might not be consumed; should the answer then be different? Furthermore, the extent to which consumption might occur could depend entirely on circumstances which were unforeseen at the time; for example, the rate of progress of the ship, whether it was stuck in port awaiting orders, or whether it had simply broken down. In each of those instances, the rate of consumption might be different than that anticipated. Furthermore, the parties' anticipation may well be different: the seller might work on the assumption that the goods would be consumed within a very short period, whilst the buyer might have an entirely different intention in relation to the goods, knowing, for example, that the ship was going to be laid up but fully bunkered. So, it was argued, even though consumption of the bunkers was contemplated, the contemplation between the parties was not shared – and if this was a matter of mere coincidence, rather than any communicated position. After all, although not expressly put this way, it is wholly artificial to assume that in the real world occupied by the buyer and seller, communicating by MSM/text or email, they had a discussion as to the likely rate of consumption and destiny of the goods before the bunker supply agreement was entered into.

The Supreme Court concluded, in agreement with the arbitrators, that no part of the contract constituted a sale, and that the whole regime was outside of the Sale of Goods Act. The Supreme Court expressly disavowed the conclusions of the Court of Appeal in relation to there being a sale in relation to any residual unconsumed bunkers at the time when payment was due. This was essentially driven, from the Supreme Court's perspective, from the fact that there was one indivisible contractual obligation in relation to which one indivisible sum was payable, although the Supreme Court did leave open the concept of restitutionary remedies (to be considered in another case). The essence of the Supreme Court judgment, which is found in paragraphs 27, 28 and 29, relies very heavily on that which the Supreme Court described as 'a reality'. By that the Supreme Court meant, and I quote:

> Bunker supplies know that bunkers are for use. If they grant relatively long credit periods combined with a reservation of title pending payment in full, it is unsurprising that they do so combined with an express qualification authorising use in propulsion, since standard terms prohibiting any use would be uncommercial or in practice, no doubt, simply ignored … OWBM's (and RMUK's) contractual terms and the assumed facts (particularly paras 13, 20 and 30) – together with an admissible modicum of commercial awareness on the court's part about how ships operate (and in particular how Owners strive to keep them operating) and about the value of credit and the likelihood that full advantage of it will be taken – all point in one direction. They demonstrate that the liberty to use the bunkers for propulsion prior to payment is a vital and essential feature of the bunker supply business …
>
> In these circumstances, OWBM's contract with the owners cannot be regarded as a straightforward agreement to transfer the property in the bunkers to the owners for a price. It was in substance an agreement with two aspects: first, to permit consumption prior to any payment and (once the theory of a nanosecond transfer property is, rightly, rejected) without any property ever passing and the bunkers consumed; and, secondly, but only if insofar as bunkers remained unconsumed, to transfer the property in the bunkers so remaining to the owners in return for the owners paying the price. But in this latter connection, it is to be noted that the price does not here refer to the price of the bunkers in respect of which property was passing, it refers to the price payable for all the bunkers, whether consumed before or remaining at the time of its payment.

In §29 of the judgment, the Supreme Court pointed out some anomalies, as the Court perceived it, in the owners' argument and then at §30 said the following:

> Mr. Crow sought to avoid some of these difficulties by submitting at one point that the agreement could be analysed as one of sale, under which OWBM undertook that at the date of payment they would transfer property in any bunkers then remaining and that they could and would also have transferred property in any bunkers already consumed, had they not been consumed. That submission certainly has a metaphysical aspect. But it makes in my view neither legal nor commercial sense. All that mattered for the owners was that they should have and had the right to consume the bunkers in the vessel's propulsion as and when they did so prior to payment, and that upon payment, they would acquire the property in, and thereby an absolute right to dispose of or use as they wished, any remaining bunkers.

There can be no doubt, therefore, that the Supreme Court, as with each of the tribunals below, was heavily influenced by what can be described, in parenthesis, as the 'commercial reality'. However, it is also right to make a number of observations in relation to this approach.

Firstly, it is correct, and indeed conventional, to regard the nature of a contract entered into between parties as being defined by the obligations that are contained within it, rather than simply the labels that the parties might choose to apply. However, that can only be taken so far – certainly is a matter of English law. In the present case, the structure of each of the contracts in the chain was based, to a greater or lesser extent, on standard terms that the bunker supply industry has adopted for at least 15 years. Indeed, most are based on BIMCO terms. These standard terms, and indeed many adaptions thereof, have been prepared by sophisticated commercial parties, often with the benefit of in-house or external lawyers. The choice of English law is deliberate, as are the arbitration provisions. In the present case, the OW Group had clearly, and carefully, decided to exclude terms that would otherwise be implied under the Sale of Goods Act, and replace some of them with express provisions in relation to quality, sampling and correspondence with description by reference to those samples. So, as is often the case, it was not merely a matter of the labels that the parties applied, such as describing each as seller and buyer. We, and indeed the parties know that, commercially, a particular objective was to be realised (namely the supply of fuel), but with a permission to use the same. But the concept of destruction of physical property is not actually expressly addressed in any bunker supply contracts, and certainly was not addressed in any of the contracts in the chain. Whilst it is true that is a necessary consequence of using the bunkers for propulsion, it is also true that the parties, when seeking to achieve that particular commercial purpose, nevertheless decided to regulate the position between each other, as a matter of law, by deliberately adopting a structure – namely an English law contract of sale, to which the Sale of Goods Act would apply. The extent to which it would not apply was also expressly dealt with, by express exclusions. It is not conventional under English law to let the commercial objective, which was so heavily stressed and emphasised in each of the judgments in this case, to determine, of necessity, the legal consequences. It is an essential part of English law that, absent contravening public policy or any statutory prohibition, parties are free to agree whatever bargain they wish.

It is worth digressing at this stage to remind ourselves as to basis of agreement clauses. These are widely used. Classically these appear in sophisticated contracts, and indeed sometimes less sophisticated contracts; for example, between banks, financial institutions and purchasers of financial products (such as derivatives). Often clauses are expressly included in the contracts between the parties reciting that the buyer has formed its own view as to the suitability of the product, has exercised its own judgment, has not relied upon any statements given or made by the seller, and that any such statements made are not to constitute advice given by the seller to the buyer and the seller has not made any recommendations. Yet frequently the inclusion of such a clause is counterfactual, often providing the foundation for the very opposite to occur as a matter of commercial reality. The purpose of such a provision is to denude the factual (ie the commercial reality) of having any legal consequence. Two classic examples are *Peekay Intermark Ltd v Australia & New Zealand Banking Group Ltd*[7] and the well-known case of *Springwell Navigation Corp v JP Morgan Chase Bank*.[8] Thus, irrespective of the fact that advice and recommendations may well have been given, the purchaser of the financial instrument was not able to assert any case to the contrary. So, stripped back to its essential components, if I agree with you that, irrespective of the true factual position, the position between us is 'x' then absent fraud or some other factor that impugns our ability to enter into such an agreement, we are both stuck with 'x'. The precise jurisprudential basis behind this is not strictly relevant for today's purposes, but it is either found in straightforward freedom of contract, or that if the parties agree 'x' then the other is estopped from asserting to the contrary, either because it is unconscionable to allow one party to rely on the agreed represented position or because the conventional behaviour of the party thereafter estops them. But on any analysis, a basis clause divorces the legal reality from the factual reality. That is its primary purpose.

I suggest that in the present case, the buyers and sellers, the owners and OWM respectively, were free to agree whatever they so wished in relation to the bunkers. The contract was not illusory – after all, the bunkers did exist, in full, at the time of delivery. What would the position have been if the owners had chosen to pay, for whatever reason, two days after delivery?

[7] [2006] 2 Lloyd's Rep 511.
[8] [2010] EWCA Civ 1221.

At this point in time all the bunkers existed and none of the bunkers had been consumed. Taken against the express language of the contract, can it seriously be said that the parties neither intended a contract of sale to arise, nor that there such a contract as a matter of legal consequence? Surely the position is that the parties decided to structure the legal obligations between them ignoring whether the bunkers remained in existence of not. The basis upon which they agreed ignored the continued physical existence of the bunkers. The buyer would not be permitted to turn to the seller at the point of payment, and say, 'I have no obligation to pay because I have consensually consumed the bunkers', and nor would the seller be able to say 'I owe you no obligations qua seller, because you have consensually, physically destroyed the goods,. Surely they would each be estopped from making such contentions. It might be said that this is far removed from the reality – it is unlikely that both parties intended for the goods to be physically destroyed. But what else did they intend? It is not as extreme in its application as a basis clause in the sale of a complex derivative involving $100m. In the present case, the Court only had to consider the basis upon which the parties contracted, as between themselves: by this I mean not in relation to the wider world. Matters of property generally give rise to rights of ownership that can be asserted against the rest of the world. However, in the present case the property rights that we are concerned with need only be considered along the chain. In other words, as between the immediate contracting parties rather than the whole world. This is because all parties seeking to make a claim, or who had an interest in payment, were involved as participants in that contractual chain.

A similar conclusion could have been reached by what, for convenience's sake, I will label 'putative property'. By this I mean that the parties contracted to convey property in goods that had been destroyed, but retrospectively. This means, therefore, that at the point of payment (assuming that the owners are prepared to pay) the seller, OWBM, has to be able to furnish the buyer with all the rights and privileges that normally accompany an outright transfer of property. Thus, at day 60 (the end of the relevant credit period, and due date for payment in *The Res Cogitans*), the sellers would have to be able to confer, notionally, upon the buyers all the rights and privileges pertinent to an outright sale; in other words, an outright transfer of the property of the goods. The practical (and, indeed, legal) effect of this would be that at day 60, the buyer would then be treated as having exercised all dominion, use and control over the goods in the period between delivery and payment as if it was the outright owner. This does not require the transfer of non-existent property, but rather the retrospective furnishing of the buyer with a particular legal status, by agreement, at an earlier stage. In passing, the Sale of Goods Act does not prohibit the passing of property retrospectively and also contains provisions dealing with non-existent goods.

Both these approaches mean that the contract works according to its terms, all along the chain, and also gives effect to the commercial purpose that each party intended to achieve. The parties are, to put it colloquially, all bound by the express terms of their bargain.

These points were not argued in the Supreme Court, but might, I suggest, feature in the future. There are a number of reasons for this. Firstly, the Supreme Court decision extends far beyond the maritime sector. In any case involving the supply of goods, on retention terms, where there is a liberty to use the goods, whether by incorporation or consumption, which results in the original subject matter being destroyed, the contract is now not one of sale. The whole regime under the Sale of Goods Act 1979 does not apply. Whilst the Supreme Court observed that implied into such a contract would be many of the terms that arise under the Sale of Goods Act, that still leaves the position particularly uncertain. It may well necessitate a substantial and wholesale reappraisal of the efficacy of Romalpa clauses as well. One can think of a number of market sectors that will immediately be affected by this judgment: chemicals, pharmaceuticals and foodstuffs, to name but a few.

The approach taken by each of the arbitrators and the judges culminating in the Supreme Court decision approached the question of determining the nature of the contract by construing its content. They sought to identify the obligations contained within it. They each concluded, although approached from slightly different perspectives, that it could not (and I stress *could not*) have been the intention of the party to enter into a contract providing for the conveyance of property, when that property may well have ceased to exist at the time when the transfer is to take place. But in so doing, surely they were letting the tail wag the dog? They were looking at anticipated post-contractual events and using them as an aid to the construction of the contract. It might be said that the post-contractual events were sufficiently anticipated before the contract was entered into, to be regarded as pre-contractual. In other words part of the factual matrix. But even this doesn't answer the question as to what that contemplation actually was – as I have pointed out earlier, the parties' actual contemplation may well be very different – and doubtless is never expressed between them. However, the one constant invariable are the terms they have expressly chosen in their contract, and the framework they have deliberately sought to impose upon their commercial arrangements.

One classic difference between civil and common law systems in relation to contractual construction is that English law does not permit recourse to post-contractual events as an aid to construction. Civil law systems do. The way the English courts accommodate post-contractual conduct is, classically, by recourse to estoppel by convention. But this simply precludes the parties from placing reliance upon the express terms of the contract under circumstances where their conventional behaviour has been different, by reference to objective factors that crossed the line between them. Even here, it can be noted, the fact that the parties may embark upon the same course of conduct does not of itself give rise to an estoppel by convention – not least because any assumptions that cross the line between them may in fact be different, and not shared – although they may coincide in their effect. This is rather the point I was making in relation to expectations and assumptions that are pre-contractual.

A further observation is also pertinent. You will remember how the Supreme Court, in the judgment of Lord Manse, referred to the owners' submissions that 'the agreement could be analysed as one of sale, under which OWBM undertook that at the date of payment they would transfer property in any bunkers then remaining and that they could and would also have transferred property in any bunkers already consumed, had they not been consumed', and he then referred to that as metaphysical. But perhaps its true significance was not fully pressed home: if all the bunkers exist, and are expressly delivered under and in accordance with the OW terms and conditions, and they are ascertainable and appropriated to the contract, then why should there not be an agreement to sell, in relation to those goods delivered, but with the obligations upon the seller being discharged, by (1) complying with its obligations under s 12 insofar as they apply to an agreement to sell[9] and (2) transferring actual property in

[9] Under an agreement to sell the seller has to have the right to transfer property in the goods at the point in time that it is meant to pass under the contract. This is a 'timing' point and says nothing about physical existence of the goods.

the bunkers that physically exist at the point of payment. In other words, the agreement always remains an agreement to sell – and, accordingly, a contract of sale at all times, but it only crystallises into an outright sale in relation to the bunkers that actually exist at the time when payment is due. Providing the seller at all times had the right to transfer property, then it has discharged its obligations. So, whilst Lord Mance observed that there was an element of the metaphysical about this sort of submission, it did not perhaps, I suggest, do full justice to the consequences of the argument.

At the start of the chapter I said that the Supreme Court judgment was in two parts. The second part concerned the decision of the Court of Appeal in *Caterpillar v Holt*. Here, after analysing a number of cases, the Court concluded that s 49 was not, in fact, an exhaustive code setting out the only circumstances under which a claim for the price could be maintained under a contract of sale. In so finding, the Supreme Court disagreed with every one of the judges in *Caterpillar v Holt*, each of whom had concluded both at first instance and in the Court of Appeal, that s 49, having as its genesis a consolidating Act of Parliament, was clearly intended to be the exhaustive code. The precise parameters of this form of judicial relaxation are yet to be worked out, as the Supreme Court recognised. However, the Supreme Court justices nevertheless concluded that whatever those parameters might be, under circumstances where property is reserved, but risk passes, and the goods are consensually destroyed, then, in principle a seller ought to be able to maintain a claim for the price.

You will recollect my observations that one classic difference between civil and common law systems in relation to contractual construction is the extent to which recourse can be had to post-contractual events. It might also be observed that the Supreme Court's approach both in relation to construing the nature of the subject contract in *The Res Cogitans*, *and* the width and ambit of s 49 signals a purposive approach to solving legal conundrums, particularly in a commercial context. It is true that the courts have been prepared to adopt such an approach in relation to provisions of the Sales of Goods Act; this can be seen, for example, in relation to s 52 of the Sale of Goods Act 1979, which gives the buyer, expressly, a remedy of specific performance. The courts have, however, apparently without question, proceeded on the assumption that such a remedy, under this provision, may also be available in favour of the seller: see, for example,

Astro Exito Navagacion SA v Chase Manhattan Bank NA (The 'Messiniaki Tolmi' No 2).[10]

III. Conclusion

I suggest that the decision of the Supreme Court provides a platform for arguing that the proper approach to contractual construction in English law is becoming more flexible and, whilst not mirroring that in civil law systems, in that it does not go quite so far as to expressly state that post-contractual behaviour is relevant, nevertheless takes into account likely post-contractual conduct particularly if it appears to coincide with the Court's identification of the true commercial purpose of the contract, irrespective of the express language used. Whether this is to be welcomed is questionable, because although it allows the Court to respond to the ad hoc situation before it, it also, surely, creates scope for greater uncertainty. It can also lead to a divergence between the parties' freedom to agree the extent to which their commercial objectives are inhibited by the deliberate choice of a contract that does not fit all of those commercial objectives, and the Court's approach to that very contract. After all, in the present case, the most substantial body of opinion within the relevant market (the bunker supply industry) all worked on the premise that the agreements were agreements to sell that may or may not mature into outright sales, and had done so for many years, and that was what they intended. The Court, however, did not agree.

[10] [1983] 2 AC 787.

8

Marine Insurance and the Duty of Disclosure: Common Law and Civil Law Perspectives

PETER MACDONALD EGGERS QC*

I. Introduction

A distinguishing feature of the English law governing insurance contracts is the duty of disclosure which rests on the assured. It is a duty which applies with rigour to contracts of marine insurance. It has been a long-lasting facet of insurance business and the negotiation of insurance contracts. The duty has for a long time been impressed with the grand title 'the duty of utmost good faith' (*uberrimae fidei*).[1] Indeed, it is this description which is provided by section 17 of the Marine Insurance Act 1906. The 1906 Act

* Barrister, 7 King's Bench Walk; Visiting Professor, UCL. This paper was prepared for a conference in the summer of 2016. Where practicable, the paper has been updated, but it has not always been possible to confirm that all updates to the law (especially those referred to in other jurisdictions) have been included.

[1] RA Hasson, 'The Doctrine of Uberrima Fides in Insurance Law – A Critical Evaluation' (1969) 32 *Modern Law Review* 615, states: 'To give a legal rule a certain rubric is of course a very important way of determining the fate in the future of that particular rule'. For the view that the words 'utmost good faith' should be cast away, see H Bennett, 'Mapping the doctrine of utmost good faith in insurance contract law' [1999] *Lloyds Maritime and Commercial Law Quarterly* 165, 221 at note 300 and S Derrington, 'Non-disclosure and misrepresentation in contracts of marine insurance: a comparative overview and some proposals for unification' [2001] *Lloyds Maritime and Commercial Law Quarterly* 66, 85. The benefits of an over-arching duty of utmost good faith have been questioned: C Butcher, 'Good Faith in Insurance Law: A Redundant Concept?' [2008] *Journal of Businness Law* 375. Intriguingly, the terms 'utmost good faith' and '*uberrima fides*' were not used until the early 19th century. The earliest uses of these terms may be found in *Sturz v de la Rue* (1828) 5 Russ 322, 324 (Lord Lyndhurst LC) and *Williams v Rawlinson* (1825) 3 Bing 71, 77 (Best CJ).

was passed to codify the state of the common law as it stood at the turn of the twentieth century based on a draft Bill prepared with the industry of Sir Mackenzie Chalmers.[2] The Marine Insurance Act 1906 underwent fundamental amendment in respect of the duty of utmost good upon the entry into force of the Insurance Act 2015 on 12 August 2016. In this respect, the 2015 Act applies to insurance contracts and variations agreed on or after that date, and the unamended 1906 Act applies to contracts and variations agreed before that date. Even with such amendment, section 17 will continue to provide that 'A contract of marine insurance is a contract based upon the utmost good faith'.[3]

Section 18 of the Marine Insurance Act 1906 provides, in some detail, for the assured's duty of disclosure which must be complied with before and at the time of the conclusion of the insurance contract.[4] The existence and performance of the assured's duty of disclosure allows the insurer who sits in London to entertain business and to evaluate and assume risks in respect of marine adventures around the world. Unlike many businesses, given the volume of risks insured, underwriters in London do not usually have the resources to evaluate every risk by reference to their own investigations and inquiries and so must rely on the assured, and a professional insurance broker, to provide an account of material information relating to the risk to the insurers. It is this original imbalance in the knowledge and information available to the assured on the one hand and the insurer on the other hand which is said to give rise to the duty of disclosure.[5] It is possible that if the insurer does undertake a full due diligence investigation of a particular risk, relying on its own surveyors and consultants, that the rationale for the duty of disclosure would disappear and, with it, the duty of disclosure.[6] The assured's duty of disclosure requires the assured

[2] P MacDonald Eggers, 'The Marine Insurance Act 1906: judicial attitudes and innovation – time for reform?' in R Thomas (ed), *Marine Insurance: Law in Transition* (Informa, London, 2006) paras 10.1–10.11.

[3] Section 14(3)(a) of the Insurance Act 2015. In the explanatory notes accompanying the legislation, at para 116, it is stated that 'The intention of [s] 14 is that good faith will remain an interpretative principle, with section 17 of the 1906 Act and the common law continuing to provide that insurance contracts are contracts of good faith'.

[4] Section 19 deals with the broker's duty of disclosure and s 20 deals with pre-contractual misrepresentations.

[5] *Pan Atlantic Insurance Co Ltd v Pine Top Insurance Co Ltd* [1995] 1 AC 501, 542 (Lord Mustill).

[6] *Coronation Insurance Co v Taku Air Transport Ltd* [1991] 3 SCR 622 (Sup Ct Canada); *Manifest Shipping & Co Ltd v Uni-Polaris Insurance Co Ltd (The Star Sea)* [2001] UKHL 1,

to provide to the insurer information which is both material (in the sense that the information is of the type which a prudent insurer would wish to take into account in assessing and rating the risk)[7] and within the assured's actual or deemed knowledge. There are established exceptions to this duty set out in section 18.

The Insurance Act 2015 made amendments to the assured's duty of disclosure, but fundamentally the duty of disclosure remains unchanged. Indeed, it may fairly be said that the assured assumed a more burdensome duty of disclosure upon the 2015 Act's entry into force. It is a more burdensome duty because, although the materiality of information is defined in the same way as under the 1906 Act,[8] the manner in which the knowledge of the assured is defined is such as to capture a more expansive perimeter of information which must be disclosed.[9] The exceptions to the duty of disclosure are broadly the same as those provided for under the 1906 Act. The important point is that the duty of disclosure will continue to exist. The 2015 Act is the result of a long process of review and consultation undertaken by the Law Commission. The Law Commission concluded that the assured's duty of disclosure remains an integral factor in the operation of the insurance market, although remarked that reform of the duty was required to ensure a more co-operative approach between the assured and the insurer.[10] The Law Commission said in this respect:[11]

> An insured often knows more than the insurer about the risk to be insured. It is therefore important to encourage a full and frank exchange of information before the insurance contract is made. Under the current law, the onus is on the prospective policyholder to disclose information to the insurer. This obligation to 'present the risk' enables the UK insurance market to provide insurance for

[2001] 2 WLR 170, [76] (Lord Hobhouse). See also *Geest plc v Fyffes plc* [1999] 1 All ER (Comm) 672, 683, 685 (Colman J).

[7] Section 18(2) of the Marine Insurance Act 1906. As to the meaning of materiality, see *Pan Atlantic Insurance Co Ltd v Pine Top Insurance Co Ltd* [1995] 1 AC 501, 531, 538 (Lord Mustill).

[8] Section 7(3) of the Insurance Act 2015.

[9] Section 4 of the Insurance Act 2015.

[10] Interestingly, the result of the amendments introduced by the 2015 Act is the effective abrogation of the insurer's duty of utmost good faith allowed by s 17 of the Marine Insurance Act 1906 in that while the duty of utmost good faith remains, the 2015 Act abolishes the remedy of avoidance for any breach of the duty (s 14) and provides for no other remedy in the event of the insurer's breach.

[11] Law Commission, 'Insurance Contract Law: Business Disclosure; Warranties; Insurers' Remedies for Fraudulent Claims; and Late Payment' (Law Com No 353), July 2014, paras 3.1–3.3.

> a wide variety of large and specialist risks, efficiently and cost-effectively. We think that this fundamental pre-contract duty is important to the successful operation of the UK insurance market. However, the law which governs the duty is more than 100 years old. It no longer works as well as it should. The law pre-dates the information revolution, before which the volume of data that firms stored, analysed and accessed was much smaller. The law is unclear and difficult to comply with, and the consequences of breaching the duty are harsh. Good disclosure requires co-operation between both parties: the policyholder knows how the business is run; the insurer knows which facts are relevant to assessing the risk. We think that the law should do more to encourage both sides to work together to exchange information.

English law is therefore in the process of reform, but the bedrock requirement of disclosure from the assured will retain a secure place in English marine insurance law. The major factor which has driven reform in England and in other countries was the perceived unfairness of the remedy of avoidance of the insurance contract, which remedy was available to the insurer in the event of any breach of the assured's duty of disclosure, no matter whether the breach was fraudulent, negligent or innocent, or whether the non-disclosure was of information which was of crucial importance to a sound assessment of the risk or of marginal relevance (albeit enough to have resulted in different terms or premium).[12] The remedy has repeatedly been described as 'draconian'.[13] In place of a single remedy for breach of the assured's duty of disclosure, the Insurance Act 2015 imposes a number of different remedies depending on whether the breach of duty was 'deliberate' or 'reckless' (as defined by the Act) and on the extent of the inducing effect of the relevant non-disclosure on the insurer in deciding whether to enter into the insurance contract.[14]

It is striking that within the commercial law systems of many countries – both common law and civil law countries – the assured's duty of disclosure continues to play an important part in the negotiation and

[12] P MacDonald Eggers, S Picken and P Foss, *Good Faith and Insurance Contracts*, 3rd edn (London, Informa, 2010), paras 16.23–16.26.

[13] For example, *Drake Insurance plc v Provident Insurance plc* [2003] EWCA Civ 1834, [2004] 1 Lloyd's Rep 268 at [145] (Clarke, LJ). See also *Manifest Shipping Co Ltd v Uni-Polaris Shipping Co Ltd (The Star Sea)* [2001] UKHL 1, [2001] 2 WLR 170 at [51], [79] (Lord Hobhouse) ('penal'); *K/S Merc-Scandia XXXXII v Certain Lloyd's Underwriters (The Mercandian Continent)* [2001] EWCA Civ 1275, [2001] 2 Lloyd's Rep 563 at [26] (Longmore, LJ) ('extreme').

[14] Section 8 and Sch 1.

conclusion of a marine insurance contract. Indeed, as discussed below, in a number of countries, insurance law is more demanding on the assured in respect of marine insurance contracts than in respect of non-marine insurance contracts. This may be because of the nature of the risks and the subject matter which are insured under a marine policy: the risks are inherently more volatile and the subject matters insured, which are often of a high value, are mobile and necessarily encounter different types and scales of risk in different countries (and on the high seas) within relatively short periods of time. Nevertheless, under English law, the assured's duty of disclosure is the same in respect of all non-consumer insurance contracts, whether marine or non-marine.[15]

The purpose of this chapter is to review the law governing the assured's duty of disclosure in a number of common law and civil law jurisdictions with a view to determining the similarities and differences between the legal systems. In preparing this paper, I am conscious of being a common lawyer (and familiar with only a few common law legal systems) and not a civil lawyer. Accordingly, the review of the legal position in each of the jurisdictions referred to below is necessarily brief and more prone to error than I am used to. Nevertheless, I have been greatly assisted by the input of a number of lawyers experienced in civil law jurisdictions.[16]

II. Common Origins: The Law Merchant

Many sophisticated commercial legal systems make provision for the assured's duty of disclosure which must be discharged prior to the conclusion of the insurance contract. This is reflected in both common law and civil law jurisdictions. It should not come as a surprise that marine insurance contracts attract a duty of disclosure because it serves a valuable

[15] The assured's duty of disclosure in respect of consumer insurance contracts was abolished by the Consumer Insurance (Disclosures and Representations) Act 2012 which entered into force on 6 April 2013.

[16] In particular, Dr George C Panagopoulos and Angeliki Kofopoulou of Reed Smith LLP, Athens; Stinne Taiger Avø, Vice President, Head of FDD, Assuranceforeningen SKULD (Gjensidig), Copenhagen; Prof Dr Frank Smeele, Professor of Commercial Law, Erasmus University, Rotterdam; Prof Baris Soyer, Head of Department of Shipping and Trade Law, Swansea University.

commercial purpose to allow the insurer to judge the nature and degree of a risk before deciding to commit to the insurance of that risk. It therefore should not come as a surprise that both common law and civil law legal systems give effect to the imposition of a duty of disclosure which has an important commercial rationale. This is because commercial law tends to follow commercial practice rather than obstruct or frustrate the conduct of business, unless there is, exceptionally, a palpable injustice inherent in the commercial practice.

English commercial law has long prided itself on the notion that it has developed in accordance with the practices of merchants. Indeed, in the eighteenth century, the redoubtable commercial judge, Lord Mansfield, not only took steps to prepare a logical (or at least a coherent) basis for English commercial law as a whole, and insurance law in particular,[17] but also made it his business to consult merchants, whether they were jurymen in his court, or more informally at his home in Bloomsbury Square.[18] In formulating the commercial law, including insurance law, Lord Mansfield embraced the law merchant which he held formed part of the law of England.[19] At around the same time, Blackstone explained the law merchant as follows:[20]

> [T]he affairs of commerce are regulated by a law of their own, called the law merchant, or lex mercatoria, which all nations agree in and take notice of. And in particular it is held to be part of the law of England, which decides the causes of merchants by the general rules which obtain in all commercial countries; and that often even in matters relating to domestic trade …

The law merchant reflected a customary law recognised across national boundaries applicable to particular types of commercial transactions. The evolution of the law merchant appears to have followed a particular pattern: a specific commercial transaction was developed and pursued; a practice or custom was developed in relation to that transaction; there might be

[17] *Anderson v Pitcher* (1800) 2 Bos & Pul 164, 168 (Lord Eldon, CJ).

[18] E Heward, *Lord Mansfield* (London, Sweet & Maxwell, 1979) 104; NS Poser, *Lord Mansfield: Justice in the Age of Reason* (Montreal, McGill-Queen's University Press, 2013) 227–28. In *Pawson v Watson* (1778) 2 Cowp 785, 788, Lord Mansfield refers to his advice given to insurance brokers, at Guildhall, to record their representations to insurers in a book.

[19] *Pillans v van Mierop* (1765) 3 Burr 1663, 1669 (Lord Mansfield CJ).

[20] Blackstone, *Commentaries on the Laws of England*, 9th edn (London, W Strahan, T Cadell, 1783), vol 1, 273. See *The Girolamo* (1834) 3 Hagg 169, 185–86 (Sir John Nichol).

conflicting practices or customs until one recognised custom prevailed; at which point it might be regarded as binding on the parties to the transaction. A custom might be applicable in a particular place or internationally. Until it was regarded as binding, any such custom might not yet form part of the law merchant.[21] However, once the relevant commercial practice was recognised as binding under the law of nature or nations (in other words, the law merchant), English common law was ready to engraft that law as part of its own.[22]

There is no clearly identifiable body of law known as the law merchant. Indeed, it has been said that the law merchant was a fiction developed by the commercial judges in the eighteenth century and that the law merchant was little more than the development of the common law dealing with mercantile cases.[23] It is true to say that the law merchant has an ethereal quality: it is often referred to but never adequately defined, other than referring to it as a body of custom or practice, or the law of nations, or the law of nature or universal law,[24] or representing the principles of equity introduced to temper the inflexible approach of the common law.[25] Thus, in *Master v Miller*,[26] Buller, J said that 'The law-merchant is a system of equity, founded on the rules of equity, and governed in all its parts by plain justice and good faith'. There was also an apparent procedural element to the law merchant.[27]

There is, however, much to be said for the view that the law merchant represented a body of a well-established commercial practice which was both notorious and applicable over a defined area, often internationally,

[21] *Stevenson v Snow* (1761) 1 Bl W 318, 320 (Wilmot J); *Pillans v van Mierop* (1765) 3 Burr 1663, 1675 (Aston J).

[22] Blackstone, *Commentaries* (1783), vol 1, 75, said that the law merchant 'however different from the general rules of the common law, is yet ingrafted into it, and made a part of it; being allowed for the benefit of trade, to be of the utmost validity in all commercial transactions: for it is a maxim of law, that *cuilibet in sua arte credendum est*'. In *The Juliana* (1822) 2 Dod 504, 515, Lord Stowell said that the common law 'adopts the law merchant as its guide upon the subjects which it regulates'.

[23] JH Baker, 'The Law Merchant and the Common Law before 1700'(1979) 38 *Cambridge Law Journal* 295.

[24] *Anon v The Sheriff of London (The Case of the Carrier who Broke Bulk)*, Select Cases in the Exchequer Chamber, vol ii (London, Selden Society, 1945), vol 64, 30, 32.

[25] Baker, 'The Law Merchant' (1979) 295–96.

[26] (1791) 4 TR 320, 342 (Buller J). See also J Oldham, *English Common Law in the Age of Mansfield*, (Chapel Hill and London, University of North Carolina Press, 2004) 102, fn 124.

[27] Baker, 'Common Law before 1700' (n 23) 301–02.

and which was regarded as binding. There are numerous references to the law merchant in the early decisions both of mercantile or local courts and superior courts.[28] It is also referred to by sixteenth- and seventeenth-century commentators.[29] Mercantile practice or custom must have been influential in the development of the law to be applied by the English courts, whether that law was described as an independent law merchant, or whether it was part of the common law. In either case, as the law was being developed to deal with new commercial instruments and transactions and the new ways of conducting business, and in the context of shipping and marine insurance, international business, the universally accepted practices of merchants would have explained the transaction and informed the development of the law. If a judge had to determine a dispute by the application of one of two competing rules, it is probable – and makes sense – that the judge would apply that rule which was consistent with or based upon the rule of commercial practice applied by the merchant community, especially if the rule was clear, universally applied and well known to the commercial market.[30]

Insurance contracts developed in this way. Thus, principles of English insurance law from the sixteenth century were recognised as emanating from the customs and practices which originated with the relevant commercial instrument and transaction, often in the Italian city states, and developed in what is now The Netherlands and Belgium.[31] Thus, Park stated that 'insurances are founded upon the great principles of natural justice, rather than upon any municipal regulations; and that consequently the law must be nearly the same in all countries'.[32] In *Barclay v Cousins*,[33] Grose, Le Blanc and Lawrence JJ referred to 'Foreign writers upon insurance,

[28] See eg Selden Society, *Select Cases on the Law Merchant, vol I* (1908), vol 23; *Select Cases on the Law Merchant, vol. II* (1929), vol 46.

[29] J Selden, *Notes upon Sir John Fortescue* in *De Laudibus Legum Angliae* (Companie of Stationers, 1616), Ad Cap III, 39; G Malynes, *Consuetudo, Vel, Lex Mercatoria, or, The Antient Law-Merchant*, 2nd edn (1636); Zouch, *The Jurisdiction of the Admiralty of England Asserted, against Sr. Edward Coke's Articuli Admiralitatis* (1663) 8–9.

[30] Baker (n 23) 298–99, refers to the 'logical trap' associated with merchant practice influencing the development of common law rules, as opposed to explaining or construing commercial contracts.

[31] Select Pleas of Admiralty (SS) ii, 76, a petition to the Council.

[32] J Park, *A System of the Law of Marine Insurances*, 8th edn (London, Saunders and Benning, 1842) xvi–xvii. At 403, Park cites Grotius, Pufendorf, Bynkershoek.

[33] (1802) 2 East 544, 548.

whose doctrines form the greatest part of our law on this subject'. In the early twentieth century, in *Moore v Evans*,[34] Lord Atkinson said that:

> Marine insurance grew out of the necessities of maritime trade and commerce. It dealt with the hazardous enterprise of the navigation of the sea by ships carrying cargo for reward. The law dealing with it is a branch of the law maritime as well as of the law merchant. It is founded upon the practices of merchants who were themselves for long the expounders of its principles, which principles general convenience had established in order to regulate the dealings of merchants with each other in all countries.

The beginnings of insurance transactions have been traced to the Italian city states, such as Genoa, Palermo and Florence, by reference to documentary evidence of such transactions in the fourteenth century.[35] Shipments between Italy and Antwerp and Bruges were undertaken at this time. This led to the emergence of an underwriting market in these cities by the fifteenth century.[36] From the fourteenth to sixteenth centuries, trade between the Italian city states and England led to the development of insurance business in England, often undertaken by Italian merchants resident in London (such as Lombard Street).[37] Indeed, by the 1540s, most insurance contracts written in London were in the Italian language; thereafter, they were written in English, reflecting the probable nationality of the underwriters.[38] In 1577, the City of London established a court to deal with insurance disputes, such court being manned by merchants

[34] [1918] AC 185, 193.

[35] WS Holdsworth, 'The Early History of the Contract of Insurance' (1917) 17 *Columbia Law Review* 85, 88–92; Piccino, 'Genoa, 1340–1620: Early Development of Marine Insurance' in AB Leonard (ed), *Marine Insurance: Origins and Institutions, 1300–1850* (London, Palgrave Macmillan, 2016) 30–35. See also *Gibbs v Mercantile Mutual Insurance (Australia) Ltd* [2003] HCA 39 at [47]–[53] (McHugh J dissenting).

[36] D De ruysscher, 'Antwerp 1490–1590: Insurance and Speculation' in Leonard, *Marine Insurance* (2016). See also M Huybrechts, 'Comparative marine insurance law: Highlighting the significant features of marine insurance law in Belgium and other selected European legal systems' in Thomas, *Marine Insurance* (2006) paras 8.1–8.7.

[37] G Rossi, 'England 1523–1601: The Beginnings of Marine Insurance' in Leonard (n 35) 132–36.

[38] WS Holdsworth, 'The Early History of the Contract of Insurance' (1917) 17 *Columbia Law Review* 85, 96–101; Rossi, 'England 1523–1601' (2016) 137, 140. See *Mayne v De Gozi* (1538) KB 27/1107 m 37, referred to in J Baker, *The Oxford History of the Laws of England* (Oxford, Oxford University Press, 2003) 215, fn 51; 859, fn 117; note also 612, fn 132. See also *Broke v Maynard* (1547) Select Pleas of Admiralty, vol ii, 47; cf *Emerson v De Sallanova* (1545), Select Pleas of Admiralty, vol ii, 46 (Selden Society, vol 11, 1897).

and it appears lawyers.[39] By this stage, the London Insurance Code had been developed.[40] In 1601, Parliament passed a statute providing for the determination of disputes relating to policies of assurance, by a commission comprising merchants and lawyers.[41] The practice of assurance was attested to by that statute (43 Eliz c 12), providing that by means of policies of insurance

> it cometh to pass upon the loss or perishing of any ship, there followeth not the undoing of any man, but the loss lighteth rather easily upon many than heavily upon few, and rather upon them that adventure not than those that do adventure, whereby all merchants, especially of the younger sort, are allured to venture more willingly and more freely.[42]

Therefore the practices which governed insurance transactions and which were developed in the Italian city states and Antwerp and Bruges, and elsewhere in Europe, applied to the legal aspects of insurance transactions, including the insurer's rights of salvage, the unavailability of an indemnity in the event that the vessel was lost at the time of the insurance contract, and the requirement of abandonment in the case of a claim for an indemnity for a total loss. Most importantly, the obligation of the assured to disclose information to the insurer prior to the underwriting of the risk was a practice recognised as binding by the law merchant.[43] The application of the law merchant was secured by provisions in policy documents that the policy would have as much force and effect as the 'surest writing' in Lombard Street (or later the Royal Exchange).[44] By this time, the wording of insurance policies was well settled.[45]

[39] D Ibbetson, 'Law and Custom: Insurance in Sixteenth-Century England' (2008) 29 *Journal of Legal History* 291, 297–99.

[40] G Rossi, *Insurance in Elizabethan England* (Cambridge University Press, Cambridge, 2016).

[41] ibid 305–07.

[42] See *Moore v Evans* [1918] AC 185, 193 (Lord Atkinson). The statute was re-enacted and amended by 13, 14 Charles II c 23.

[43] Rossi (n 37) 132–36. As to abandonment, see *Case v Davidson* (1816) 5 M&S 79, 83–84 (Lord Ellenborough CJ), 86–87 (Abbott, J); *Rankin v Potter* (1873) LR 6 HL 83, 123–26 (Blackburn J); FE de Roover, 'Early Examples of Marine Insurance' (1945) 5 *Journal of Economic History* 172, 198–99; AB Leonard, 'England 1523–1601: The Beginnings of Marine Insurance' in Leonard (n 35) 161.

[44] WH Holdsworth, 'The Early History of the Contract of Insurance' (1917) 17 *Columbia Law Review* 85, 98; Leonard, 'England 1523–1601' (n 43) 155.

[45] de Roover, 'Marine Insurance' (1945) 198.

III. English Law

The first references to the assured's duty of disclosure by the English courts occur during the late seventeenth century.[46] However, it was not until 1766 that the assured's duty of disclosure received a sustained examination. The major exposition of the assured's duty of disclosure was explained by Lord Mansfield CJ in *Carter v Boehm*.[47] In that judgment, the Court of King's Bench was concerned with the assured's alleged non-disclosure relating to the insurance of Fort Marlborough on the Island of Sumatra. In reviewing the law, Lord Mansfield explained the nature of the duty of disclosure:

> Insurance is a contract upon speculation. The special facts, upon which the contingent chance is to be computed, lie most commonly in the knowledge of the insured only; the under-writer trusts to his representation, and proceeds upon confidence that he does not keep back any circumstance in his knowledge, to mislead the under-writer into a belief that the circumstance does not exist, and to induce him to estimate the risque, as if it did not exist. The keeping back such circumstance is a fraud, and therefore the policy is void. Although the suppression should happen through mistake, without any fraudulent intention; yet still the under-writer is deceived, and the policy is void; because the risque run is really different from the risque understood and intended to be run, at the time of the agreement ... Good faith forbids either party by concealing what he privately knows, to draw the other into a bargain, from his ignorance of that fact, and his believing the contrary ... The reason of the rule which obliges parties to disclose, is to prevent fraud, and to encourage good faith. It is adapted to such facts as vary the nature of the contract; which one privately knows, and the other is ignorant of, and has no reason to suspect.

The Court explained that, in order for the assured to be bound to disclose information to the insurer prior to the agreement of the insurance contract, the information in question had to be known to the assured and had to

[46] *Whittingham* v *Thornburgh* (1690) 2 Vern 206. See also *Wakeham* v *Carter* (1680), *Lord Nottingham's Chancery Cases*, vol II (Selden Society), 818, referred to by H Bennett, 'Mapping the Doctrine' [1999] 189. See also Molloy, *De Jure Maritimo et Navali*, 6th edn (London, Walthoe and Wotton, 1707) 284, referring to *Stockden's Case* (1686) and *The Mayflower* (1692). See also Park, *Law of Marine Insurances* (1842) 405, referring to a decision before Lord Holt CJ during the reign of William and Mary (Skin 327, 90 ER 146).

[47] (1766) 3 Burr 1909, 1909–1911. There were a number of decisions which applied the duty of disclosure during the earlier part of the 18th century, but none with an equivalent sustained analysis of the duty of utmost good faith.

be material.[48] Furthermore, the Court explained the exceptions which exist to the duty of disclosure, including information which lessened the risk, information already known or which ought to have been known to the insurer, and information as to which the insurer has waived disclosure.[49]

This duty of disclosure has been applied and refined on innumerable occasions since the seminal decision in *Carter v Boehm*. In 1906, the Marine Insurance Act 1906 was passed. Sir Mackenzie Chalmers had drafted that statute based on a review of all of the relevant insurance cases which had been heard up until that time. In preparing the draft Bill, Chalmers had published a *Digest of the Law relating to Marine Insurance*,[50] in which he said that he had identified over 2,000 relevant authorities.[51] Section 18 of the 1906 Act set out the assured's duty of disclosure and followed the principle explained by Lord Mansfield in *Carter v Boehm*. This duty reflects both the common law governing marine and non-marine insurance contracts.[52]

Section 91(2) of the Marine Insurance Act 1906 provides that 'The rules of the common law including the law merchant, save in so far as they are inconsistent with the express provisions of this Act, shall continue to apply to contracts of insurance'.[53] Indeed, in 1994, in *Pan Atlantic Insurance Co Ltd v Pine Top Insurance Co Ltd*,[54] the House of Lords relied on section 91(2) in order to import the common law requirement of inducement applicable to misrepresentations to a misrepresentation by the assured within section 20 of the 1906 Act. The House of Lords introduced a similar requirement of inducement for non-disclosures, but recognised that it could not rely on section 91(2) for that purpose. By this decision, the insurer could not avoid the insurance policy unless

[48] (1766) 3 Burr 1909, 1911, 1916.

[49] There is a fourth exception: there is no need to disclose information where disclosure is rendered superfluous by reason of the existence of a warranty in the policy: s 18(3)(d) of the Marine Insurance Act 1906; *Haywood v Rodgers* (1804) 4 East 590.

[50] London, William Clowes & Sons, 1901.

[51] P MacDonald Eggers, 'The Marine Insurance Act 1906: judicial attitudes and innovation – time for reform?' in Thomas (n 2) para 10.10.

[52] *Pan Atlantic Insurance Co Ltd v Pine Top Insurance Co Ltd* [1994] 2 Lloyd's Rep 427, 452 (Lord Mustill); *Avon Insurance plc v Swire Fraser Ltd* [2000] 1 All ER (Comm) 573, [17] (Rix J); *Manifest Shipping Co Ltd v Uni-Polaris Shipping Co Ltd (The Star Sea)* [2001] UKHL 1, [2001] 2 WLR 170 at [47] (Lord Hobhouse); *HIH Casualty and General Insurance Ltd v Chase Manhattan Bank* [2003] UKHL 6, [2003] 2 Lloyd's Rep 61 at [5] (Lord Bingham).

[53] Chalmers and Owens, *The Marine Insurance Act 1906*, 2nd edn (London, Butterworth & Co, 1913) 142–43.

[54] [1995] 1 AC 501, 549–50 (Lord Mustill), 571 (Lord Lloyd).

the insurer was induced by the assured's non-disclosure to enter into the insurance contract; if the insurer would not have entered into the contract on the same terms had full and accurate disclosure been made, the insurer would have been induced.

If the insurer had been induced to enter into a marine insurance contract, by sections 17 and 18 of the Marine Insurance Act 1906, the insurer was entitled to avoid the insurance contract such that the contract would be unwound and all benefits (premiums and claims proceeds) which have been transferred under the contract would have to be returned, save that in the event of the assured's fraud or in the event of illegality, the insurer would be entitled to retain the premium.[55]

Accordingly, under the Marine Insurance Act 1906, the insurer would be entitled to avoid the marine insurance contract, if the assured has failed to disclose to the insurer, prior to the conclusion of the contract, a material circumstance which the assured either knows or ought to have known in the ordinary course of business, and by reason of that non-disclosure, the insurer has been induced to enter into the contract.

After the Insurance Act 2015 entered into force on 12 August 2016, the assured remains obliged to disclose material information to the insurer prior to the conclusion of the insurance contract. Under the 2015 Act, the duty of utmost good faith remains but the pre-contractual aspect of the duty is now to be called the 'duty of fair presentation'.[56] In large measure, the duty of disclosure which forms part of the duty of fair presentation is the same as that provided for by the common law and under the 1906 Act. The test of materiality is the same, the requirement of inducement remains, and the exceptions to the duty of disclosure are broadly the same.[57] There are two fundamental changes brought about by the 2015 Act. First, the assured's duty of disclosure is determined not only by materiality but also what the assured knows or is deemed to known. What counts as the assured's knowledge has been redefined by the 2015 Act in a manner which appears to enlarge the assured's knowledge by reason of a duty of reasonable search and by reason of the attribution of knowledge to corporate assureds by reference to what is known to any one member of the assured's

[55] Section 84(3)(a) of the Marine Insurance Act 1906.

[56] Section 3(2) of the Insurance Act 2015.

[57] The exception in s 18(3)(d) of the Marine Insurance Act 1906 will no longer exist, however, because of the change to the law of warranties introduced by the 2015 Act in ss 10 and 11.

'senior management' (which itself benefits from an expansive definition).[58] Similarly, the insurer's knowledge – which delineates an exception to the assured's duty of disclosure – has been redefined in a manner which is narrower than the definition of the assured's knowledge.[59]

Second, the insurer's remedies in the event of a material and inducing non-disclosure by the assured are the right to avoid the contract (if the assured's breach of duty were deliberate or reckless or if the insurer would not have entered into the contract at all had the requisite disclosure been provided)[60] or the right to rewrite the insurance contract to include or omit provisions which would have been included or removed had the requisite disclosure been provided[61] or, if the insurer would have increased the premium, the right to reduce any recoverable claim by that proportion represented by the amount which the insurer did charge by way of premium and would have charged by way of premium had full disclosure been provided.[62]

IV. Development in Common Law Countries

The passage of the Marine Insurance Act 1906 was influential throughout the common law world. In US federal maritime law and New York law, the law of marine insurance historically is based upon English law. In the case of marine insurance, the Supreme Court of the United States has held that maritime disputes are governed by US federal law and that insurance disputes are governed by state law, but in the case of marine insurance disputes, state law should govern the dispute, unless there is a judicially established federal admiralty rule governing the issue.[63] In *New York Marine*

[58] Section 4 of the Insurance Act 2015.

[59] Section 5 of the Insurance Act 2015.

[60] The insurer is obliged to return the premium to the assured if the assured's breach of duty is not deliberate or reckless, but the insurer is entitled to retain the premium if the assured's breach is deliberate or reckless.

[61] J Davey, 'Proportionality, Fair Presentation of the Risk and the Hypothetical Bargain: the Law Commission's Remaking of Commercial Insurance Law' [2019] *Lloyd's Commercial and Maritime Law Quarterly* 360.

[62] Section 8 and Sch 1 of the Insurance Act 2015.

[63] *Wilburn Boat Co v Fireman's Fund Insurance Co*, 348 US 310 (1955). See M Sturley, 'Restating the Law: A Workable Solution to the *Wilburn Boat* Problem' (1998) 29 *Journal of Maritime Law & Commerce* 41; J Dunt, *International Cargo Insurance* (London, Informa, 2012) para 8.5.

and General Insurance Company v Continental Cement Company LLC,[64] the United States Court of Appeals for the Eighth Circuit concluded that there was such a judicially established federal admiralty rule governing marine insurance disputes:

> We conclude that the doctrine of utmost good faith is such a judicially established federal admiralty rule. The Supreme Court has long recognized the doctrine. See McLanahan v. Universal Ins. Co., 26 U.S. (1 Pet.) 170, 185 (1828) (The contract of insurance has been said to be a contract uberrimae fidei, and the principles which govern it, are those of an enlightened moral policy.); Phoenix Mut. Life Ins. Co. v. Raddin, 120 U.S. 183, 189 (1887); Stipcich, 277 U.S. at 316. In fact, by the time of the Court's Stipcich decision in 1928, the doctrine was referred to as a 'traditional' aspect of insurance law. 277 U.S. at 316. Acknowledging this tradition in insurance law, we discussed the doctrine in the context of a fire insurance case in 1931. *Springfield Fire & Marine Ins. Co. v. Nat'l Fire Ins. Co.*, 51 F.2d 714, 719 (8th Cir. 1931). In Springfield, we explained that the doctrine of uberrimae fidei was a "cardinal rule of insurance contracts … early adopted as to marine insurance contracts." Id. Other circuits have long acknowledged this doctrine in the maritime insurance context as well … Although the Fifth Circuit rejected the doctrine of utmost good faith in favor of state law in *Albany Insurance Co. v. Anh Thi Kieu*, 927 F.2d 882 (1991), a number of circuits which have addressed the question since then, including our own, have concluded that the doctrine remains established federal precedent. In *Shipley v. Ark. Blue Cross and Blue Shield*, we recognized in 2003 that "insurance policies are traditionally contracts uberrimae fidei," in upholding a right of rescission where material information had been withheld on a health insurance application governed by ERISA. 333 F.3d at 903 (quoting Stipcich, 277 U.S. at 316). The Ninth Circuit pointedly rejected the approach of the Fifth Circuit while deciding a maritime insurance case, explaining that 'in the face of 200 years of precedent, it takes more than a single circuit case and spotty citation in recent years to uproot an entrenched doctrine.'

[64] 761 F 3d 830, 2014 AMC 2063 (8th Cir 2014). See also *AIG Centennial Insurance Company v O'Neill* 782 F 3d 1296 (11th Cir 2015); *Catlin at Lloyd's v San Juan Towing & Marine Services, Inc*, 778 F 3d 69 (1st Cir 2015). In *New York Marine & General Insurance Company v Tradeline LLC* 266 F 3d 112, 123 (2d Cir 2001), the United States Court of Appeals for the Second Circuit said that '[P]arties to a marine insurance contract are held to the highest degree of good faith. Under this obligation, called uberrimae fidae, the party seeking insurance is required to disclose all circumstances known to him which materially affect the risk.' *Puritan Ins Co v Eagle Steamship Co SA*, 779 F 2d 866, 870 (2d Cir 1985). *Uberrimae fidae*, the duty of utmost good faith, requires an assured to disclose any information that materially affects the risk being insured, because the assured is more likely to be aware of such information. See *Knight v US Fire Ins Co*, 804 F 2d 9, 13 (2d Cir 1986). A non-disclosed fact is material if it would have affected the insurer's decision to insure at all or at a particular premium. See *Mutual Benefit Life Ins Co v JMR Elecs Corp*, 848 F 2d 30, 32–33 (2d Cir 1988).

> Certain Underwriters at *Lloyds, London v. Inlet Fisheries, Inc.*, 518 F.3d 645, 653 (9th Cir. 2008) … Based on its lengthy history, we conclude that "no rule of marine insurance is better established tha[n] the utmost good faith rule." *Inlet Fisheries*, 518 F.3d at 653–54 (quoting Thomas J. Schoenbaum, The Duty of Utmost Good Faith in Marine Insurance Law: A Comparative Analysis of American and English Law, 29 *Journal of. Maritime Law & Commerce* 1, 11 (1998)).

Under US federal jurisdiction, the duty of disclosure has been held to apply as part of the duty of utmost good faith based on the English common law principle. The assured is obliged to disclose material circumstances known to the assured, whether or not the assured in fact appreciates the materiality of that information. In the event of a material non-disclosure, the insurer is entitled to avoid the marine insurance policy, even if the assured's breach of duty was entirely innocent.[65]

In most common law jurisdictions, however, the marine insurance law governing pre-contractual disclosure is codified or regulated by statute based on the UK's Marine Insurance Act 1906. In New Zealand, the Marine Insurance Act 1908 adopted many provisions of the 1906 Act, including section 18, which provided for the assured's duty of disclosure. Interestingly, however, the New Zealand Act omits section 17, which imposes the duty of utmost good faith in general terms. The New Zealand Insurance Law Reform Act 1977 was passed in order to set out the requirements of an actionable misrepresentation inducing an insurance contract, and the Marine Insurance Act 1908 is subject to the 1977 Act, which will prevail in the event of any inconsistency.[66] However, the 1977 Act does not affect the assured's duty of disclosure under the Marine Insurance Act 1908.

In Australia, the Marine Insurance Act 1909 was passed following the provisions of the UK statute. Section 23 is in terms similar to section 17 of the 1906 Act, providing that the contract of marine insurance is based upon the utmost good faith. Section 24 is in terms similar to section 18 of the 1906 Act providing for the assured's duty of disclosure.[67] In 1984, the Insurance Contracts Act 1984 was passed with the effect of altering

[65] *Grande v St Paul Fire and Marine Insurance Company*, 436 F 3d 277 (1st Cir 2006); *St Paul Fire and Marine Insurance Company v Halifax Trawlers Inc*, 495 F Supp 2d 232 (D Mass 2007). See also Dunt, *International Cargo Insurance* (2012) paras 8.7–8.10.

[66] Sections 5, 6, 14.

[67] See Australian Law Commission Report 91 on 'Review of the Marine Insurance Act 1909' (2001).

the scope of the assured's duty of disclosure (by altering the test of materiality, now referred to as 'relevance', and by limiting the disclosure to information 'known' to the assured, there being no express reference to deemed knowledge) (section 21), and with the effect of modifying the remedies available to the insurer in the event of a relevant non-disclosure (section 28). Under the 1984 Act, the insurer may avoid the insurance contract if the insurer was induced to enter into the insurance contract by reason of the non-disclosure and if the non-disclosure was fraudulent. If the non-disclosure induced the insurer to conclude the insurance contract, but was not fraudulent, the insurer is not entitled to avoid the insurance contract, but the liability of the insurer is reduced to the amount that would place the insurer in a position in which the insurer would have been had the non-disclosure not occurred.[68] However, by section 9, the 1984 Act does not apply to contracts of marine insurance to which the 1909 Act applies. Thus, in the case of marine insurance contracts, the common law position set out in section 18 of the Marine Insurance Act 1906 continues to apply.

It is therefore often critical to determine whether the relevant insurance contract is a marine insurance contract (to which the 1909 Act applies) or a non-marine insurance contract (to which the 1984 Act may apply). In *Gibbs v Mercantile Mutual Insurance (Australia) Ltd*,[69] the issue was whether a policy on a riverboat which operated on the River Swan was a marine or non-marine insurance policy. The majority of the High Court of Australia held that the policy was a marine policy, which meant that the law governing non-disclosure under the 1909 Act applied. The High Court recognised that the 1909 Act was 'virtually identical' to and 'based wholly on' the UK legislation. In a dissenting judgment, McHugh, J said that:

> Subject to public policy – particularly in respect of gaming, illegality and enemies – or statutory prohibitions, an insurer can insure against any risk. If the risk eventuates, the insured is entitled to an indemnity in accordance with the terms of the policy. Classification of a policy as a marine or non-marine

[68] *Permanent Trustee Australia Limited v FAI General Insurance Company Limited (In Liq)* [2003] HCA 25, (2003) 214 *CLR* 514, [60]–[73] (Gummow and Hayne JJ dissenting). See R Merkin, *Reforming Insurance Law: Is there a case for reverse transportation? A Report for the English and Scottish Law Commissions on the Australian Experience of Insurance Law Reform* (London, Law Commission, 2006).

[69] [2003] HCA 39, (2003) 214 *CLR* 604 at [38], [41] (McHugh, J, dissenting), [173] (Hayne and Callinan JJ).

> policy is of practical importance only where legislation adds to or detracts from the terms of the policy or adds to the obligations of a party. Early in the history of marine policies, for example, classifying a policy as a marine policy meant that stamp duty was payable on it, and such policies were a large source of revenue for the United Kingdom government. In Australia today, classifying a policy as a marine policy has important consequences. It means, in the absence of an indication to the contrary in the policy, that non-disclosure of material matters may entitle the insurer to set aside the policy in circumstances that are not available if the policy is governed by the Insurance Contracts Act.'

In Hong Kong, the Marine Insurance Ordinance (Cap 329) was enacted in 1961, again following the UK's 1906 Act. *In Hua Tyan Development Ltd v Zurich Insurance Co Ltd* (*The Ho Feng 7*),[70] the Hong Kong Court of Final Appeal noted that 'The MIO follows almost word for word the provisions in the Marine Insurance Act 1906' and said that:

> The MIO was enacted in Hong Kong in 1961. Prior to that, although there was undoubtedly much marine insurance cover underwritten in Hong Kong, the insurance industry was content to follow the law and practice of marine insurance in the United Kingdom to govern the position here. In the United Kingdom, the law of marine insurance was codified by the Marine Insurance Act 1906. Underwriters and others in the marine industry in Hong Kong followed the Act but only as a matter of custom … The MIO (and the Marine Insurance Act) state they are codifications of the existing law. It is perhaps a tribute to the skill of the draftsman of the Marine Insurance Act – Sir Mackenzie Chalmers (also the draftsman of the Bills of Exchange Act 1882 and the Sale of Goods Act 1893) – that the Act and our Ordinance have remained almost wholly unamended since enactment.

In India, the Marine Insurance Act 1963 is also modelled on the UK legislation. Section 19 states that the marine insurance contract is a contract of the utmost good faith and section 20 provides for the assured's duty of disclosure in the terms of section 18 of the 1906 Act. In *Contship Container Lines Ltd v DK Lall*,[71] the Supreme Court of India asserted that the duty of disclosure was applicable both to the assured and the insurer and in doing so relied on the decision of Lord Mansfield in *Carter v Boehm*.

[70] [2014] HKCFA 72, [2015] Lloyd's Rep IR 14 at [14]–[16], [19]–[20] (Ma, CJ).

[71] [2010] INSC 206 at [23]–[26] (TS Thakur J). See also *United India Insurance Company Ltd v MKJ Corporation* (1996 (6) SCC 428); *Modern Insulators Ltd v Oriental Insurance Co Ltd* (2000 (2) SCC 734) ('It is the fundamental principle of insurance law that utmost good faith must be observed by the contracting parties and good faith forbids either party from non-disclosure of the facts which the parties know').

In 1993, Canada passed the Marine Insurance Act 1993,[72] which was modelled on the UK legislation,[73] although it adopted a more reader-friendly structure. Section 20 recognises the marine insurance contract as a contract based upon the utmost good faith and section 21 allows the insurer to avoid the marine insurance contract in the event that there has been a non-disclosure of a material circumstance by the assured. Section 21 recognises the same exceptions to the duty of disclosure as the 1906 Act.

In the same year, by section 4 and the First Schedule of the Application of English Law Act 1993, the English Marine Insurance Act 1906 was declared to apply in Singapore as it stood on 12 November 1993,[74] so that any subsquent amendments to the English statute passed by the UK Parliament would not result in the amendment of the statute as it applied in Singapore. A Singapore statute was passed in 1993 based on the then 1906 Act, sections 17 and 18 being in identical terms to the same provisions in the unamended 1906 Act.[75]

V. Civil Law Countries

Civil law, in particular continental, jurisdictions make provision for the assured's duty of disclosure which must be discharged before the marine insurance contract is agreed.[76] In many jurisdictions, the obligation on the

[72] Before this federal Act, much of marine insurance law was regulated by provincial legislation: Noussia, *The Principle of Indemnity in Marine Insurance Contracts: A Comparative Approach* (Berlin & Heidelberg, Springer, 2007) 20–21.

[73] *Peracomo Inc v Telus Communications Co (The Realice)* 2014 SCC 29, [2014] 2 Lloyd's Rep 315 at [70] (Sup Ct Canada).

[74] Dunt (n 63) para 5.4.

[75] In *Stansfield Group Pte Ltd v Consumers' Association of Singapore* [2011] SGHC 122, [186] (Judith Prakash J), the Singapore High Court said that 'It is established insurance law that the duty of good faith which is expressly stated in section 17 of the Marine Insurance Act (Cap 387, 1994 Rev Ed) (which is the Singapore enactment of the English Marine Insurance Act 1906) is applicable to all contracts of insurance and reinsurance and applies both before a contract is concluded and during the performance of the contract'.

[76] In 1979–1980, there was a proposal for a European Council Directive co-ordinating the laws regulating provisions in insurance contracts dealing with, amongst other things, the assured's duty of disclosure (31/12/79 OJ C355, 31/12/80 OJ C255/30) (Art 3). However, the proposed Directive excluded marine insurance from its operation, see MacDonald Eggers, Picken and Foss, *Good Faith* (2010) paras 5.12–5.16. By contrast, under Art 2.101 of the voluntary Principles of European Insurance Contract Law (2010), the assured must inform

assured is to disclose information which is known to the assured and which is relevant to the risk being insured. In many instances, before the insurer is entitled to a remedy, the insurer generally must have been induced by the non-disclosure to enter into the contract. There is, however, a greater emphasis on the remedy being dependent on the degree of blameworthy fault on the part of the assured, especially if the non-disclosure was fraudulent or deliberate, but in many cases the insurer has a remedy even if the non-disclosure was innocent. The obligation need not be observed if the insurer is already aware of the relevant information. A common remedy available to the insurer is the nullification, avoidance or termination of the marine insurance policy, or being excused from payment of a claim. Unlike the common law jurisdictions, there is a greater variety of regimes applicable in civil law jurisdictions.

In Belgium, there is an ancient tradition of marine insurance business. There is a Statute of 11 June 1874 which applies to all types of insurance business, including marine and transport insurance.[77] Article 9 of that Statute provides that a non-disclosure by the assured, even when made without bad faith, nullifies the insurance contract when the assessment of the risk is modified in such a way that the insurer would not have contracted had disclosure been made. It appears that the obligation of disclosure is limited to actual knowledge, rather than constructive, knowledge.[78] The 1874 Statute has been repealed and its provisions have largely been incorporated into the Insurance Act of 4 April 2014.

the insurer of circumstances of which they are, or ought to be, aware and which are the subject of clear and precise questions. Under Art 2.102, the breach of that duty allows the insurer remedies depending on whether the breach was negligent or innocent and whether an insured event has occurred. If no insured event has occurred, the insurer may propose a reasonable variation of the contract, to continue the contract or to terminate the contract; if, however, the breach was innocent, the insurer may terminate the contract only if it would not have entered into the contract at all had full and accurate disclosure been provided. However, if an insured event has occurred before the termination of the contract, the insurer will be liable in respect of that event unless the breach was negligent, in which case the insurer does not have to pay the claim if it would not have entered into the insurance contract at all; if the insurer would have entered into the contract, but only on different terms, had the negligent non-disclosure not occurred, the insurer may rewrite the contract or pay a proportionately reduced amount in respect of the claim. Under Art 2.104, the insurer may avoid the contract in the case of fraud.

[77] There is another insurance statute of 25 June 1992, which applies only to land-based insurance contracts; see M Huybrechts, 'Comparative marine insurance law: Highlighting the significant features of marine insurance law in Belgium and other selected European legal systems' in Thomas (n 2) para 8.19.

[78] Huybrechts (ibid) paras 8.19–8.25.

There is a similar duty of utmost good faith in France. By Law No 92-665 of 26 July 1992, marine insurance law is dealt with under the *Code des Assurances* (*Livre I, Titre VII*). By Article 172.19.3 of the *Code des Assurances*, the duty of utmost good faith requires the assured to disclose material information to the insurer. By Article 172.2, the insurer may annul the insurance contract in the event of a non-disclosure, where the non-disclosure was capable of significantly minimising the insurer's risk assessment, whether or not that non-disclosure caused damage or loss of the subject matter insured. If, however, the assured demonstrates that they acted in good faith, the insurer may avoid the policy if the insurer would not have entered into the contract at all had full disclosure been made; otherwise, the insurer may reduce any recoverable claim by that proportion represented by the premium charged to the premium which would have been charged had there been no non-disclosure.[79]

This is in contrast to the law governing non-marine insurance. In cases of non-marine insurance, if the non-disclosure is intentional, the insurer is entitled to avoid the policy and is entitled to retain the premium. If the non-disclosure is not intentional, the remedy available to the insurer depends on whether the non-disclosure was discovered by the insurer after a relevant loss which would otherwise fall for cover under the policy. If the non-disclosure is discovered before the loss, the insurer may require an increased premium, which will not be effective unless the assured agrees, or the insurer may terminate the policy but must also make a *pro rata* return of premium. If the non-disclosure is discovered after a relevant loss, the insurer is entitled to reduce the claim payment on the basis of that proportion represented by the premium which was originally agreed to the premium which would have been charged had there been full disclosure.[80] The legal regime applicable to non-marine insurance contracts in France is similar to the regime which applies to marine and non-marine insurance contracts in Turkey.[81]

[79] A Ziegler, 'The Utmost Good Faith in Marine Insurance Law on the Continent' in Huybrechts (ed) *Marine Insurance at the Turn of the Millennium* (Cambridge, Intersentia. 2000), Vol 2, 23–25; Dunt (n 63) paras 11.8–11.9.

[80] See Arts 113.8 and 113.9 of the *Code des Assurances*. See also J Henrot and P Talbourdet 'France' in N Brook (ed), *Insurance and Reinsurance* (London, Sweet & Maxwell, 2012) 132–33.

[81] Sections 1435 and 1439 of the Turkish Commercial Code. I am grateful to Prof Baris Soyer, Head of Department of Shipping and Trade Law, Swansea University for this information concerning Turkish law, provided in 2016.

In Germany, there is an Insurance Contract Act 2008 (VVG), section 19 of which imposes a duty of disclosure on the assured prior to the contract's conclusion in respect of information relevant to the insurer's decision to underwrite the risk and which the insurer has requested in writing; there is no wider duty of disclosure. If the assured fails to observe this duty and the breach is either intentional or grossly negligent, the insurer may withdraw from (ie avoid) the contract. If, however, the assured's breach of duty is neither intentional nor grossly negligent, the insurer may terminate the contract on notice. However, in such cases, other than in the case of an intentional breach of duty, the insurer's remedy exists only if they would not have entered into the contract at all. The insurer must have informed the assured of the consequences of any non-disclosure by the assured in writing. However, the 2008 Act does not apply to marine insurance (sea-going carriage). Marine insurance law is technically governed by the German Commercial Code (HGB) at Articles 806–811, which imposes a duty of disclosure on the assured and which allows the insurer to annul the insurance contract if there has been a non-disclosure of information of significance in assessing the risk. However, most marine insurance transactions are in practice governed by the German General Rules of Marine Insurance (ADS), which are standard conditions incorporated into marine insurance contracts. By sections 19 and 20, if the assured fails to disclose material information to the insurer, which is not within the insurer's knowledge, the insurer will be discharged from liability.[82]

In Denmark,[83] the assured's duty of disclosure is governed by the Danish Insurance Contracts Act (consolidating Act no 1237 of 9 November 2015). Under section 4 of the Act, the insurance contract is not binding if the assured has been guilty of a fraudulent misrepresentation or non-disclosure or if the assured's reliance on the contract is inconsistent with general principles of good faith. Under section 5, the insurer will be liable under the contract in the event of a non-fraudulent and non-negligent misrepresentation, but may terminate the contract on the provision of one week's notice. In the case of a negligent misrepresentation, the insurer will not be liable if it is established that the insurer would have refused the

[82] A Ziegler, 'The "Utmost Good Faith" in Marine Insurance Law on the Continent' in Huybrechts (2000) Vol 2, 25–26; Dunt (n 63) paras 10.42–10.51.

[83] I am grateful to Stinne Taiger Avø, Vice President, Head of FDD, Assuranceforeningen SKULD (Gjensidig), Copenhagen for information relating to Danish law, provided in 2016.

insurance if full disclosure had been made. In the case of marine insurance, the insurer will be liable only if there was no causal connection between the circumstance misrepresented and the loss or the extent of loss. Under section 7, if there has been a grossly negligent non-disclosure, that will be treated as a misrepresentation. Under section 9, the insurer cannot exercise a remedy if the information not fully and accurately disclosed was known to the insurer or if it was not material.

In Norway, the Norwegian Marine Insurance Plan is often incorporated into marine insurance contracts. There have been a number of Plans, the most recent being 1996 and 2013.[84] Marine insurance contracts are not subject to Norway's mandatory insurance legislation.[85] Section 3-1 of the Plan imposes a duty upon the policyholder to disclose all circumstances that are material to the insurer when deciding whether and on what conditions the insurer is prepared to accept the insurance. If the assured's non-disclosure is fraudulent, the contract is not binding on the insurer (section 3-2). Under section 3-3, where the non-disclosure is not deliberate, the contract is not binding on the insurer if the insurer would not have entered into the contract at all had full disclosure been provided; if, however, the insurer would have entered into the contract, but on different terms, the insurer is liable only to the extent that it is proved that the loss being claimed is not attributable to such circumstances as the person effecting the insurance should have disclosed. By section 3-4, if the non-disclosure is innocent, meaning without any blame attaching to the assured, the insurer is entitled to cancel the contract on 14 days' notice. However, the insurer is not entitled to rely on non-disclosure if they were aware, or ought to have been aware, of the information not disclosed.[86]

In the Netherlands,[87] as from 1 January 2006, the Dutch Civil Code introduced a new regime in respect of the assured's duty of disclosure prior to the conclusion of the insurance contract.[88] Article 7:928 of the Civil Code provides that, prior to the conclusion of the insurance contract, the assured must inform the insurer of all circumstances of which they are

[84] There is a 2019 version of the 2013 Plan. As to cargo insurance, see Dunt (n 63) ch 12.

[85] HS Lund, 'Comparative lessons derivable from the Norwegian Marine Insurance Plan 1996' in Thomas (n 2) paras 9.1–9.11.

[86] ibid paras 9.16–9.33.

[87] I am grateful to Prof Dr Frank Smeele, Professor of Commercial Law, Erasmus University, Rotterdam, for this information relating to Dutch law, provided in 2016.

[88] Prior to 2006, the assured's duty was governed by Art 251 of the Dutch Commercial Code.

aware or ought to be aware and of which they know or ought to know that the insurer's decision whether or not to enter into the insurance agreement, and if so, on which terms and conditions, depends or may depend on it. The assured's duty, however, does not arise in respect of circumstances which the insurer already knows or ought to know or circumstances which could not lead to a more unfavourable decision for the assured. The assured cannot rely on this exception of the insurer's knowledge if the assured has given an incorrect or incomplete answer to a specific question that the insurer has asked. When the insurance contract has been concluded on the basis of a questionnaire formulated by the insurer, the insurer cannot rely on the fact that other questions are not answered or that circumstances about which no questions were asked are not mentioned by the assured or the fact that a question which was formulated generally has been answered incompletely, unless this is done with the wilful intent to mislead the insurer.

Under Article 7:929, the insurer who discovers that the pre-contractual information duty has not been observed may only invoke the effects thereof if they have notified the assured of this non-observance within two months after it has been discovered, mentioning as well the possible consequences thereof. The insurer who discovers that the assured has misled them with wilful intent, or who would not have entered into the insurance contract had there been full disclosure, may terminate the insurance agreement with immediate effect within two months of such a discovery. This appears to suggest that the termination will take effect only from the date of notice of termination without affecting rights to an indemnity which accrue before the date of termination. If this is the case, the right of termination would appear to give little practical protection to the insurer. Under Article 7:930, no insurance benefit is payable when the insurer, who would not have entered into the insurance contract at all had there been full disclosure, or if the assured has misled the insurer with wilful intent. However, if the undisclosed circumstances are of importance for the assessment of the risk that has materialised (ie this is a causation requirement),[89] and the insurer would have stipulated a higher insurance premium or have closed the insurance for a lower insurance sum, had full disclosure been provided,

[89] G Kamphuisen, 'Important Differences between the Old and New Insurance Contract Law' in JH Wansink, JGC Kamphuisen and WMA Kalkman, *New Dutch Insurance Contract Law* (Amstelveen, deLex, 2006) 31.

the insurance benefit is reduced in proportion to the amount that the insurance premiums would have been increased or to the amount that the insured sum would have been decreased. Where the insurer would have stipulated other conditions in the insurance contract had full disclosure been provided, the insurance benefit will be paid out as if these conditions would have been included in the insurance contract.

In Greece,[90] the assured's duty of disclosure, which is part of the duty of utmost good faith, is regulated by Article 3 of the Law on Private Insurance 2496/1997. The duty of disclosure relates to information or circumstances which are material and which are known to the assured. However, as with Dutch law, the insurer is entitled to answers to questions put by the insurer to the assured, who must answer the questions truthfully. Indeed, it is presumed that the information and circumstances in relation to which the insurer has set clear written questions constitute the sole grounds on which the insurer based its assessment and acceptance of such risk. If the insurer concludes the contract upon the basis of written questions, the insurer cannot rely on the fact that some questions were unanswered, circumstances which were not the subject of written questions was not disclosed and an obviously incomplete answer given to a general question.[91] The insurer cannot rely upon inadequate or defective answers to a questionnaire unless they were supplied deliberately by the assured (ie with the intention of deceiving the insurer). If there has been a non-disclosure of material information not known to the insurer, the insurer may terminate the insurance contract within one month of discovering the non-disclosure or propose a variation to the contract, which if not accepted by the assured will constitute a termination.

In the case of an innocent or negligent breach of duty, the termination of the contract will take effect after 15 days from the notice of termination and immediately in the event of an intentional breach of duty. If the insured risk occurs after the termination of the contract, the insurer is not liable. In the case of a negligent breach, if the insured risk occurs before the termination of the contract, the insurer may proportionately reduce a recoverable claim by reference to the premium which would have been charged had full disclosure been provided. In the case of an intentional

[90] I am grateful to Dr George C Panagopoulos and Angeliki Kofopoulou of Reed Smith LLP, Athens for the information relating to Greek law, provided in 2016.

[91] cf Court decision of the Greek Supreme Court 1014/1991.

breach of duty, the insurer will be excused from paying an insurance claim if the insured event occurs during the period between the insurer becoming aware of the breach and the termination of the contract. In addition, the assured is liable in damages for any loss suffered by the insurer.

VI. Conclusion: Common Themes

The common law and civil law jurisdictions referred to above, without exception, recognise that the assured is subject to a pre-contractual duty of disclosure when negotiating a contract of marine insurance. The duty embraces the disclosure of information which is known to the assured and is material or relevant to the insurer's assessment of the risk. In addition, the assured is not under any duty to disclose information to the insurer if the information is already known to the insurer. There is an inducement requirement before any relief is granted to the insurer, at least in most cases.

There is a remarkable similarity between the English common law (reflected in the Marine Insurance Act 1906) and the law governing marine insurance contracts in New Zealand, Australia, Hong Kong, India and Singapore and in the federal jurisdictions in the US and Canada. In England, with the passage of the Insurance Act 2015, the common law position has been tempered to reflect a greater range of proportionate remedies dependent on the blameworthy conduct of the assured and the extent of the insurer's inducement. There is greater diversity among the civil law jurisdictions. The position governing marine insurance law in Belgium and Germany is most similar to the English common law position. In the other civil law jurisdictions, the law governing marine insurance contracts is dependent on a variety of factors, differing in each jurisdiction, such as the blameworthy conduct of the assured, the extent of the insurer's inducement, and – in some cases – the discovery of the non-disclosure and the termination of the contract relative to the occurrence of an insured event.

Perhaps the striking aspect of the various approaches to the insurer's remedy in the case of non-disclosure is that the remedies are structured to apply whenever the relevant blameworthy conduct or inducement is established, and does not generally allow the court a discretion to tailor a remedy to suit the case before it (for example, as is the case under the English Misrepresentation Act 1967).

There had been greater unease, at least in the common law world, with respect to the remedy of avoidance available to the insurer for a non-disclosure by the assured. Avoidance was often seen too harsh and draconian a remedy for what might constitute a relatively minor failure on the part of the assured. In consequence, different legal systems have developed different responses which are designed to impose what is perceived to be a fairer and more proportionate remedy for any vitiation of the insurer's consent by reason of the assured's non-disclosure.

This state of affairs is not surprising. The duty of disclosure has long been recognised as serving an important function in respect of the conclusion of insurance contracts, and marine insurance contracts in particular. This reflects not only a judicial and legislative recognition of the importance of disclosure; it also reflects a commercial practice which emerged centuries ago soon after the regular use of marine insurance policies, a practice which no doubt influenced the creation of binding legal duties of disclosure. In this way, the early modern law merchant still continues to influence the postmodern business of insurance.

9

The Doctrine of *Res Judicata* in Commercial Maritime Arbitration

DR MELIS ÖZDEL*

I. Introduction

There is an understandable tendency to conceptualise the different legal traditions around the world with reference to the civil law and common law divide. This is perhaps an oversimplification, particularly in the context of international maritime arbitration, where the divisions between the common law and civil law traditions are much less visible than in court proceedings. As a dispute resolution process, international arbitration usually presents itself as a blend of common law and civil law traditions regardless of where the arbitration is seated. Although international arbitration is a private dispute resolution method that is designed to be self-contained and self-sufficient, it is not possible, at least in common law jurisdictions,[1] to speak of it as an autonomous legal order that is completely independent from national courts.[2]

When considering the true value of international arbitration to its users, it is important to bear in mind that the enforcement of a favourable

* Director of UCL Centre for Commercial Law, Lecturer in Maritime and Commercial Law at University College London.

[1] *Bank Mellat v Helliniki Techniki SA* [1984] QB 291 at [301], per Kerr LJ, where he said that the common law 'does not recognise the concept of arbitral procedures floating in the transnational firmament unconnected with any municipal system of law'.

[2] It is widely accepted that commercial arbitrations are anchored in one particular jurisdiction, although there are also proponents of the view that arbitration is a component of a plurality of national legal orders. See J Paulsson, *The Idea of Arbitration* (Oxford, Oxford University Press, 2013) 35ff.

award is as crucial as obtaining the award itself. A party may pursue a case successfully and obtain a favourable award, but all this will be of no value if they cannot collect the award from their counterparty. With the adoption by more than 150 countries of the New York Convention on the Recognition and Enforcement of Foreign Arbitration Awards 1958 ('the Convention') arbitration awards are, in most cases, more readily enforceable than court judgments.[3] Undoubtedly, the so-called 'pro-enforcement bias',[4] which has been duly observed by most of the Convention states, has also played an instrumental role in facilitating the enforcement and recognition of awards under the Convention.[5]

The crucial question is, therefore, not *whether* awards can be recognised and enforced, but *which* awards should be recognised and enforced by national courts under the Convention. If arbitration is to be taken as a final determination of the rights of the parties, how much deference should national courts give to awards? National courts do not speak with one voice, particularly on the question of whether arbitration awards should owe their force to the laws of the seat of an arbitration. The lack of uniformity among the Convention states on this matter has given rise to two practical issues. Firstly, where a court located at the seat of the arbitration (the 'primary jurisdiction') sets aside the award or dismisses a challenge against the award, does the decision of that court have a preclusive effect on the enforcement of the award by the courts in other 'secondary jurisdictions')?[6] Secondly, where a court in a secondary jurisdiction refuses

[3] On the recognition and enforcement of judgments in civil and commercial matters within the EU, see Regulation (EU) No 1215/2012 of the European Parliament and of the Council of 12 December 2012 on jurisdiction and the recognition and enforcement of judgments in civil and commercial matters (recast). In this paper, this Regulation will be referred to as 'the Brussels Regulation'.

[4] *Parsons & Whittemore Overseas Co v Société Generale de L'Industrie du Papier (RAKTA)*, 508 F 2d 969 (2nd Cir 1972).

[5] For US law, see *American Const Mach & Equip Corp v Mechanised Const of Pakistan Ltd*,659 F Supp 426, 428 (SDNY 1987).

[6] These terms, 'primary jurisdiction' and 'secondary jurisdiction', are used by the US Court of Appeals for the Fifth Circuit in *Karaha Bodas v Perusahan Pertambangan*, 335 F 3d 357 (5th Cir 2003). This division of primary/secondary jurisdictions has attracted much criticism, and the use of these terms is not widely recognised. The main objection to this division is based on the premise that the secondary jurisdictions usually have a more tangible interest in the enforcement of an award than the primary jurisdiction. Giving primacy to the seat of an arbitration can also appear unnecessary, particularly since the seat is usually chosen either fortuitously or because of its lack of connection to the dispute and the parties. On this matter, Paulsson, *The Idea of Arbitration* (2013) 35 ff.

or accepts to enforce the award, does that decision have a preclusive effect, preventing the parties from re-litigating the issues determined by that court in the enforcement proceedings?

If the pillars of the Convention are international comity and uniformity,[7] both questions should be answered in the affirmative. Further, and perhaps more persuasively, support for an affirmative answer can be drawn from two Latin maxims: *nemo debet bis vexari pro una et eadem causa* ('no one should be vexed twice for the one and the same cause') and *interest reipublicae ut sit finis litium* ('it is in the public interest that there should be an end to litigation').[8] Embedded in almost every legal system, these Latin maxims have brought about 'the rules of preclusion', which differ materially from jurisdiction to jurisdiction.

This chapter discusses the extent to which the rules of preclusion apply to the question of recognition and enforcement of arbitration awards by national courts. With these discussions, the paper will conclude, inter alia, that the rule of issue estoppel is conducive to the public policy of finality and the pro-enforcement bias under the Convention.

II. The Rules of Preclusion in Common Law

The rules of preclusion in common law have a broader application than those under civil law. Under English law, the concept of *res judicata*[9] in essence covers the defences[10] of cause of action estoppel, issue estoppel and merger of judgment.[11] The rule of cause of action estoppel dictates that once a court of competent jurisdiction determines a particular cause of action, no subsequent proceedings on the 'same cause of action'[12] can be

[7] MB Holmes, 'Enforcement of Annulled Arbitral Awards: Logical Fallacies and Fictional Systems' (2013) 7 *Arbitration* 244–55.

[8] S Sime, '*Res Judicata* and ADR' (2015) 34 *Civil Justice Quarterly* 35.

[9] See *Virgin Atlantic Ltd v Zodiac Seats UK Ltd* [2013] UKSC 46, [2013] 4 All ER 715, where Lord Sumption said at [17] that 'res judicata is a portmanteau term which is used to describe a number of different legal principles with different judicial origins'.

[10] The application of the cause of action or issue estoppel also allows a plaintiff to defeat the defences that are inconsistent with earlier judgments or that are rejected in earlier proceedings, see KR Handley, 'A Closer Look at Henderson v Henderson' (2002) 118 *Law Quarterly Review* 397. See also *Man v Haryanto* [1991] 1 Lloyd's Rep 161.

[11] *The Indian Grace* [1993] AC 410, 417–418 per Lord Goff of Chieveley.

[12] A cause of action is the key minimum facts that a claimant is required to plead and prove in order to obtain remedy, see *Letang v Cooper* [1965] 1 QB 232, 243. When interpreting the

brought by the same parties or their 'privies'.[13] For the doctrine to apply, the judgment must be final and conclusive on the merits.[14]

At common law, the judgment of a non-English court was capable of giving rise to a cause of action estoppel where the judgment is in the defendant's favour. However, if the judgment is in favour of the plaintiff, it did not amount to a bar against English proceedings brought on the same cause of action.[15] This was because the principle of merger of judgment did not apply in the case of a non-English judgment.[16] The principle of merger prevents a claimant who has already obtained a favourable judgment from bringing subsequent proceedings on the same cause of action even in cases where the judgment remains unsatisfied. The rationale behind the principle is that once decided, the cause of action becomes merged in the judgment. In respect of the preclusive effect of foreign judgments, section 34 of the Civil Jurisdiction and Judgments Act 1982 now provides that:

> No proceedings may be brought by a person in England and Wales or Northern Ireland on a cause of action in respect of which a judgment has been given in

phrase 'cause of action', English courts tend to avoid a narrow and technical interpretation of the phrase; see *The Indian Grace* [1994] 2 Lloyd's Rep 354, per Clarke J at 354, reversed on other grounds. On competing estoppels see the decision in *Air Foyle v Centre Capital* [2003] 2 Lloyd's Rep 753.

[13] *Thoday v Thoday* [1964] P 181 (CA), per Lord Diplock at 197. See also *Thrasyvoulou v Sectretary of State for the Environment* [1989] 2 AC 273 (HL). A modern approach to the issue of who might be considered as privy is elucidated by Sir Robert Megarry in *Gleeson v J Wippel & Co Ltd* [1977] 1 WLR 510, at 515C–515D, where he said that there would normally be sufficient privy between the trustees and their beneficiaries in the case of a trust property. Moreover, a person can also be treated as privy to proceedings if they have 'a concrete interest in the outcome'; see *Resolution Chemicals Ltd v H Lundbeck A/S* [2013] EWCA Civ 924, per Floyd LJ at [47].

[14] *Jacobson v Frachon* (1927) 138 LT 386 (CA). For the purposes of cause of action estoppel, a default judgment is considered to be a final judgment, see *Virgin Atlantic Airways v Zodiac Seats* [2013] UKSC 46, [2013] 3 WLR 299. However, default judgments do not give rise to the defence of issue estoppel. A judgment is usually considered to be final if it is incapable of being reviewed by the same court giving the judgment. A judgment does not lose its *res judicata* effect due to a mere possibility of an appeal to a higher court, see *The Irini A* [1999] 1 Lloyd's Rep 189.

[15] *The Indian Grace* [1993] 1 Lloyd's Rep 387, 391 (HL), per Lord Goff of Chieveley.

[16] ibid. Notably, the non-merger rule also applies in the case of *in rem* admiralty proceedings, see the decision in *The Rena K* [1979] QB 377, where Brandon J established the rule that a cause of action *in rem* does not merge in a judgment *in personam* and remains available to the extent that the judgment remains unsatisfied. He also held that the principle was also applicable in the case of arbitration awards. The Hong Kong court in *The Alas* [2014] 6 HKC 239 followed the decision when allowing an action *in rem* that was brought by an award creditor to recover the unsatisfied part of the award.

> his favour in proceedings between the same parties, or their privies, in a court in another part of the United Kingdom or in a court of an overseas country, unless that judgment is not enforceable or entitled to recognition in England and Wales, or as the case may be, in Northern Ireland.

As interpreted by Lord Goff of Chieveley in *The Indian Grace (No 1)*, the above provision does not expressly abolish the non-merger rule. Rather, it creates a plea against 'reassertion' founded upon the same cause of action and therefore provides a 'bar against proceedings by the plaintiff rather than excluding the jurisdiction of the court'.[17] In essence, it prevents a claimant having a second bite at the cherry.[18]

A. Issue Estoppel under English Law

The other branch of the doctrine of *res judicata* is the rule of issue estoppel. The rule prevents parties, or their privies,[19] from denying or rearguing an issue of fact[20] or law that was previously determined by a 'competent'[21] court.[22] In essence, issue estoppel bars subsequent proceedings brought in relation to points that were not raised in the earlier proceedings[23] as well as those that *were* raised, but unsuccessfully. To establish an issue

[17] *The Indian Grace* [1993] 1 Lloyd's Rep 387, 395 (HL), per Lord Goff of Chieveley. See also L Collins, *Illogical Survivals and Astonishing Results* (1992) 108 *Law Quarterly Review* 393.

[18] On the issue of what constitutes the same cause of action, English courts tend to engage in the process of characterisation with reference to the rules of the forum. See the decision in *Black v Yates* [1991] 1 Lloyd's Rep 181. Furthermore, characterisation of the claim is also considered to be a step towards deciding the law governing the claim; see [1985] 1 Lloyd's Rep 521.

[19] See *Littlewoods Retail Limited v The Commissioners for HMRC* [2014] EWHC 868 (Ch), where Henderson J said at [214]: 'an issue estoppel binds not only the parties to the earlier determination but also their privies in blood, title or interest'.

[20] See KR Handley, *Res Judicata*, 4th edn (London, LexisNexis Butterworths, 2009) para 1.06.

[21] The foreign court must have jurisdiction to determine the issue 'both by its own law and in the eyes of English law'; see *Tracomin v Sudan Oil* [1983] 1 Lloyd's Rep 560, per Staughton J at 566.

[22] The operation of issue estoppel is not limited to cases where a tribunal has given a reasoned decision on the issues of fact and law in the first litigation, see *Barber v Staffordshire CC* [1996] ICR 379, per Mummery J at 388.

[23] As regards those points that was not raised in previous proceedings, the bar is usually absolute if they could with reasonable diligence have been raised. See the decision in *Arnold and Other Respondents v National Westminster Bank* [1991] 1 AC 93 at 106.

estoppel, the earlier judgment given by a competent court must be final[24] and conclusive[25] on the merits.

On the question of what constitutes an issue on the 'merits', the decision in *The Sennar (No 2)*[26] is worthy of note. There, the buyers of a cargo of Sudanese groundnut expellers commenced proceedings in Rotterdam against the sister ship of *Sennar* in relation to their claim in tort for fraudulent or negligent misrepresentation under the bill of lading. The defendants put up security, while also obtaining a stay of the action relying on the jurisdiction clause under the bill of lading. Thereafter, the buyers brought English proceedings claiming damages in tort while also arguing that their tort claim was not subject to the jurisdiction clause. However, the defendants contended that this issue had already been decided by the same parties in Dutch proceedings.

The main ingredients of the decision of the Dutch court were (a) that the buyers' claim was contractual and (b) that the jurisdiction clause was applicable to the claim. The decision went to the substance of the claim with a view to deciding whether the jurisdiction conferred by the Arrest Convention was to be exercised. The decision was not on a procedural issue, nor was it just a preliminary point declining to accept jurisdiction.[27]

It is clear that issue estoppel can be derived from a decision on a preliminary point provided that the relevant issues are fully argued and decided with reasons.[28] What is not clear is the precise boundaries of the expression 'on the merits'. There appears to be two main difficulties in ascertaining the boundaries. Firstly, the question of jurisdiction is not treated in the same way in every legal system.[29] While accepting or refusing to exercise jurisdiction is a matter of legal discretion in some legal systems (particularly under English law), it is usually considered to be a matter of obligation in civil

[24] Thus the judgment must not be subject to subsequent review, discharge or modification by the court giving the judgment, see *Carl-Zeiss-Stiftung v Rayner & Keeler Ltd (No 2)* [1967] 1 AC 853 at 538G–539B, 541A–542B, although it may be subject to appeal to a court of higher jurisdiction. See *The Sennar* [1985] 1 Lloyd's Rep 521 (HL) at 523 per Lord Diplock.

[25] See *Carl-Zeiss-Stiftung v Rayner & Keeler Ltd (No 2)* (ibid).

[26] *The Sennar (No 2)* [1985] 1 Lloyd's Rep 521 (HL), [1984] 2 Lloyd's Rep 142 (CA).

[27] Had this been the main issue decided, there would not have been identity of issues because the issue of whether Dutch courts had jurisdiction was not the same as the issue of whether English courts had jurisdiction.

[28] *Tracomin v Sudan Oil* [1983] 1 Lloyd's Rep 560.

[29] See A Briggs, 'The Hidden Depths of the Law of Jurisdiction' (2016) 1 *Lloyd's Maritime and Commercial Law Quarterly* 238ff.

law countries.[30] Secondly, an interlocutory judgment of a foreign court on a procedural or jurisdictional issue can even give rise to issue estoppel. It is accepted in *Desert Sun Loan Corp v Hill*[31] that issue estoppel could arise following an express submission of the procedural or jurisdictional issue to the foreign court provided that the relevant issue of fact had been decided by the court.[32] Following the decision, there is no set guidance on what particular procedural or jurisdictional issues could in practice give rise to issue estoppel. Nonetheless, the decision makes it clear that the scope for a plea of issue estoppel arising from a procedural decision would be very small on the grounds that the necessary degree of certainty could rarely arise on an application for summary judgment.[33]

When determining whether a foreign judgment is final and conclusive, the courts do not just look at English law. They also consider the nature of the judgment in the eyes of the foreign court that gave the judgment.[34] For this reason, once a foreign judgment is recognised by an English court, the court will give the judgment the same effects that a comparable domestic judgment would have. However, it will do so only if the foreign judgment is capable of creating that effect in the foreign country (ie the country of origin).[35] The rationale behind this approach can be found in Lord Reid's judgment in *Carl-Zeiss-Stiftung v Rayner & Keeler Ltd*, where his Lordship said:

> [I]t seems to me to verge on absurdity that we should regard as conclusive something in a German judgment which the German courts themselves would not regard as conclusive. It is quite true that estoppel is a matter for *the lex fori* but *the lex fori* ought to be developed in a manner consistent with good sense.[36]

There is also another important requirement regarding the application of issue estoppel: only the particular issues that have formed 'the necessary

[30] See *The Sennar (No 2)* [1984] 2 Lloyd's Rep 142 (CA) at 154, per Kerr LJ.

[31] [1996] CLC 1132.

[32] ibid at 1142.

[33] ibid at 1144.

[34] *The Irini A (No 2)* [1999] 1 Lloyd's Rep 189, 193. This approach is also followed in Singapore, see *The Bunga Melati 5* [2012] 4 SLR 546 at 86; *Manharlal Trimkamdas Mody and Another v Sumikin Bussan International (HK) Ltd* [2014] 3 SLR 1161 at 141.

[35] *Charm Maritime v Kyriakou* [1987] 1 Lloyd's Rep 433, 450.

[36] [1967] 1 AC 853, 919.

ingredients' of the judgment of the court can give rise to issue estoppel.[37] Thus, issues that are ancillary and collateral can be reopened in subsequent proceedings.[38]

All these explanations clearly point out the importance of characterising the issues previously determined by a competent foreign court: for a previously determined issue to give rise to issue estoppel, it should be 'identical' to the issue raised in the subsequent English proceedings. As Lord Wilberforce in the *Zeiss* case stated, caution must be exercised when establishing the identity of the issue previously decided by a foreign court. In this context, the important factors to consider are as follows:

- a party against whom the issue estoppel is invoked might not have had an opportunity to defend the particular issue in the foreign jurisdiction;
- the issue might not have been brought into full contestation;
- there may not be a clear decision by the foreign court on that issue; and
- the decision-making techniques, procedural rules and the substantive law of the foreign country can make it difficult to ascertain the particular issue decided.[39]

It is to be observed that these factors cannot be determined without giving any consideration to the laws and proceedings in the relevant foreign jurisdiction. However, the question as to the identity of the relevant issue is ultimately decided with reference to the *lex fori*. It this context, the decision in *The Good Challenger* is worthy of note.[40] The case was concerned with the enforcement of a 20-year-old award. In June 1983, the claimant ('the owners') obtained an arbitration award in their favour. The owners sought to enforce the award against the defendant ('charterers') in Romania. After lengthy enforcement proceedings, the Romanian Supreme Court decided in 1998 that the proceedings were time-barred both under the Romanian limitation period (three years) and under the English limitation period (six years). The English Court of Appeal held that the Romanian

[37] *Arnold v NatWest Bank* [1991] 2 AC 93, per Lord Keith at 104–05. Hence, the discovery of a new factual matter that could not have been found out by reasonable diligence does not permit subsequent proceedings on the same cause of action. See also the decision *Virgin Atlantic Ltd v Zodiac Seats UK Ltd* [2013] UKSC 46, [2013] 4 All ER 715 at [26].

[38] ibid. See also, *The Good Challenger* [2004]1 Lloyd's Rep 67.

[39] [1967] 1 AC 853, 967.

[40] [2004] 1 Lloyd's Rep 67 (CA).

Supreme Court's finding on the English limitation period was not a 'fundamental' and 'essential' determination on which the Romanian judgment was based. Consequently, the owners were not issue estopped from submitting before the English court that the enforcement proceedings were brought in time.

In addition to the process of characterisation, English courts have a tool to remove the harshness that may arise from the application of issue estoppel: the overarching principle on the application of issue estoppel is that it must be applied to bring about justice, not injustice.[41] Therefore, the courts have discretion not to apply the issue estoppel if doing so would lead to injustice.[42]

B. The Legal Position in Other Jurisdictions

In other common law jurisdictions, the doctrine of *res judicata* is applied in a wider sense. In *Armacel Pty Limited v Smurfit Stone Container Corporation*,[43] an issue estoppel arose from the decision of the US Federal Court that the jurisdiction clause in favour of the New South Wales courts was non-exclusive. In the eyes of the Federal Court of Australia, the US court's determination was, in fact, wrong, in that it failed to apply Australian law on the effect of the jurisdiction clause. Nonetheless, following the English decision in *The Sennar (No.2)*, the Federal Court of Australia held that the claimant be bound by the decision of the US court on the effect of the jurisdiction clause.

[41] For this reason, issue estoppel allows an issue to be re-examined if there is new evidence that changes substantially particular aspects of the case and that could not by reasonable diligence have been determined previously. Re-examination is also possible if there a change in the law in relation to the original decision or if fraud or collusion is alleged. *Arnold v NatWest Bank* (n 37) per Lord Keith at 109. Nonetheless, English courts exercise caution on the issue of whether new evidence should be allowed in an action for the enforcement of an arbitration award. This is particularly the case where the supervisory court (the court of primary jurisdiction) has refused to set aside an award. From the perspective of English courts, this usually brings with it a 'very strong policy consideration' that the award should be enforced. Hence, if the award has not been set aside despite the admission of additional evidence, the 'public policy of finality' require that the English courts should not permit the further evidence to be adduced at the stage of enforcement. See the decisions in *Westacre Investments Inc v Jugoimport-SPDR Holding Co Ltd* [1999] QB 740 at 784 (per Colman J), *Minmetals Germany GmbH v Ferco Steel Ltd* [1999] 1 All ER (Comm) 315 and *Eastern European Engineering Ltd v Vijay Construction Ltd* [2018] EWHC 2713 (Comm) at [48]–[49].

[42] *The Sennar (No 2)* [1985] 1 Lloyd's Rep 521 (HL), [1984] 2 Lloyd's Rep 142 (CA).

[43] [2008] FCA 592.

In the US, the *res judicata* principles are applied in a much wider sense. While issue estoppel requires mutuality under English law,[44] the US law also accepts the concept of 'collateral estoppel', which allows a third party to the previous proceeding to rely on a prior finding as a defence and/or ground for dismissal[45] when it is 'fair' to do so.[46]

In civil law jurisdictions, the courts also adopt the principle of finality in litigation.[47] However, the finality of a judgment given by a competent court does not usually extend to the conclusions of the competent court on the necessary issues of law and fact.[48] Only the dispositive part of the judgment has the *res judicata* effect on the parties.[49] The finality of the judgment has the further effect of preventing a party from arguing in subsequent proceedings legal and factual issues existing at the time of the proceedings.[50]

Despite the material differences between the *res judicata* principles applied in common law and civil law jurisdictions, it is widely accepted that, just as with court judgments, arbitration awards also have *res judicata* effects.[51] Based on party consent, the arbitral process results in an award that contains a definitive determination of the dispute between the parties, who promised to abide by the resulting award.[52] Particularly in countries

[44] *Carl-Zeiss-Stiftung v Rayner & Keeler Ltd (No 2)* (n 24) 511. See also *Lincoln National Life Insurance Co v Sun Life Assurance Co of Canada* [2004] EWCA Civ 1660, [2006] 1 All ER 675 (CA).

[45] *Parklane Hosiery Co v Shore*, 439 US 322 (1979).

[46] ibid.

[47] C Soderlund, '*Lis Pendens, Res Judicata* and the Issue of Parallel Judicial Proceedings' (2005) 4 *Journal of International Arbitration* 301.

[48] ibid.

[49] Swedish Procedural Code, c 17, Art 11; German Civil Procedure (ZPO), Art 322; French New Code of Civil Procedure (NCPC), Art 480, all quoted in Soderlund, '*Lis Pendens*' (2005). In the context of the mutuality principle, the effect of the *res judicata* principle extends to the parties' successors, assignors and executors, see ZPO Arts 326–27, cited in S Brekoulakis, 'The Effect of an Arbitral Award and Third Parties in International Arbitration: Res Judicata Revisited' (2005) 16 *The American Review of International Arbitration* 9. In Swiss law, the *res judicata* effect of a foreign judgment is decided by reference to the law of the country in which the judgment is given, see the decision of the Swiss Federal Trubunal, 140 III 278 [4A_508/2013, *The South Railways decision*, cited in N Voser and J Raneda, 'Recent Developments on the Doctrine of Res Judicata in International Arbitration from a Swiss Perspective: A Call for a Harmonised Solution' (2015) 4 *Journal of International Arbitration* 742.

[50] Soderlund (n 47).

[51] *Fidelitas Shipping Ltd v V/O Exportchleb* [1965] 1 Lloyd's Rep 13, where the court held that an arbitration award can give rise to an issue estoppel; for German Law; see ZPO, Art 1055.

[52] An appellate procedure is usually not provided in the rules of arbitration agreed by the parties.

where the Model Law[53] is adopted, an award can be challenged in the primary jurisdiction in only exceptional circumstances. Under English law, the grounds for challenge of the awards rendered in the jurisdiction are exhaustively set out under the English Arbitration Act 1996.[54]

At the enforcement stage, where an award-debtor can usually avail itself of the passive remedy of resisting enforcement pursuant to the Convention,[55] it is generally accepted that the merits of an award are not reviewed.[56] The review envisaged by the Convention is founded on the need to ensure that there is no significant departure from the main tenets of the Convention.[57] In Convention states, an award on an arbitration agreement can, by leave of the court, be enforced in the same manner as a judgment, and the grounds for refusal of enforcement under the Convention are considered to be exhaustive.[58] Under the Convention, the rules of preclusion are not expressly provided as a ground for refusal of enforcement, but does this constitute a bar to application of the rules of preclusion to the question of enforcement of an award?

III. Can an Enforcement Judgment have Any Preclusive Effect on the Enforcement of the Award in Another Jurisdiction?

On this matter, our attention must initially be drawn to one specific ground for refusal provided under Article V(1)(e) of the Convention. Under this provision, recognition and enforcement of an award 'may' be refused, at the request of the party resisting recognition and enforcement, if that party proves that the award has not yet become binding on the parties, or has been set aside or suspended by a court of primary jurisdiction. The plain

[53] See the UNCITRAL Model Law on International Commercial Arbitration 1985, as amended in 2006.

[54] See ss 67, 68 and 69 of the English Arbitration Act 1996.

[55] *Astro Nusantara International v PT Ayunda Prima Mitra* [2013] SGCA 57 (Singapore).

[56] See *Scherk v Alberto-Culver Co* (1974) 417 US 506, 519 (US); *Westacre Investments Inc v Jugoimport SDBR Holding Co Ltd* [2000] QB 288 (CA); *Minmetals Germany GmbH v Ferco Steel Ltd* [1999] CLC 647; *Honeywell International Middle East Ltd v Meydan Group LLC* [2014] 2 Lloyd's Rep 133.

[57] *Dallah Real Estate and Tourism Holding Co v The Ministry of Religious Affairs, Government of Pakistan* [2010] 2 Lloyd's Rep 691 (SC).

[58] *Rosseel NV v Oriental Commercial Shipping* [1991] 2 Lloyd's Rep 625.

reading of the provision allows a court to recognise and enforce an award that has been set aside or suspended. Because of the use of the word 'may', enforcing courts thus have discretion to enforce such an award.[59] Under English law, it is accepted that the discretion cannot be used arbitrarily.[60] In particular, in *Swenska AB v Republic of Lithuania*, Teare QC said:

> [T]he Court's discretion to refuse recognition of a foreign arbitration award … could only be exercised where 'despite the original existence of one or more of the listed circumstances, the right to rely on them had been lost, by for example, another agreement or estoppel' or where there were circumstances which might on some recognisable legal principle affect the prima facie right to have an award set aside arising in the cases listed in s. 103(2) [of the English Arbitration Act 1996].[61]

It will be observed that the common law rule of issue estoppel can have a significant impact on the question of what issues can be argued or re-argued in the enforcement proceedings under the Convention. In *Yukos Capital SARL v OJSC Rosneft Oil Company*,[62] the English Court of Appeal was concerned with the question of whether the decision of a court in the secondary jurisdiction could give rise to issue estoppel. The relevant arbitration awards were set aside by the courts in Moscow, but the Court of Appeal in Amsterdam gave leave to enforce the awards. The question before the English Court of Appeal was whether the decision of the Dutch court, which was based on Dutch public policy, created an issue estoppel. While accepting that the decision of a court in secondary jurisdiction could create an issue estoppel, the Court of Appeal held that an issue estoppel did not arise from the decision of the Dutch court since each country's public policy is different from one another.[63] On characterising the identity of the issues brought in both jurisdiction, the Court of Appeal took the view that English public policy cannot be equated with the public policy of another country.

[59] *Dowan Holding SA v Tanzania Electric Supply Co Ltd* [2011] EWHC 1957 (Comm) 820.

[60] See *Dardana Limited v Yukos Oil Company* [2002] 2 Lloyd's Rep 326, per Mance LJ at [8] and [18].

[61] See *Svenska Petroleum Exploration AB v Government of the Republic of Lithuania and Another* [2005] 1 Lloyd's Rep 515 at [19].

[62] [2014] EWHC 2188.

[63] See also the decision in *ED & F Man v Yani Haryanto* [1991] 1 Lloyd's Rep 161. There, the English Court of Appeal accepted that illegality could amount to such special circumstances where the 'nature' of illegality outweighed the countervailing public policy in support of the finality of awards.

The decision in *Yukos* brings to mind the question of how the jurisdictional issues can be characterised for the purposes of issue estoppel. A jurisdictional issue decided in an interlocutory judgment would potentially be incapable of giving rise to identity of the issues as required for the application of issue estoppel.[64] One of the main reasons for this is that the question of whether the courts located in state A have jurisdiction is not identical to the question of whether those located in state B have jurisdiction.[65] Where the courts of state A decide that the courts in state B should have jurisdiction or that the latter courts are most suitable for the ends of justice, such a decision does not necessarily give rise to issue estoppel, even in cases where it is brought before a court in state B. Although such a decision may overcome the test on identity of the issues it is highly unlikely that it can form 'the necessary ingredients' of state A's judgment regarding its own jurisdiction.

Nonetheless, the explanations above should not be taken to mean that a jurisdictional issue previously determined by a competent foreign court is incapable of giving rise to issue estoppel. As has been discussed above, the decision in *The Sennar (No 2)* is authority for the proposition that such issues are indeed capable.[66] It will be recalled that the decision of the Dutch court did more than just hold that the Sudanese courts had jurisdiction: it held that the exclusive jurisdiction clause was applicable to the parties and the dispute at hand. Hence, where an issue that forms the basis of a court's jurisdiction is decided conclusively, it can give rise to estoppel.

For present purposes, the observations above support the proposition that the rule of issue estoppel can apply to enforcement judgments that have determined the jurisdictional issues regarding the existence, scope and validity of arbitration agreements. Indeed, this was recognised by the English Supreme Court in *Dallah Estate v Pakistan*.[67] There, the English Supreme Court conceded that jurisdictional issues previously determined by a competent court, particularly by courts located at the seat of the

[64] See, however, the decision in *Desert Sun Loan Corp v Hill* [1996] CLC 1132.

[65] This is also because the decision on jurisdiction may not at that stage be final and conclusive on the merits.

[66] There, the Dutch court's decision on jurisdiction was held to be a judgment 'on the merits' for the purposes of application of the rule of issue estoppel; see [1985] 1 Lloyd's Rep 521.

[67] [2010] 2 Lloyd's Rep 691 (SC).

arbitration, could give rise to issue estoppel.[68] although the arbitrators' decision on jurisdiction would be subject to review by the courts.[69]

A. The Decision in *The Wadi Sudr*

The extent to which the jurisdictional issues regarding the existence, scope and validity of arbitration agreements can give rise to issue estoppel is further illustrated in *The Wadi Sudr*.[70] On discharge of the short-delivered cargo, the cargo interests applied to the Spanish court for the arrest of the vessel. After the Spanish court's order for the arrest of the vessel, the carrier objected to the jurisdiction of the Spanish court on the grounds that there was a valid and binding arbitration agreement between the parties under the bill of lading. Later on the same day, the shipowners commenced English proceedings before the Commercial Court for a declaration of non-liability. Following these sets of litigation proceedings, the carrier also commenced (i) arbitration proceedings in London for a declaration of non-liability and (ii) a second action before the Commercial Court to obtain a declaration that the dispute was subject to an arbitration agreement.

Through the eyes of the English courts, the dispute was subject to arbitration in London, with the bill of lading effectively incorporating the charterparty arbitration clause pursuant to English law, which was the putative applicable law of the Bill of lading.[71] However, the Spanish court made a preliminary decision that the cargo interest was not bound by the arbitration clause on the grounds that it was not incorporated into the Bill of lading under Spanish law. In so holding, the Spanish judgment clearly stated why the court had not applied English law to the incorporation issue.[72]

On the question of whether the preliminary decision of the Spanish court created an issue estoppel, the English Court of Appeal held unanimously that it did. Through the application of the rule of issue estoppel, the

[68] ibid at [98].

[69] ibid at [104] and [160].

[70] [2009] EWCA Civ 1397.

[71] M Ozdel, *Bills of Lading Incorporating Charterparties* (Oxford, Hart Publishing, 2015) ch 1.

[72] [2009] EWCA Civ 1397 at [19].

English court was thus precluded from deciding afresh the formal validity of the arbitration agreement. Since the Spanish court had competent jurisdiction as the court first seised under the regulation, the mere fact that an English court would have come to a different decision did not constitute a bar to application of the rule of issue estoppel.[73] The English Court of Appeal also refused to hold that the public policy exception had any role to play. This was founded upon the premise that the question of validity of arbitration agreements did not fall outside the scope of the previous regulation where it was tied up with a dispute that falls within the ambit of the regulation.[74] For present purposes, the following conclusions can be drawn from the decision:

(a) Whether a jurisdictional issue that was previously determined by a foreign court should be recognised depends mainly on the English conflict of laws rules.[75]
(b) If the foreign court is a competent court under the English conflict of laws rules, the decision of the foreign court on a jurisdictional issue can give rise to issue estoppel.[76]
(c) At English common law, a jurisdictional issue determined by a foreign court can therefore be binding upon English courts. It can be binding even in cases where, through the eyes of English courts, the foreign proceedings are in breach of a forum selection clause.[77]
(d) By and large, the effect of the rule of issue estoppel, stated in (c) above, is diminished with the enactment of section 32 of the Civil Jurisdiction and Judgments Act 1982, which provides, inter alia, that: 'a judgment given by a court of an overseas country in any proceedings shall not be recognised or enforced in the United Kingdom if the bringing of those proceedings in that court was contrary to an agreement under which the dispute in question was to be settled otherwise than by proceedings in the courts of that country'.

[73] [2009] EWCA Civ 1397 at [62] and [125].
[74] This was the opinion of the Advocate-General in *The Front Comor* Case C-185/07, [2009] ECR I-663.
[75] [2009] EWCA Civ 1397 at [125].
[76] ibid.
[77] ibid. In this context, the decision clearly suggests that it will not be against English public policy to recognise a foreign judgment provided that it had not been obtained by commencing or continuing foreign proceedings in defiance of an injunction; see [125].

On the more intriguing issue of the law governing the validity of the arbitration agreement, there is not much practical guidance that can be drawn from the decision in *The Wadi Sudr*. This may be partly for the reason that a governing law issue does not usually present itself as an issue on the merits. On the application of the rule of issue estoppel, English courts are usually not concerned with the governing law chosen by the foreign court. As long as the foreign court is competent, an issue estoppel may arise from a judgment that arrives at a conclusion that is wrong according to English law.[78]

A final point to note is the effect of the decision within the EU. The decision in *The Wadi Sudr* was effectively reversed by Recital 12 of the Brussels I Regulation (Recast),[79] which provides that:

> This Regulation should not apply to arbitration. Nothing in this Regulation should prevent the courts of a Member State, when seised of an action in a matter in respect of which the parties have entered into an arbitration agreement, from referring the parties to arbitration, from staying or dismissing the proceedings, or from examining whether the arbitration agreement is null and void, inoperative or incapable of being performed, in accordance with their national law.

A ruling given by a court of a Member State as to whether or not an arbitration agreement is null and void, inoperative or incapable of being performed should not be subject to the rules of recognition and enforcement laid down in this Regulation, regardless of whether the court decided on this as a principal issue or as an incidental question.

Consequently, the courts of each Member State should now have complete freedom to examine whether there is a valid and binding arbitration agreement between the parties. For present purposes, the key question is: in an enforcement action under section 103 of the Arbitration Act 1996,[80] would an English court be issue estopped by the determination of a European court on the validity of an arbitration agreement? Since the Brussels I Regulation (Recast), including its recital, is not applicable to the

[78] See *Carl-Zeiss-Stiftung v Rayner & Keeler Ltd (No 2)* [1966] 2 All ER 536, per Lord Wilberforce at 966. See also *Tracomin v Sudan Oil*, above, per Staugthton J at 569 and 674.

[79] See Regulation (EU) No 1215/2012 of the European Parliament and of the Council of 12 December 2012 on jurisdiction and the recognition and enforcement of judgments in civil and commercial matters.

[80] The section reflects the wording in Art V of the New York Convention.

enforcement of arbitration awards, this question should still be answered with reference to English common law.

Following Brexit, the recognition and enforcement of judgments on civil and commercial matters will be subject to a different legal framework. However, the extent to which the rules of preclusion can apply in the present context will remain the same particularly since this matter has already been ring-fenced away from the relevant European legal framework.

B. The Decision in Diag Human SA v Czech Republic[81]

Although the decisions in *Dallah Estate* and *Yukos* recognised that the rule of issue estoppel can in principle apply in the context of the enforcement of arbitration awards, the decision in *Diag* was the first to apply the rule in the context of the Convention. There, Eder J considered the issue of whether a Czech award was binding for the purposes of enforcement. The relevant arbitration agreement provided for an internal appeal process, and the losing party had the right to appeal by serving a valid notice. When the award was first brought before an Australian court for enforcement, the court refused to enforce the award on the grounds that the award was not binding. When the award was later brought before Eder J for enforcement, the question arose as to whether the Austrian decision gave rise to an issue estoppel. Eder J refused to enforce the award for two reasons.

Firstly, he concluded that the award was not binding. In reaching this conclusion, he observed the abolition of the 'double exequatur' under the Convention. Since under the Convention the party seeking to enforce an award is no longer required to prove that the award has become binding in the country in which the award is rendered, he decided the question by reference to the autonomous interpretation of the Convention.[82] With this interpretation, he found that the award was not binding. His second ground for the decision was based on the rule of issue estoppel. He took the view that the Austrian court's decision that the award was not binding gave

[81] [2014] 2 Lloyd's Rep 283.

[82] This interpretation was suggested by Professor Van den Berg in *The New York Arbitration Convention of 1958: Towards a Uniform Judicial Interpretation* (1981) 266. See also *Dowans Holding SA v Tanzania Electric Supply Co Ltd* [2011] 2 Lloyd's Rep 475 at [24].

rise to an issue estoppel. Although the issue of whether one of the grounds under Article V of the Convention applies is one for the *lex fori*, the decision shows that a previous decision of a foreign court on this matter can give rise to issue estoppel in English enforcement proceedings.

Forum shopping can be considered as a fundamental characteristic of the Convention regime. However, applying the rule of issue estoppel in enforcement proceedings would appear to be conducive to the attainment of uniformity of approach.[83] The tension between these two conflicting policy considerations can perhaps be better understood by considering the effects of each policy. Had the determination of the issue by the Austrian court in *Diag* been erroneous in the eyes of the English court, would the English court have been bound by the Austrian court's determination? Considering the pro-enforcement bias reflected in the Convention, would the English court have exercised its discretion not to apply the rule of issue estoppel and enforce the award? In these circumstances, there appears to be two countervailing policies: the policy in support of the finality of litigation and the pro-enforcement policy towards arbitration awards.

At the other extreme is the decision in *Karaha Bodas Companu v Perusahaan Pertambangan Minyak Dan Gas Bumi Negara*. There, a Swiss award was sought to be enforced in various jurisdictions including Canada, the US, Hong Kong and Indonesia. The award was initially enforced in the US.[84] It was later annulled by the Central Jakarta District Court in Indonesia, although the court was not a court of primary jurisdiction. Thereafter, the Hong Kong High Court granted an order enforcing the award on the ground that the US court decision gave rise to an issue estoppel.[85] In the US, the award went up to the Supreme Court, which refused the petition of the party resisting enforcement. Shortly afterwards, the Indonesian Supreme Court reversed the Jakarta District Court decision and confirmed the validity of the award.[86] At a later stage, the award was brought before a Canadian court for enforcement in Canada. The resisting party's failed attempts ended with the Canadian court's

[83] See [2014] 2 Lloyd's Rep 283, 299.

[84] 264 F. Supp 2d 490 (SD Tex 2003).

[85] [2003] HKCU 1. See also the *dicta* in *Yat Tung Investment Co Ltd v Dao Heng Bank Ltd*, which suggests that, to prevent any abuse of process, the courts should not permit a party to re-open an issue, if that issue could have been raised in earlier proceedings in another jurisdiction.

[86] The chronology of the actions brought is stated in the decision of the Court of Queen's Bench of Alberta in *Karaha Bodas* [2004] ABQB 918.

decision to grant leave for enforcement of the award.[87] The Canadian court did not apply issue estoppel to the grounds for refusal that had already been decided during the earlier proceedings, but it gave some weight to the determination of the US Court of Appeals for the Fifth Circuit Court that failure to produce evidence of political risk insurance did not violate public policy.

Lengthy and complex enforcement proceedings in various jurisdictions would leave no room for sufficient recovery of wasted costs and time. For the finality and effectiveness of arbitration awards, the courts should perhaps be justified in considering the rules of preclusion in enforcement proceedings and in not permitting parties to contest the enforcement of an award on a ground that has already been rejected by a foreign court. The application of the rule of issue estoppel in the context of the enforcement of awards under the Convention would thus be in line with the general policy under the Convention that the enforcing courts should only conduct a limited review of the award at the enforcement stage.

Following the decision in *Diag*, English courts have been receptive to the application of the rule of issue estoppel in the enforcement proceedings. Recently, the decision in *Eastern European Engineering Ltd v Vijay Construction Ltd*[88] has followed the decision in *Diag* and applied the rule of issue estoppel in respect of a ruling made by a foreign court in the course of enforcement proceedings under the Convention. There, the party resisting the enforcement of the award was issue estopped from alleging that the award and the conduct of the arbitration were defective after the supervisory court had already ventilated and rejected the same arguments.

IV. Conclusion

In light of the discussions above, it can be concluded that although there is no express provision to that effect, the Convention permits the use of the rules of preclusion, which can be treated as part of 'the public policy of finality'.[89] Every country is justified in applying its own preclusive rules

[87] ibid.

[88] [2019] 1 Lloyd's Rep 1.

[89] See the decision in *Eastern European Engineering Ltd v Vijay Construction (Pty) Ltd* [2018} EWHC 2713 (Comm). Although the principle of issue estoppel can at first seem just

in the enforcement proceedings. Hence, a previous decision of a foreign court on the enforcement of an award under the Convention is capable of giving rise to issue estoppel in English enforcement proceedings.[90]

As is clear from the decision in *Diag*, issue estoppel is a matter for the *lex fori*. Thus, a national court applies its own laws when characterising the issue previously determined in a conclusive manner by a foreign judgment. However, the question of whether the issue determined in a foreign judgment is final and conclusive should be decided with reference to the law of the foreign jurisdiction. This matter, which is related to the application of issue estoppel, is separate and distinct from the issue as to whether an award has become binding for the purposes of Article V(1)(e) of the Convention. The latter issue is, in essence, one for the *lex fori*. Nonetheless, a previous decision of a foreign court on the application of Article V(1)(e) can give rise to issue estoppel in enforcement proceedings.

Maritime claims are vulnerable to forum shopping, and it is not a coincidence that one of the landmark decisions on issue estoppel, namely the decision in *The Sennar*, is a shipping case, where the court emphasised the need to prevent parties from re-litigating the same issue in different jurisdictions and applied the rule of issue estoppel as a solution to prevent double jeopardy.[91] When the same principle was deployed in disputes between parties from EU Member States, it was used as a delay tactic mainly to undermine the enforcement of arbitration agreements. These events have shown that to use issue estoppel with a view to precluding a multiplicity of successive proceedings in different jurisdictions may not be an ideal solution, particularly in the case of a litigant wishing to 'torpedo' the enforcement of an arbitration agreement. The preamble to the Brussels I Recast Regulation now expressly leaves no room for the application of the rule of issue estoppel in that context.

an evidential matter for the courts and tribunals, it is considered as a substantive right under English law that courts as well as arbitral tribunals are expected to observe. See *Associated Electric and Gas Insurance Services Ltd v European Reinsurance Co of Zurich* [2003] 1 WLR 1041 (PC), 1047, per Lord Hobhouse.

[90] An arbitration award itself can also give rise to an issue estoppel. The net result of this is that an award that has not been challenged bars any claim in relation to the matters dealt with by the arbitrators in their award. See *Fidelitas Shipping Co Ltd v V/O Exportchleb* [1965] 1 Lloyd's Rep 223 and *Emirates Trading Agency LLC v Sociedade de Fomento Industrial Pte Ltd* [2015] EWHC 1452 (Comm).

[91] See [1985] 1 Lloyd's Rep 521, 523, per Lord Diplock.

Under the Brussels Regulation particularly, each Member State is required to decide the issue of validity of arbitration agreements.[92] This restriction on the use of the rules of preclusion does not appear to have an effect on the recognition and enforcement of arbitration awards under the Convention, since the Regulation does not apply to the recognition and enforcement of arbitration awards. The net result of this is that in an action for the recognition and enforcement of an award, a court in an EU Member State should be able to rely on an earlier determination of an issue (eg the validity of an arbitration agreement) by a competent court whether or not the latter court is in another EU Member State. Consequently, whatever consequence Brexit may bring on the recognition and enforcement of judgments on civil and commercial matters, the extent to which the rules of preclusion can apply in the present context will remain the same.

For present purposes, a more relevant question is whether the use of issue estoppel can have the effect of undermining the pro-enforcement bias widely recognised by the Convention states. It is also highly unlikely that the rule of issue estoppel will serve those wishing to 'torpedo' the enforcement of arbitration agreements and awards, particularly since the overarching principle on the application of issue estoppel is that it must be applied to bring about justice, not injustice.

Multiplicity of successive proceedings in different jurisdictions is a fundamental characteristic of the Convention regime, and the use of issue estoppel can at first seem irreconcilable with the Convention regime. Nonetheless, at least so far as English law is concerned, the balance comes down in favour of using issue estoppel in the interest of public policy on finality, even in the case of enforcement proceedings under the Convention. This is particularly the case where a party resisting enforcement seeks to raise substantially the same challenges to the award in different jurisdictions.

On the whole, in the context of the enforcement of arbitration awards, the rules of preclusion, particularly the rule of issue estoppel, do more than just strengthen judicial comity. The recent cases have shown that the rules can be deployed with a view to giving teeth to the pro-enforcement policy for the recognition and enforcement of arbitration awards, while also helping to promote the finality of international arbitration awards under the Convention.

[92] See para 12 of the Preamble to the Recast Regulation on Jurisdiction and the Recognition and Enforcement of Judgments in Civil and Commercial Matters (Regulation (EU) No 1215/2012).

INDEX

www.ingramcontent.com/pod-product-compliance
Ingram Content Group UK Ltd.
Pitfield, Milton Keynes, MK11 3LW, UK
UKHW020812290926
15470UKWH00003B/1104

9 781849 466752